PASCAL

BLAISE PASCAL
Sanguine drawing by Domat

PASCAL

by
JEAN STEINMANN

Translated by
MARTIN TURNELL

A Helen and Kurt Wolff Book
Harcourt, Brace & World, Inc.
NEW YORK

Foreword

PASCAL not only divides the critics; he divides them more sharply than most great writers. The divisions do not follow any particular pattern; they transcend the boundaries of language, race and creed. Friendly and unfriendly voices are heard inside and outside the fold. Newman, the religious thinker with whom Pascal is perhaps most often compared, remarked tartly that "the gifted Pascal, in the work on which his literary fame is mainly founded, does not approve himself to a Catholic judgment". Claudel with his granite-like faith spoke disparagingly of him as a "sick man". François Mauriac's devotion to "the prodigious genius" is well known, and Charles Du Bos is not the only literary critic to have described Pascal quite simply as "the greatest French writer". Among those who do not or did not share Pascal's faith, Valéry once wrote a violent diatribe which was based on an elementary misreading of one of the most celebrated sentences in the whole of the *Pensées*. More recently one Marxist critic has declared that he reads him with a "sacred horror", while another has hailed him as "the first modern man . . . an original thinker in the strongest sense of the term".

The Marxist tributes are of special interest. Pascal's primary concern was a lay apostolate to the unbeliever. The *Pensées* were written for the sceptical man of the world and for the earnest seeker after truth who cast a longing glance at the Church with the secret wish that it were all true. Pascal has always had a large audience among the descendants of the cultivated seventeenth-century unbeliever. The fact that he was a layman has been of great importance as enabling him to speak to the educated unbeliever in his own language. His place in European thought is less with the professional apologists than with independent crusaders like Kierkegaard and Simone Weil.

The Abbé Jean Steinmann, who unhappily lost his life two

v

years ago in a flood disaster while visiting the Holy Land,
was a well-known writer on the Bible as well as on other
subjects ranging from Richard Simon, the founder of modern
biblical exegesis, to whom he pays a warm tribute in the
present work, to Léon Bloy and Danilo Dolci. His study of
Pascal first appeared in 1954, the tercentenary of what is known
as Pascal's second conversion and the writing of the *Memorial*.
A revised edition followed in 1962, the tercentenary of Pascal's
death.

In his foreword to the first edition the Abbé proclaimed himself a lifelong devotee of Pascal. "Outside the Bible", he wrote,
"there is no book that I have read more assiduously than the
Pensées." The Abbé was something of a rebel. Pascal, he said,
acted as his "protector" against scholasticism as it was then taught.
His admiration was by no means confined to the *Pensées*. "I read
and re-read the *Provincial Letters*, amused at seeing them come to
life under my own eyes. I made a habit of re-reading them almost
every year in order to cleanse my mind by a dose of irony."
"Life", he went on, "has not cured me of Pascal. He had taught
me to scorn the great figures of the establishment and this scorn
is still with me. He taught me to love the Bible and to love and
respect Port-Royal."

For the past quarter of a century the field of Pascal studies
has been the scene of great activity and important discoveries.
Thanks to the work of scholars like Zacharie Tourneur, Louis
Lafuma and Jean Mesnard we are probably closer today to the
true meaning of the *Pensées* than at any other time. The Abbé
Steinmann's book is one of the best general studies that have so
far been written. It is also one of the most balanced and persuasive.
When he was elected in 1961 to membership of the Society of
Friends of Port-Royal, he remarked that he had the impression of
finding his family again.

There is, however, nothing Jansenist about his interpretation of
the man or his work. He is concerned to correct the false impression given by Valéry's essay, to demolish once for all the image of
the gloomy, Jansenist Pascal. There is no special pleading. He
does not tone down or remove what he calls in one passage the
"prickles". Pascal was a proud, haughty, irascible man who was

given to violent outbursts of temper. His violence not infre-
quently carried him too far. His biographer rightly blames him
on occasion for harshness and lack of charity in controversy.
He does not minimize the serious danger of schism which existed
immediately before Pascal made his sudden decision to withdraw
from all public controversy, but his last word on the man is fair
and generous. He calls him "a saint like another". "He was not a
canonized or, indeed, a canonizable saint, but an anonymous one
lost in the crowds which swarm into the churches on feast days. A
saint like millions of other saints."

His commentary on the religious writings is equally balanced.
He does not embroil us in the controversies over the order in
which the fragments of the *Pensées* should be presented. He
simply directs our attention to the main themes and expounds
them: the mentality of the unbeliever, the nature of man, the use
of thought, the infinite, the meaning of faith, the Bible and Jesus
Christ. The message which emerges from his exposition is one of
hope and encouragement. After quoting an appalling passage
from Jansen's *Augustinus*, he observes:

"It is easy to see the distance that separates the harmless picture
of the *Pensées* from the hell of screams of rage and slaughter. It is
commonly said that Pascal exaggerates the wretchedness of man.
That is absurd. Compared with the picture presented by Lucretius,
Sade, Dostoevsky, Proust or Kafka, Pascal's vision of humanity
is that of a choirboy. He never concerns himself with the evil
done by man, but simply with the ridiculous spectacle of his
activities. In the *Pensées* man never assumes the appearance of a
savage and lubricious ape whose instincts civilization tries in vain
to camouflage. He finds man merely grotesque and not wicked
. . . he suppresses the sight of blood and tears, and only preserves
the comic element."

The present translation has been made from the revised edition
of the Abbé Steinmann's book, which has been somewhat abridged
to make it more suitable for the English-speaking public. Part V,
which deals with the different views of Pascal's work taken by
Frenchmen from the seventeenth to the twentieth centuries,
has been omitted altogether. Some of the chapters recounting
religious and other controversies in the seventeenth century

have been shortened and a number of footnotes in which the author attacks the views of other Pascal specialists have been suppressed.

MARTIN TURNELL

Contents

ix

PART III

GETHSEMANE
(1658–1662)

PART IV

THE "PENSÉES"

Illustrations

Acknowledgements

Frontispiece, 3, 10, Desclée de Brouwer; 1, 2, 9, 11, 13, Giraudon; 4, Société des Amis de Port-Royal; 5, Studio Piccardy; 6, H. Roger Vidlet, print from DDB; 7, 8, Giraudon, prints from Mansell Collection.

xi

Abbreviations

G.E.
Oeuvres de Blaise Pascal in "Les Grands Écrivains de la France" series. Ed. L. Brunschvicg, P. Boutroux and F. Gazier, 14 volumes (Hachette, Paris), 1904–1925.

Lafuma, I, II or III
Pensées. Ed. L. Lafuma, 3 volumes (Éditions du Luxembourg, Paris, 1951).

Lafuma
Pensées, Ed. L. Lafuma, 1 volume (Delmas, Paris, 1952). Translated into English by Martin Turnell as *Pascal's Pensées* (Harvill Press, London, 1962). All quotations from the *Pensées* and Gilberte Périer's life of Pascal used in the present work are taken from this translation.

Laf., Br.
These abbreviations, followed by a number, refer to the numbering of the *Pensées* adopted by Lafuma (Delmas Edition) and Brunschvicg (Éditions de Cluny, 1934).

Part I

THE YOUNG ARCHIMEDES
(1623–1655)

"In the intervals of applying algebra to the second book of Euclid, we experimented with circles; we stuck bamboos into the parched earth, measured their shadows at different hours of the day, and drew exciting conclusions from our observations. Sometimes, for fun, we cut and folded sheets of paper so as to make cubes and pyramids. One afternoon Guido arrived carrying carefully between his small and rather grubby hands a flimsy dodecahedron. 'E tanto bello!' he said, as he showed us his paper crystal; and when I asked him how he had managed it, he merely smiled and said it had been so easy. . . ."

Aldous Huxley: "Young Archimedes"
in *The Little Mexican*

CHAPTER I

Two Infant Prodigies

BLAISE PASCAL'S family were natives of Cournon, a little village of two thousand inhabitants standing on a hill near the River Allier, half way between Clermont and Pont-du-Château. In 1345 Durand Paschal had undertaken to make an annual donation of three *deniers* to the chapter canons of Cournon and two *deniers* to the minor canons on the anniversary day of his ancestors.[1]

In his later years Jehan Pascal, Pascal's great-grandfather on his father's side, settled at Clermont where he became an alderman. His son, Martin Pascal, was an important personage. He was inspector of taxes in 1584, "then secretary to Queen Louise, wife of Henri III", and in 1586 was appointed treasurer of France, the King's Counsellor and general administrator of finance for the district of Riom.[2] He had joined the Reformers, but abjured Protestantism shortly after St Bartholomew's Eve.[3]

About 1586 he married Marguerite Pascal of Mons, who belonged to another family of the same name which had been raised to the nobility by Louis XI.[4]

Martin Pascal was the father of seven children. His descendants were so numerous that, according to Fléchier, one of his daughters had fifteen hundred grandchildren, nephews and great-nephews.

Étienne, the eldest of Martin Pascal's children, studied law in

[1] *Archives départ.*, chap. Cournon, No. 196. Cf. *Les Pascal en Basse Auvergne* (Imprimerie Paul Vallier, Clermont-Ferrand, 1923), p. 11.
[2] Cf. J. Mesnard, *Pascal: His Life and Works* (London, 1952), p. 2.
[3] Cf. E. Jovy, *Études pascaliennes*, vol. VII (Paris, 1930), pp. 217-24.
[4] The Pascals of Mons and the Pascals of Clermont did not belong to the same family. Blaise was a descendant of the first through his paternal grandmother and of the second through Martin Pascal.

3

Paris during the reign of Henri IV. On his return to Clermont he purchased the post of "counsellor nominated by the king for the district of Lower Auvergne at Clairmont", and in 1616, at the age of twenty-eight, he married twenty-year-old Antoinette Begon. In 1624 he purchased, at the cost of 30,000 *livres*, the post of deputy president of the Cour des Aydes at Montferrand.

He lived with his young wife at a house known as the Hôtel de Vernines in upper Clermont. The house, which was already a hundred years old, stood in the Rue des Gras close to the cathedral. It survived until the beginning of the twentieth century. Maurice Barrès paid it a visit and has left a description of it. The 'connoisseur of souls' had to hold his nose when he went through the corridors of the filthy, insalubrious, dilapidated building. In the courtyard there was a leaking, foul-smelling drain.[5] But in 1616 the ancient mansion had not yet fallen into ruin. If it was already gloomy— life by daylight is after all a modern invention—we must not forget that in the seventeenth century towns were still built in the medieval style with narrow sordid streets which rain and filth transformed into bogs. Comfort was unknown, but people lived neither better nor worse than they do today.

We have no portrait of Étienne Pascal or his wife. All we have of Étienne's are some autograph manuscripts.[6] His handwriting, to which his son's came later to bear a strange resemblance, is that of a learned, haughty, imperious individual. The wealthy judge, who was obsessed with his own importance, an able mathematician and well versed in dead languages, wrote a judicial French,[7] that is to say, his style was ponderous and retained a pronounced Auvergnat flavour. Apart from this he was, without being bigoted, a very good man and a very good Catholic.[8]

Like her husband Antoinette Begon came of a family of public

---

[5] Maurice Barrès, *Les Maîtres* (Paris, 1927), pp. 143 *et seq.* "Les Deux Maisons de Pascal à Clermont-Ferrand", cf. E. Jovy, *Explorations circumpascaliennes* (Paris, 1928). Drawings of the house in which Pascal was born will be found in V. Giraud, *La Vie Héroïque de Blaise Pascal* (Paris, 1923), p. 8, and in L. Brunschvicg, *Pascal*, n.d. ("Maîtres des Littératures "); also in A. Béguin, *Pascal par lui-même* (Paris, 1952), pp. 7–8.

[6] Brunschvicg, *op. cit.*, Plates VII and VIII.

[7] As an example of Étienne Pascal's style, see his letter to Père Noël, *G.E.*, I, pp. 254–79.

[8] On Étienne Pascal, see Marguerite Périer's memoir, *G.E.*, I, pp. 5–22.

servants. She seems to have been gentle, kind to the poor, pious, intelligent and sensitive, but suffered from poor health and was probably tubercular.

The Pascals had four children: Antonia, a daughter who died shortly after birth; Gilberte, Blaise and Jacqueline.

In 1623, the year before Richelieu came to power, when the twenty-seven-year-old Descartes was a soldier in the Comte de Bucquoy's army and Pierre Corneille was finishing his schooldays with the Jesuits at Rouen, Blaise Pascal was born on 19th June. He was baptized on 27th June in the parish of Saint-Pierre.

Marguerite Périer, known as Margot, one of the daughters of his sister Gilberte, tells us in her memoirs that she had heard it said that, as soon as he was born, the child was seized with convulsions. On to this she grafted the story of the witch who was supposed to have applied a compress compounded of medicinal herbs gathered by the light of the full moon. This produced a catalepsy and everyone thought the child was dead. In a moment of exasperation Étienne slapped the witch, but the baby regained consciousness and the convulsions gradually disappeared.[9] A strange century in which medicine hovered between magic and mumbo-jumbo! Trials for witchcraft were still common. A few years later Urbain Grandier was burnt alive at Loudon; Monsieur Olier, parish priest of Saint-Sulpice, discovered signs of witches' dens in his parish; the Montespan attended black masses; Racine was nearly implicated in the Poisons Case. In 1623 Shakespeare, the poet of the witches in *Macbeth* and the fairies in *The Tempest*, had been dead only seven years.

But Étienne Pascal treated witches as a joke. He was after all a mathematician. Unfortunately his son's health was delicate and he was subject to nervous disorders.

In 1626 Antoinette Begon died at the age of thirty. We know nothing about Blaise Pascal's earliest years. Dr. Roux has left a list of the neighbours and relatives of his vast family. "I know his neighbours: they were the Peghouxs, the Chardons and the Montorciers. The first two were his cousins, the third friends and

---

[9] *G.E.*, I, p. 125. Lafuma, III, pp. 59–67. On Marguerite Périer's reliability, see J. Mesnard, *op. cit.*, p. 7: "M. Périer's stories should be treated with the greatest reserve."

supporters of his family. To these should probably be added a dozen little Pascals and an incalculable number of first cousins or the descendants of first cousins who were related to Blaise on his mother's side: the Begons, Fontfreydes, Lavilles, de Bretats, Lecourts, Benosts, Charriers, Dalmas, Rochettes, Savarons, Tailhandiers, Perreyrets, etc."[10]

Five years after the death of his wife President Pascal, like so many of his fellow Auvergnats, settled in Paris, where he had been educated. He did not sell his office to his brother Blaise until 1634 and was not paid until several years later, if at all.

Blaise was eight when he came for the first time to the Paris of Louis XIII. From the carriage which took him through the maze of famous streets—the tortuous, muddy, foul-smelling streets— the child missed nothing: the houses with turrets and gables huddled together near the barges, with their show windows projecting from their black bellies, and the citadels: the Bastille, the Temple, the Louvre, the Châtelet, the numerous churches often standing awry; the Seine hidden by the stalls which cluttered up the bridges and the quays. Everywhere there was the bustle of the spruce, good-humoured, lively crowd. You breathed a gayer, brisker, lighter atmosphere than in the sour, austere Puy de Dôme. The Pascal family went to live in the Rue de la Tisseranderie in the Temple district: one of the most thickly populated and even today one of the best preserved parts of the old city. Two years later the family moved to the Rue Neuve-Saint-Lambert, then to the Rue Brisemiche. In fact, they seem to have spent their lives moving house.[11]

Étienne Pascal engaged a housekeeper to run his home and look after his children. The housekeeper, Louise Delfault, came of a lower middle-class family from Coulommiers which was related

---

[10] Les Entretiens des Amis de Pascal (Jan.–Feb. 1930), vol. VII, No. 21, p. 87.

[11] The following is a list of Blaise Pascal's homes in Paris: 1st January 1632, Rue de la Tisseranderie; 1634–5, Rue Neuve-Saint-Lambert (at present Rue de Condé); 1645–48, Rue Brisemiche (the stay at Rouen); 1651, Rue Beaubourg; October 1654–62, Rue des Francs-Bourgeois-Saint-Michel (at present 54 Rue Monsieur-le-Prince). Cf. Lafuma, III, p. 50. Pascal died at his sister's home in the Rue des Fossés-Saint-Victor between the Porte Saint-Marcel and the Porte Saint-Victor close to the Fathers of Christian Doctrine (at present 77 Rue du Cardinal-Lemoine), Lafuma, III, p. 50.

to the La Fontaine family.[12] She acted as mother to the President's two youngest children.

Having given up the law, Étienne Pascal had nothing to occupy him in Paris except the management of his capital, mathematics, and supervising the education of his son and his two daughters. Like a good middle-class family man who favoured sound investments guaranteed by the State, he invested all his ready money—*livres* and *pistoles*—which would be worth several million today, in city bonds, Richelieu having inspired confidence.[13]

He was a keen mathematician who found that he now had leisure in which to take up mathematics seriously and so he devoted the greater part of his time to it. When it came to the education of his children, Paris could offer him a selection of high-class convents for his daughters, while for his son there were famous schools like Harcourt and Clermont, which was run by the Jesuits. But their methods of education did not commend themselves to him because in his opinion they were not sufficiently based on reason. Besides, he was worried about his son's poor health. Being very fond of his children, he was anxious to have them at home with him and feeling that he had a vocation as a schoolmaster, was bursting with impatience to test a rational method of teaching languages and science on a son who appeared to be really gifted. He still retained something of the thirst for knowledge of the Renaissance, the burning enthusiasm with which a hundred years earlier the humanists had set out on their voyage of discovery of Antiquity, the sciences and all the "novelties" of which Rabelais and Montaigne had spoken. Everybody was anxious to achieve for himself that intellectual freedom for which René Descartes was to provide a charter in his *Discours de la méthode*.

We may have our doubts about amateur pedagogues, but Pascal was one of those children with whom any method of education was bound to succeed. His genius would have triumphed over anything.

In the task of educating his son, Étienne Pascal steered a middle

[12] J. Mesnard, *op. cit.*, p. 14.
[13] In *Pascal mondain et amoureux* (Paris, 1923), p. 167, E. Chamaillard puts Pascal's capital at three hundred thousand gold francs. Charles de Beaurepaire, in *Blaise Pascal et sa famille à Rouen* (Paris, 1902), puts it at double this figure (cf. V. Giraud, *op. cit.*, p. 249).

course between the method used by Montaigne's father and the one employed by a Descartes to refurbish his own mind. He wanted Blaise to acquire a sound knowledge of Latin and Greek, but a knowledge which was founded on rational principles rather than something which was a simple matter of habit. He preferred philology to languages and poetry. At an age when, parrot-like, the little Montaigne was trotting out his declensions, the little Pascal sought to demonstrate them. By a method of education which was more that of a critic than of a humanist, Pascal felt that he was turning his son into a person with the least bookish of minds. He brought him up, in the most natural way in the world, to be a scientist; the miracle is that the little boy was one day to become, most unexpectedly, a poet, but a poet and a writer who almost alone in his century did not imitate the ancients or borrow any of the literary forms of the classics of Greco-Roman Antiquity. Corneille took the subjects of his tragedies from Latin and Spanish authors; Molière imitated Plautus and the Italians; Boileau, Horace; La Bruyère, Theophrastus; La Fontaine, Aesop and the Isopets; Racine was the new Euripides. Pascal was the creative artist.

Étienne Pascal had sensed his son's inclination for the experimental sciences and mathematics, but in his opinion they were pastimes for grown-ups who discoursed indefatigably in Latin about the least theorem. He was therefore satisfied if he could occasionally lead the conversation, when the family were together, to the simple and picturesque aspects of science, to amusing and entertaining little problems. At meal times they discussed the explosion of gunpowder, the way water rises in pumps, the effects of lightning, the refraction of light, and the reason why certain objects float on the surface of water. Blaise experimented with sound by tapping with his spoon on a pewter plate, then on a copper jug and a silver plate. He discovered that sound is produced by vibrations, and as soon as he had learnt to write, attempted a short treatise on acoustics. But when the child questioned his father about mathematics, which he often heard discussed, he received only the evasive answer that it was the science of producing "accurate figures". Fuller information was refused and all geometry books locked away.

At the age of twelve the child's passionate interest got the better of his father's reticence. In the memoirs of Gilberte, the elder sister, an incident which illustrates the mathematical precocity of the child assumes a quasi-miraculous aura. In a brilliantly gloomy short story Aldous Huxley has described the brief childhood of a little Italian Archimedes.[14] He has simply transposed and dramatized a page from Blaise Pascal's biography which inspired one of Chateaubriand's most celebrated flights of rhetoric.

Gilberte relates that, coming one day into the room tiled with red bricks where the children used to play, Étienne Pascal found his son sitting on the floor absorbed in the contemplation of circles, angles and parallel lines. He asked him what he was doing and the little boy admitted that he was in the process of proving that the sum of the angles of a triangle is equal to that of two right angles. Gilberte has been made to say that her brother had discovered all the propositions of Euclid up to the thirty-second. That is not correct. She simply declares that with the help of axioms that he had worked out for himself the child had reached this proposition.[15] It needed no more than this to fill his father's eyes with tears of joy and send him off to describe his amazement to his friend Le Pailleur.

People have dismissed this incident as legendary. In his *Historiettes* Tallemant des Réaux argues that the child admitted that he had read the first six books of Euclid on the sly. Others have assumed that the budding mathematician had had a glimpse of a treatise on geometry, but not knowing Latin well enough to read it had simply copied the figures from it and invented names for them— "rounds" and "bars"—in order to feel his way to the theorems. Gilberte has suggested a different interpretation. She asserts that before being caught by his father, her brother had spent a long time practising accurate figures: perfect circles, triangles whose sides were dead straight, parallel lines. Being an imaginative person, he approached geometry as a draughtsman and it was a study of the proportions of his figures that led him, fumblingly and by flashes of intuition, to the discovery of a few theorems; in particular, thanks to the empirical method of parallel lines, the

[14] *The Little Mexican* (London, 1924), pp. 271–340.
[15] Lafuma, p. 31. Eng. tr., p. 34.

sum of the three angles of a triangle. It would be an exaggeration to say that he reinvented Euclid. For a child of twelve to have discovered on his own what he did discover is already enough to remind us of Mozart's precocity in music. Above all else the mathematical ecstasy of the child Pascal is the most remarkable indication of what he was to become in the future. How closely the little boy resembles Huxley's young Archimedes, the tragic and charming Guido! In future, geometry was to be his holiday reward. Just as Guido goes into a state of abstraction when drawing squares in the sand, so Blaise Pascal deciphering the Euclid that his father lent him experienced a sort of ultimate joy of a mystical nature and murmured to himself: "How beautiful it is!"

It may equally have been that in the case of Pascal the precocity of his gifts as a mathematician was accompanied, as so often happens, by a real appreciation of music. He was able to satisfy it. The family were not always taken up with mathematics; they were not always serious in the house in the Rue Brisemiche in 1636. They laughed and they sang.

Le Pailleur, poet, mathematician, melomaniac, dancer and an intimate friend of Pascal senior, was a jovial fellow. After a rakish and adventurous youth he had become the official lover of the Protestant Maréchale de Thémines. He delighted in practical jokes, composed light verse in which he made fun of "the corny syllogisms" of the pedants, and mixed with the company of musicians and poets like Benserade as well as the scholars. He was devoted to the young Pascal. When visiting Étienne he used to bring with him the poet Dalibray and his sister, Mme Saintot, who was the mistress of Voiture, dictator of preciosity at the Hôtel de Rambouillet. Mme Saintot came with her daughters who played with Gilberte and Jacqueline Pascal. They used to take the happy bunch of children to the carnival or the fair, so that they could enjoy the knockabout of the performers in front of the booth where Scapin was beating Gorgibus. There were other days when they visited the Maréchale de Thémines and listened to sixteenth-century melodies based on the poems of the Pléiade, Benserade or Voiture and accompanied on the harpsichord.

Then they would go to the theatre. The Pascals and their friends had no intention of being stuffy about the most fashionable

form of entertainment offered by the capital which was as keen
on the theatre as the London of Elizabeth I. In 1636 the *Comédie
des Tuileries*, Scudéry's *Comédie des comédiens*, Du Ryer's *Vendanges
de Suresnes* and La Calprenède's *Mithridate* were all performed in
Paris. And first and foremost people queued at the Théâtre du
Marais, which always had a full house, in order to greet the *Cid*
with frantic applause. The part of Rodrigue was played by the
Auvergnat, Mondory, who was a friend of the Pascals. Jacqueline,
a child of eleven who had been taught how to read poetry, was
carried away by her emotions. Like the youth of the day she knew
by heart long passages of the brilliant and fiery tragi-comedy. She
was as wildly enthusiastic about Corneille—and in precisely the
same way—as her brother, Blaise, was about Euclid, and she
longed to act herself.

That year Jacqueline's father went on a short visit to Clermont
with Blaise and Gilberte. He left his daughter in the care of Mme
Saintot whose own daughters were also avid readers and passionate
declaimers of poetry. The bevy of twelve-year-old poetesses set
to work to amuse themselves by composing a comedy in verse.
"They performed it twice with other actors, whom they selected
personally, in the presence of a large audience. Everyone was
astonished that the children had had the stamina to write a full-
length play and discovered many delightful things in it; with the
result that for a considerable time it was the talk of all Paris."[16]

To a far greater extent than her brother, Jacqueline gave the
impression of being the infant prodigy of the family. She was
graceful and pretty; a "sweetie", said Tallemant des Réaux. She
was the spoilt child, petted and made a fuss of by everybody.
Between the hours spent putting her doll to bed she composed
pieces of verse: sonnets, *dizains*, quatrains, rondeaux, songs,
improvisations. Her whole girlhood, indeed, unfolds to the sound
of poems, rhymes and celebrations. Her "versifying vein", as
Sainte-Beuve calls it, was curious and at times if not actually
scabrous, was certainly daring, more in keeping with the gifts of a
Le Pailleur or a Dalibray than those of a young girl. She wrote
some lines for "a lady in love with a man who knew nothing
about it".[17] It is evident from Benserade's reply that Jacqueline's

[16] *G.E.*, I, p. 145.   [17] *Ibid.*, p. 232.

lines were a declaration of love intended for him. She was
thirteen; he was twenty-six.[18] This is his reply:

> *Que vos vers sont ardents! Que leur pompe est brillante*
> *   Et qu'ils sont radoucis!*
> *Il n'en faut douter, vous êtes l'Amarante*
> *   Et je suis le Thyrsis.*
>
> *Ils sont de vous à moi ces vers que chacun loue,*
> *   Et ne le niez plus.*
> *Pensez à la rougeur qui vous a peint la joue*
> *   Dès que je les ai lus.*
>
> *. . . J'ai honte qu'une fille ait été la première*
> *   A me parler d'amour.*

> Your lines are burning! Their style is brilliant
>   And how chastened they are!
> There can be no doubt about it: you are Love-lies-bleeding
>   And I am Thyrsis.
>
> These lines which everyone praises were written by you for me,
>   So don't deny it any longer.
> Think of the blushes that dyed your cheek
>   As soon as I'd read them.
>
> . . . I'm ashamed that a girl should have been the first
>   To speak to me of love.

A game if you like, but a somewhat precocious one. Later in
"Lines on a Metal Vase Containing Flowers", she was to write:

> *A bas, à bas, ces fleurs!*
> *   Vous profanez ce verre.*
> *Le fade émail de ces couleurs*
> *   N'est bon que pour des pots de terre.*
> *C'est pervertir l'ordre des choses.*
> *   Un métal si divin*
> *   N'est pas fait pour des roses·*
> *   Il est fait pour du vin!*[19]

[18] G.E., I, pp. 235–6.   [19] Ibid., p. 266.

Down, down with these flowers!
You profane the glass.
The stale enamel of the colours
Is only fit for earthenware pots.
It's a perversion of the order of things.
A metal so divine
Is not made for roses:
It's made for wine!

If we have dwelt on the poetic talent of the little Pascal girl, which seems modest enough to modern eyes, it is because it was ultimately responsible for the events which followed: the favours enjoyed by her father; the removal of the entire family to Rouen, and the circumstances which led to the invention of the adding machine. But we are interested in Jacqueline first and foremost because she explains her brother. Twenty years later the most intoxicating and the most magical of poetry will suddenly well up from the *Pensées*. Where did it come from except the same mysterious source which produced the thin trickle of the innocent *bouts-rimés* of the little sister?

Only one portrait survives from this period. At the time of the journey of father and son to Rouen, the lawyer Jean Domat, a friend of the family and the father of the man who was to be one of Pascal's closest friends, did an admirable sketch in red chalk of the fourteen-year-old boy on the fly-leaf of a law compendium. The head is slightly hunched into the shoulders, the face full, the forehead square and slightly protruding. The dark eyes with their clear pupils are wide open under strongly arched brows. The nose is faintly curved without being thick; the mouth small with a pronounced upper lip under the slight moustache; the chin divided by a dimple. The youth's face beneath the curly hair is handsome with a hint of naïveté in expression and attitude. His friends remained under the charm of the young Archimedes.

CHAPTER II

The Benjamin of the Academy

A<small>T THE</small> beginning of the year 1638 the happiness and tranquillity of this middle-class family were shattered by momentous events. When we look back at it across the centuries, the reign of Richelieu appears to have been an age of prosperity and renown. When we examine it more closely, we see that beneath the surface of a France ruined by wars and invasions the Fronde was hatching. Peasants, the nobility, the bourgeoisie were weary to the point of disgust and rebellion due to the iron rule of the Cardinal-Minister and of his merciless rigidity in the service of the State.

In the middle of the Thirty Years' War, the government needed gold to pay the armies which were fighting in Germany and to finance the plots which were being woven by Père Joseph. It resorted to the classic methods of money raising: increasing taxation, reducing the rate of interest on the national debt, converting loans and even failing to pay interest at all. Étienne Pascal thought himself ruined and was beside himself with rage. On 21st March he was present at a meeting at the Hôtel de Ville of four hundred investors in government securities who uttered strong threats against Chancellor Séguier and browbeat him. "They even did things which were rather violent and seditious", as Gilberte admitted.[1] Richelieu reacted like lightning. He had those primarily responsible arrested and imprisoned in the Bastille. Étienne Pascal fled in disguise to his native Auvergne. But the authorities took hostages and the police started to look for him. His children remained in Paris. They wondered how many years their father would have to live like a hunted man who was

[1] *G.E.*, I, p. 147.

lucky to have escaped imprisonment in the Bastille because no one knew how long it would be before the Cardinal's victims were released.

Étienne Pascal's Parisian friends were soon busy trying to obtain a pardon for him. It was more than a year before they succeeded.

In May it became known that the Queen was pregnant, which produced an immense surge of joy throughout the country. The succession to the throne seemed assured. People imagined that it removed the risk of civil war which had drenched the last years of the Valois in blood. Jacqueline was at once called upon to express the loyalty of the family to the throne in verse. She wrote this sonnet:

> Sus, réjouissons-nous, puisque notre princesse,
> Après un si long temps rend nos voeux exaucés
> Et que nous connaissons que par cette grossesse
> Nos déplaisirs sont morts et nos malheurs cessés.

> Que nos coeurs à ce coup soient remplis d'allégresse
> Puisque nos ennemis vont être renversés,
> Qu'un Dauphin va porter dans leur sein la tristesse,
> Et que tous leurs desseins s'en vont bouleversés.

> Français, payez vos voeux à la Divinité,
> Ce cher Dauphin, par vous si longtemps souhaité,
> Contentera bientôt votre juste espérance.

> Grand Dieu! je te conjure avec affection
> De prendre notre Reine en ta Protection
> Puisque la conserver, c'est conserver la France![2]

Come let us rejoice because our Princess,
After so many years, has provided an answer to our prayers,
And we know that by this pregnancy
Our anxieties are over and our unhappiness past.

---

[2] G.E., I, pp. 209–10. Was the poem written before March 1638 as Gilberte suggests (G.E., I, p. 145) or in May as the documents and the manuscript (ibid., p. 209) state? The date is of some importance as on it depends whether the poem was anterior or not to Étienne Pascal's flight.

With what joy our hearts are filled by the news
Since our enemies are about to be vanquished,
And a Dauphin will bring sorrow to their breasts,
And all their plans will collapse.

Frenchmen, pay tribute to the Divinity,
The dear Dauphin whom you have so long desired
Will soon fulfil your righteous hopes.

Great Lord! I call upon you with affection
To take our Queen under your Protection
Because to preserve her is to preserve France!

Her tribute to the future Louis XIV was no masterpiece, but the family eventually decided to present it to the Queen in the hope of obtaining a pardon for M. Pascal. "At that time", wrote Gilberte, "we were living quite close to Monsieur and Madame de Morangis [he was a *maître des requêtes* and a counsellor of state] who were so delighted by the charm of the child that scarcely a day passed without her going to their house. Mme de Morangis was enchanted to learn that she had written a poem on the royal pregnancy and said that she would like to take her to Saint-Germain so that she could present it to the Queen. She did in fact take her there and as the Queen was busy in her private apartments when they arrived everyone crowded round the little girl to ask her questions and see her poem. Mademoiselle [de Montpensier], who was still very young,[3] said to her: 'Since you write such good poems, do one for me'. Jacqueline withdrew very calmly into a corner and composed an epigram for Mademoiselle":[4]

> *Muse, notre grande Princesse*
> *Te commande aujourd'hui d'exercer ton adresse*
> *A louer sa beauté; mais il faut avouer*
> *Qu'on ne saurait la satisfaire,*
> *Et que le seul moyen qu'on a de la louer*
> *C'est de dire, en un mot, qu'on ne le saurait faire.*[5]

---

[3] She was eleven.   [4] *G.E.*, I, pp. 145-6.   [5] *Ibid.*, p. 212.

Muse, our great Princess
Bids you show your skill today
In praising her beauty; but it must be confessed
That you will not be able to satisfy her,
And that the only way of praising her
Is to say in one word that it cannot be done.

"Mademoiselle," adds Gilberte, "seeing that she had so soon
done, said to her: 'Write one for Madame d'Hautefort as well.'"[6]
Mme d'Hautefort was one of the great beauties of her time.
Jacqueline performed with grace:

> *Beau chef-d'oeuvre de l'univers,*
> *Adorable objet de mes vers,*
> *N'admirez pas ma prompte poésie.*
> *Votre oeil, que l'univers reconnaît pour vainqueur,*
> *Ayant bien pu toucher soudainement mon coeur,*
> *A pu d'un même coup toucher ma fantaisie.*[5]

Lovely masterpiece of the universe,
Adorable object of my verse,
Do not be surprised at the promptness with which I write.
Your eye, which the world recognizes as its conqueror,
Having suddenly touched my heart,
Was able at the same time to kindle my imagination.

They were then admitted to the Queen's presence. Jacqueline
was in no way intimidated by the sight of the fat, over-ripe
Spaniard plastered with jewels, whose features today evoke for
us those of Queen Victoria. She recited her lines. Anne of Austria
began by being sceptical about their authorship, but in order to
convince her she was shown the two improvisations which
Jacqueline had written in the antechamber. She made a great
fuss of the child who was presented to Louis XIII, smothered with
sweetmeats and kisses, admitted to the service of the Queen, but
on the subject of the girl's father they turned a deaf ear.

The friends of the family would not admit defeat. Jacqueline
wrote another poem on "the Queen feeling her child moving".
It was printed together with the earlier poem under the title of

[6] *G.E.*, I, p. 146.

Vers de la petite Pascal, 1638. The volume was sent to the Queen, but without result.[7]

In November 1638 the little girl fell ill with smallpox. Her father came to Paris to look after her without being discovered by the police. Jacqueline recovered, but her face was pitted like Mirabeau's. She thanked God for her recovery in lines in which from time to time we find a gleam of true poetry:

> *Ainsi l'on voit qu'en vérité,*
> *Grand Dieu! votre benignité*
> *S'est montrée en moi bien extrême,*
> *Me garantissant d'un péril*
> *Où sans votre bonté suprême*
> *Mes ans allaient finir dans leur plus bel avril.*[8]

> Thus we see that in truth,
> Great Lord! your benignity
> Towards me has been extreme,
> Saving me from a peril
> Where without your supreme goodness
> My life would have ended in its loveliest Spring.

After Jacqueline's convalescence, President Pascal's friends, particularly M. and Mme de Morangis, realized that they had started off on the wrong track by appealing to the King and Queen. The person whom they needed to win over was the Cardinal. They knew Mme d'Aiguillon, his niece. Thanks to her good offices, they organized some theatricals performed by children. Richelieu adored the theatre and had himself written seven tragedies. Jacqueline was chosen for the role of Cassandra in Scudéry's *L'Amour tyrannique*, and Mondory agreed to produce the play.

The performance, which was given at the Hôtel de Richelieu at seven o'clock in the evening beneath the blaze of the great candelabra, was a delicious occasion. The sight of the little boys and girls declaiming the *tirades*, in which emotional subtlety was mixed with preciosity, must have been enchanting.

Before the curtain rose Mondory had a long talk with Richelieu

[7] *G.E.*, I, p. 214.   [8] *Ibid.*, p. 219.

THE BENJAMIN OF THE ACADEMY

in which he warmly defended Étienne Pascal. When the audience had applauded the play the Cardinal rose to leave. Jacqueline, still wearing her stage costume, boldly left the group of little actors and with an address in verse in her hand went to meet him. "As soon as he saw me coming towards him," she said in a letter to her father, "he called out: 'Here's the little Pascal'. Then he put his arm round me and gave me a kiss and while I was reciting my poem he held me in his arms and kept kissing me with great satisfaction."[9] Here is the little girl's tribute:

> Ne vous étonnez point, incomparable Armand,
> Si j'ai mal contenté vos yeux and vos oreilles;
> Mon esprit, agité de frayeurs sans pareilles,
> Interdit à mon corps et voix et mouvement.
> Mais pour me rendre ici capable de vous plaire,
> Rappelez de l'exil mon misérable père.
> C'est le bien que j'attends d'une insigne bonté;
> Sauvez cet innocent d'un péril manifeste.
> Ainsi vous me rendrez l'entière liberté
> De l'esprit et du corps, de la voix et du geste.[10]

Do not be surprised, incomparable Armand,
If I have brought little satisfaction to your eyes and ears;
My mind disturbed by fears of which I have never known the like,
Froze body, voice and gesture.
But if you want to put me in a state to please you,
Bring my unhappy father back from exile.
That is the gift that I expect of your unparalleled goodness;
Save an innocent man from an evident danger.
In so doing you will restore completely my freedom
Of mind and body, voice and gesture.

Sainte-Beuve himself was forced to admit that for a child of her age the address was very prettily turned.

"He said to me," adds Jacqueline: "'There, there, I'll grant all you ask for. Write and tell your father that he can return in perfect safety.'[10] Whereupon Madame d'Aiguillon came up and said to the Cardinal: 'Monsieur, you really must do something for the poor man. I have heard people talk about him. He is a very worthy

⁹ G.E., I, p. 229.   ¹⁰ Ibid., p. 227.

person and very learned. It is a pity that no use is being made of him. He has a son who is marvellous at mathematics and who is still only fifteen.' When he heard this Monsieur le Cardinal told me again that I was to let you know that you could return in perfect safety. Since I found him in such a good humour, I asked whether he would permit you to go and pay your respects to him. He replied that you would be welcome and said: 'Tell your father that when he returns he is to come and see me.' And he repeated what he had said three or four times. . . . We were taken into a room where there was a magnificent collation consisting of dried fruits, fresh fruit, lemonade and such like. And in this room Mme d'Aiguillon made such a fuss of me that it passes belief."[11]

M. Pascal was at once told what had happened and hastened to Rueil where the Cardinal was staying. He was informed that he would not be received unless he brought his children with him. He came back with them. Richelieu welcomed him and congratulated him on having such a brilliant little daughter. Jacqueline recited a rather grandiloquent epigram. Étienne Pascal's fortune was made.

Richelieu was not popular with the friends of Port-Royal among whom Gilberte's memoirs were written because he had imprisoned Saint-Cyran in a dungeon at Vincennes. But this could not prevent her from recounting the splendid domestic triumph where Jacqueline is seen being fondled and embraced by the most powerful old gentleman in the world. They were the family's golden years.

At the end of 1639 Étienne Pascal learnt that he had been appointed by the government to a very senior administrative post. He had become commissioner deputed by His Majesty for the imposition and collection of taxes in Upper Normandy. He was taking up again the functions of an inspector of taxes which had brought wealth to his ancestors.

Normandy was in a state of open rebellion. Excessively heavy taxation had finished by exhausting the country and driving the inhabitants to exasperation. The armed mob of "bare-footed Jack-a-napes" had sacked the offices of the collector of taxes.

[11] G.E., I, pp. 229–30.

Richelieu had, as usual, retaliated savagely. De Gassion had been given the task of putting down the rising. On 2nd January 1640 soldiers entered Rouen with flags unfurled. In order to punish the townspeople they were compelled to billet the soldiery and pay a fine of one million eighty-five thousand *livres*. Séguier spoke of razing the Hôtel de Ville to the ground and actually had a few of the ringleaders executed. Then de Gassion and his army marched on Avranches where the bands of revolutionaries had assembled. The fighting was bloody and the repression savage. Prisoners were hanged.

When Étienne Pascal arrived at Rouen in a military truck he found a city in the grip of terror. The lower strata of the populace displayed towards him some of the hatred which had been roused by the iron hand of the central government. A contemporary has described him as "watching Rouen like a vampire and continually imposing new taxes on it".[12] On the other hand, the aldermen presented him, in the name of the city, by way of an Easter gift with a purse of silver counters stamped with the paschal Lamb which they had had specially struck.[13] For his post made Étienne Pascal one of the principal personages of the city. His children had joined him and they were all installed in a house in the Rue des Murs-Saint-Ouen.

Like Paris Rouen was a capital city with Gothic buildings, gabled and turreted houses, narrow tortuous streets, many of which had scarcely changed since the death of Joan of Arc.

The plight of the poor in these appalling times went side by side with the opulence of the cloth merchants. At Rouen, in particular, there was an endless swarm of excise officials, plaintiffs, barristers and judges who were perpetually involved in litigation which for the cantankerous Norman has a strange and irresistible attraction. Like Honoré de Balzac two hundred years later and in different circumstances, Blaise Pascal was to have an opportunity of observing at close quarters the world of lawyers and judges, spending the last years of his youth in the capital of the money-grubbing legal fraternity. Fortunately, there was quite

---

[12] According to Floquet. Cf. C. Urbain, "Un Épisode de la vie de Camus et de Pascal," in *Rev. Hist. Litt. de la France* (15th Jan., 1895).
[12] According to Marguerite Périer, *G.E.*, I, p. 21.

a vigorous intellectual life at Rouen. The administrative circles in which the King's representative moved for the purpose of levying taxes boasted an interest in poetry. A frequent visitor to the Pascals' drawing-room was a young barrister, Messire Pierre Corneille, who was at the height of his fame and who a short time previously had married the gentle Marie Lampérière. The cunning little Jacqueline, now fourteen years old, was thus able to make the acquaintance of her favourite poet. Less than a year after the Pascals had settled at Rouen, Corneille pushed her into competing for the Puis poetry prize, as he himself had competed seven years earlier.

This was the name used to describe the poetry festivals which were held every year on 8th December and which had originated in the fifteenth century. There were prizes for ballads and *stances* or "Palinodes" celebrating the glory of the Immaculate Conception of the Blessed Virgin. The prizes were a silver rose for the ballad and a silver tower for the *stances*. On 8th December 1640 Jacqueline won the tower for some violent lines against those who denied the Immaculate Conception. The Blessed Virgin is compared to the Ark which brought victory over the Philistines:

> *Exécrables auteurs d'une fausse créance,*
> *Dont le sein hypocrite enclôt un coeur de fiel,*
> *Jetez vos faibles yaux sur l'arche d'alliance*
> *Vous la verrez semblable à la Reine du Ciel . . .*[14]

Execrable inventors of a false belief,
Whose hypocritical breast contains a heart of gall,
Cast your feeble eyes on the Ark of the Covenant
And you will see that it resembles the Queen of Heaven.

Jacqueline was away from Rouen on prize-giving day. Corneille received the prize on her behalf in the Grand' Place to the sound of the music of drums and trumpets, and he improvised a message addressed to the Prince, the title he gave to the president of Le Puis:

> *Prince, je prendrai soin de vous remercier*
> *Pour une jeune muse absente,*
> *Et son âge et son sexe ont de quoi convier*

[14] G.E., I, p. 263.

A porter jusqu'au ciel sa gloire encore naissante.[15]

Prince, I shall take care to thank you
On behalf of a youthful muse who is absent,
Both her age and her sex are grounds which encourage
Us to raise to the skies her fame which is still growing.

The following year, in the Pascals' drawing-room, Corneille either read himself or got Mondory to read some scenes from *Cinna* and *Polyeucte*, the two plays on which he was working at the time. Blaise was one of the first to hear those stanzas (*stances*) which three hundred years later were to rouse the immense enthusiasm of Péguy. He retained a very lively memory of them. Apart from Homer and Martial, Corneille is the only poet who is quoted in the *Pensées*. Jacqueline more than anyone responded to the reading of this mystical poetry which carried her away. She had found her master as her brother was later to find his when reading Montaigne. In her few poems which are still readable she imitates Corneille.

In the drawing-room in the Rue des Murs-Saint-Ouen, Blaise Pascal met the pick of the girls of the Norman upper-middle class. He was invited to the Château de Gaillon, the home of Archbishop François de Harlay, who belonged to the inner circle of the Best People. As in Paris, the Pascals went to the popular fêtes at carnival time with its noisy fun and its masks, took part in the frequent religious processions, and in the celebrations of the guilds which expressed the heady provincial atmosphere by means of kermesses and Norman jollifications. The troupes from the Paris theatres came to Rouen in the course of their provincial tours. The Court went to Forges-les-Eaux. The Pascals wrote to their friends in Paris, to Mme Saintot, to Dalibray, to Le Pailleur.

Living with his comfortable pious family who enjoyed the favours of the King and the Cardinal-Minister, the young Pascal continued an education which was at once serious, worldly and Catholic. He learned to use Latin and Greek correctly and acquired the rudiments of theology which in those days represented the intellectual equipment of a cultured young Frenchman. He

[15] *G.E.,* I., p. 264.

read the Bible in a sixteenth-century folio edition, written in a crude, vigorous and archaic language which in substance went back to Lefèvre d'Étaples and more or less reproduced Pierre Olivetain's Protestant version.[16] He argued with his father about the authority of revelation to which his father submitted scrupulously in all matters pertaining to faith. They talked about the latest developments in science and philosophy: of René Descartes whose treatise on dioptics, preceded by a very exciting *Discours de la méthode*, had just been published. They exchanged views on Galileo's hypothesis. Did the stars which shone during the night high above the dark waves of the Seine revolve round the earth or not? And what were the relations between man and his fellows? Why did judges put on ermine to condemn the down-and-outs to death on the gibbet or the wheel in the market place? From time to time father and son betook themselves to Paris. Étienne Pascal was a member of several academies to which he introduced his young son.

Today, like the other branches of the Institute, the Academy of Sciences suggests a collection of gouty old gentlemen in green uniforms. In 1639, at the end of the reign of Louis XIII, there were some fifteen scientific academies in Paris, all at their peak like the sciences themselves, like French poetry and philosophy. Academies rather like Plato's, that is to say, consisting of free enquirers, amateurs who had replaced the garden of Athens by a salon or a study.

It is a pity that no one invited the young Rembrandt, who at that time was living near the Amsterdam ghetto in Joden Breestraat, to come and paint, as he had done for the Dutch aldermen, the group consisting of Père Mersenne, Bourdelot, Roberval, Petit, Gassendi, Le Pailleur, Fermat, the two Pascals and, tucked away in a corner, Descartes. He might have assembled a splendid gallery of serious, thoughtful faces round a table covered with compasses, sextants, retorts and fat tomes. First of all the astute features of Mersenne,[17] wearing the habit of the Friars Minor. The friar had a voracious appetite. He knew everybody,

---

[16] This was either the Bible known as the Louvain Bible which was reprinted in 1615, or that of R. Benoist. Cf. J. Lhermet, *Pascal et la Bible* (Paris, 1931), pp. 240ff.

[17] See R. Lenoble, *Mersenne ou la naissance du mécanisme* (Paris, 1943).

kept up an active correspondence with Descartes, Hobbes, Gassendi; acted as a sort of "post-box", a secretary to the learned world of Europe. He was informed about everything, wrote enormous folio volumes about everything: philosophy, exegesis, physics, ethics, mathematics, music, medicine. He foresaw the electric telegraph, the submarine (navis submarina), the aeroplane, the wand of the water-diviners and the ectoplasm of the spiritualists. He believed, naïvely, in ancient dragons, wondered whether spontaneous generation might not take place in warm sand, hoped to see in paradise Gyges' ring and discover the quadrature of the circle. He was a good mathematician who "possessed the special art of asking the right question", as Pascal was to say, who felt a deferential friendship for him tempered by a touch of irony.

Roberval, Professor at the Collège de France and an intimate friend of the Pascals, was an example of the tough, bohemian kind of scholar. He produced little and wrote badly. He detested Descartes, who reciprocated; their discussions always ended in squabbling.

The Abbé Bourdelot, a very curious person, appears to belong already to the eighteenth century and the age of the Encyclopaedia. He was an atheist doctor who moved in the most aristocratic circles, attached himself to the Prince de Conti, who was himself a man of very liberal views, and to Christina, Queen of Sweden, the daughter of Gustavus Adolphus, who persuaded Descartes to take up residence at her court.

Descartes was, with Blaise Pascal, the most celebrated member of the group which he visited when he was passing through Paris. He looked rather like a crafty peasant. Heavy featured, he gave an impression of dullness and obstinacy. He was touchily proud, disagreeable in his relations with people, and had a strong bent for algebra and mathematics. He thought himself infallible and could not bear to be contradicted, or to feel that anyone was ahead of him. Pascal distrusted him and though he was conscious of his genius, always sided with Roberval in their scientific arguments.

To the circle of Père Mersenne belonged Gassendi, a genuine philosopher though he was an opponent of Cartesianism, and an excellent astronomer; Girard Desargues of Lyons, a specialist in

architecture and geometry, who applied himself to the problem of
conic sections. Desargues was the master of the young Pascal who
was also an admirer of Fermat, a fat man with chubby cheeks,
long straight hair and the serious expression of a provincial judge.
Fermat was the greatest mathematician of the seventeenth century.
He lived at Toulouse where he worked as a magistrate. He
corresponded with Étienne Pascal, and later with Blaise. At
Mersenne's one would also have met Petit, inspector of fortifica-
tions, a former provincial commissioner of Artillery and Royal
engineer, who prided himself on his knowledge of physics, was a
successful experimenter, but a mediocre scientist.

Owing to its rather exaggerated enthusiasms, the circle of
academicians to which Étienne Pascal introduced his son was very
appealing. These learned men were bursting with optimism and
self-confidence. They flung themselves into their researches, were
beside themselves with excitement over the results and argued
about them in Latin, in French and in a jargon in which genuine
science mingled with astrology and occultism. From Holland to
Toulouse, from Lyons to Poland, from Sweden to Italy, there
was a stream of letters containing profound scientific problems or
childish magic. The scientists concealed their inventions because
patents did not exist. They invited one another to geometrical
jousts and mathematical duels. They asked one another questions
much as the Queen of Sheba had sent riddles to Solomon. They
argued over the least theorem with a bitterness reserved in our
own time for political differences. Science appears to have been
still bogged down by scholastic and occult terminology. Yet in
spite of all the uncertainties, what was at stake was nothing less
than the birth of modern science and its clearly mechanical
methods.

With the exception of Roberval all these gentlemen were self-
taught amateurs. Mersenne was a monk, Bourdelot and Gassendi
secular priests, Descartes a soldier, Fermat a judge and Étienne
Pascal a civil servant. Blaise himself will be a man of the same
stamp.[18] He will never be a professional in any of the sciences, still

---

[18] The leading work on the subject is P. Humbert, *Cet effrayant génie . . .
L'Oeuvre scientifique de Blaise Pascal* (Paris, 1947). It is also worth consulting the
catalogue of the exhibition at the Palais de la Découverte: *L'Oeuvre scientifique
de Blaise Pascal . . . et trois siècles après*, Paris, 22nd April till end of June 1950.

less in theology and literature. A man of the world who could talk about anything, but who had a horror of the pedantry of the learned. Thomassin, the leading scientific light of the Oratory, will say of him: "A young man with plenty of brains, but very ignorant." To which Pascal will reply: "There's a man for you who is terribly learned, but has hardly any brains."[19]

At the age of sixteen Blaise Pascal put his abilities to the test among these old fogies. The Benjamin of the Mersenne Academy soon showed his colleagues that he was someone with whom they had to reckon. He offered for discussion his *Essai pour les coniques*, which was printed in 1640 as a broadsheet on a single piece of paper. He stated clearly and simply the conclusions reached by Desargues, but added a new theorem which was named after him. He showed that the opposite sides of a hexagon inserted in the circumference of a circle meet at three points which are in a straight line. Then he went on to extend his theorem to any conic section. And he showed the gentlemen of the Academy that he could extract four hundred propositions from his theorem. With his first effort Blaise Pascal brought Desargues's calculations out of the clouds and perceived their remoter consequences.

During the years that followed he continued to work at this projective geometry, flung himself into the most complicated figures because his imagination enabled him to see things in space. P. Humbert has shown that in this field we had to wait for the brilliant discoveries of Poncelet at the beginning of the twentieth century before Pascal's work was continued in the way that he had continued the work of Desargues.[20]

Faced with this precocious genius, Mersenne was moved to admiration and Descartes grumbled.[21] But it was an accomplished fact. The beardless young geometer was recognized by his peers as a master.

P. Humbert shows that like all the scientists of his age Pascal was an amateur. "His works are works of circumstance " (p. 10). And he proves that Pascal always obtained from his entourage the statement of the problems which he set out to solve. This observation is not confined to his scientific work: it applies to everything he wrote.

[19] Remark by M. d'Etemare reported by Sainte-Beuve, *Port-Royal*, ed. L. Doyon and C. Marchesné (Paris, 1926), vol. III, p. 181 (footnote).

[20] P. Humbert, *op. cit.*, p. 47.

[21] "We shall look in vain in Descartes's letters for the least word of praise for anyone except Descartes himself" (P. Humbert, *op. cit.*, p. 41).

CHAPTER III

The Engineer and
Fashionable Lecturer

WHEN Étienne Pascal took up his appointment at Rouen,. he found himself saddled with a vast and wearisome task. In the same way as our own inspectors of taxes, he had to check the registers of taxes for all Normans. What complaints and appeals there must have been! Richelieu had chosen him not merely because he was a former member of the Cour des Aydes, who had dealt with taxation, but because of his ability as a mathematician. The President set to work with the customary determination of an Auvergnat.

He asked his son to help him with the interminable and complicated calculations of *sols*, *pistoles* and *livres*. The pair of them did their calculations by means of counters or a counting frame, and in the beginning used to sit up until two or three o'clock in the morning, working by candlelight in the gloomy rooms of the old house while the chimes of the city clocks and the shouts of the guards in the sleeping town fell on the freezing air. What a monotonous and mechanical labour! Did not the clocks perform the same sort of calculations in recording the hours? Blaise hit on the idea of a clockwork apparatus which would enable them to add and subtract by manipulating levers. He discussed the idea with his father, who thought it ingenious and encouraged him to try to construct a machine on those lines. As a journalist has remarked amusingly: "The calculating machine was born of filial love flying to the rescue of the tax man."[1]

Blaise executed a large number of drawings. It was the beginning of his long career as an engineer, for until the day of his death he

[1] P. Guth in *Le Figaro Littéraire* (12th July 1947).

28

remained passionately interested in the problems of mechanics. He constructed winches, gears, levers, with the result that legend, which only bestows gifts on the rich, credited him with the invention of the wheelbarrow which had come into use in the Middle Ages.

In Pascal's day an academician did not suffer any loss of status by becoming an engineer. Had not Archimedes in ancient times constructed catapults and mirrors for the defence of the embattled Syracuse? The learned amateurs of the seventeenth century did not fail to follow the example of this "prince of minds". Like Leonardo and Galileo they tried to turn their discoveries to practical use. In so doing they anticipated and prepared the way for the machine age. It was the source of interesting and harmless distractions which sometimes amused or startled them, and roused their enthusiasm as though they were overgrown children. Huyghens constructed clocks; Mersenne dreamed of submarines and Petit was soon to work himself up into a state of intense excitement over the diving bell.

For two years Pascal was completely absorbed by the construction of the calculating machine. The principle was perfectly simple: a few wheels with teeth moved one another. But the process of making them fit was decidedly complicated. For their construction Blaise used workmen to whom he showed his diagrams. In order to make them understand what he wanted, he had to get rid of learned jargon and return to the "bars" and "rounds" of his childhood, turn himself into a foreman. It was an exhausting task for a proud and irritable young man. How often, as he himself has told us, he had to stamp with his foot, raise his voice when he saw the blunders of his workmen, the unusable pieces of machinery, the broken or ill-made wheels. The very materials he used seemed to put up a resistance: the wheels smashed; the gears jammed; the teeth buckled. Blaise became a mechanic, sat up at night, strained his eyes, fumbled, argued, made mistakes, corrected them, but dug in and went on with his experiments. And in the end the day came when he was able to present his father triumphantly with the ebony box measuring fifteen by thirty centimetres which looked like a large-size glove box. On the lid was a series of wheels like the dial of an automatic telephone, and in front of them holes containing the numerals necessary for the calculations. The entire family were overcome by the same astonishment they had experienced years ago when the child discovered all by himself that the angles of a triangle are equal to the sum of two right angles. The new masterpiece, known as "the Pascale" or "the Pascaline", was publicly exhibited and the whole of fashionable society at Rouen filed through the President's drawing-room in order to try the machine. The young Pascal was on the verge of fame.

But he was not the sort of person to remain satisfied with the first sample. The demands that he made on himself were insatiable. His machine only had six numbers: he wanted eight. He started all over again. All his life he was to go on making fresh starts.

He tried new gears made of ivory and copper, went to the blacksmith's, watched fittings and would not leave the workshops. The President supported his son and provided the necessary funds. Pascal declared that during the space of two years he constructed more than fifty models of his calculating machine and tested its solidity by moving or banging it. He would only be satisfied with a strong, simple, perfect apparatus.

Then came the counterfeit products. Pascal has told the story of one of them with a slightly arrogant contempt:

I have seen with my own eyes one of these false products of my own idea, constructed by a workman of the City of Rouen, a clockmaker by profession. After being given a simple account of my first model which I had constructed several months previously, he was bold enough to attempt another and what is more with a different kind of movement; but since the fellow has no aptitude for anything except the skilful use of his own tools and does not even know whether there is such a thing as geometry or mechanics, the result was that (though very competent in his own line of business and very industrious in various ways unconnected with it) he simply turned out a useless object, nice enough to look at, to be sure, with its outside smooth and well polished, but so imperfect inside that it was no good for anything; but owing simply to its novelty it aroused a certain admiration among *people who knew nothing at all about such things*, and notwithstanding the fact that all the basic defects came to light when it was tested it found a place in the collection of one of the connoisseurs of this same city which was filled with rare and interesting things. The sight of this little abortion was extremely distasteful to me and so chilled the enthusiasm with which I was working at the time to perfect my own model that I dismissed all my workmen, fully intending to abandon the enterprise owing to the fear I rightly felt that others might set to work with the same boldness and that the spurious objects they might produce from my original thought would undermine both public confidence and the use that the Public might derive from it. But shortly afterwards the Lord Chancellor, who had done me the honour to inspect my first model, and express his admiration for my invention, urged me to perfect it; and in order to remove the fears which had been holding me back for some time, he was good enough to tackle the trouble at its source and prevent it from operating to the detriment of my reputation and to the disadvantage of the Public by his grace in bestowing a special licence that had the effect of smothering at birth these *illegal abortions*, which might be engendered otherwise than by the legitimate and necessary alliance of theory and practice.[2]

We feel the pronouncement bristling with the haughty pride of the young scientist who was sure of himself and of his "new idea".

Moreover, the calculating machine was something more for him than the mere exercise of his talents, or a caprice intended for the physics section of collectors of curiosities. If Pascal paid tribute to the Chancellor for obtaining a Royal Licence, that is to say, a patent, if he imposed his own trade mark in the form of his signature inside the case, it was because he intended to manufacture calculating machines in bulk and put them on sale.[3] He wanted to sell off the finished models.

The proof is to be found in a very curious paper. It is a commercial prospectus written in the purest publicity style and intended to attract customers. Pascal anticipates the customer's objections, starts a dialogue with him in which he addresses him in the familiar style, holds up to admiration the marvellous

[2] G.E., I, pp. 311–2 (*italics mine*).
[3] G.E., I, pp. 298 *et seq.* Cf. the photograph in P. Humbert, *op. cit.*, p. 16, Plate I, and the autograph dedication to Séguier in L. Brunschvicg, *Pascal* (Paris, 1932), p. 16, Plate IX.

qualities of his machine which is solid and durable and even able to stand up to the wear and tear of transport: "a simple, easy movement, convenient to open and quick to produce results". He suggests that the prospective purchaser might come and try it, thus using precisely the same sales technique as that used today by house-to-house salesmen of vacuum cleaners and radio sets.

> Those who are interested and wish to see the machine should apply to the Sieur de Roberval, Professor of Mathematics at the Royal College of France, who will demonstrate *quickly* and *without charge* the simplicity with which it works, will sell the machine and teach the purchaser how to use it.
>
> The said Sieur de Roberval lives at the Collège Maître Gervais, Rue du Foin, near the Mathurins. He is there until 8 a.m. every morning and all afternoon on Saturdays.[4]

In order to organize his sales campaign, Pascal also called upon the poet Dalibray, Le Pailleur's elderly companion, to compose a publicity sonnet. This was the result:

> Dear Pascal, you who understand with your subtle insight
> What is most admirable in mechanics,
> And whose skill gives us today
> A lasting proof of your marvellous genius,
>
> After your great intelligence, what is the point of having any?
> Calculation was the action of a reasonable man,
> And now your inimitable skill
> Has given the power to the slowest of wits.
>
> For this art we need neither reason nor memory,
> Thanks to you, each of us can do it without fame or pain
> Because each of us owes you the fame and the result.
>
> Your mind is like that fertile soul
> Which runs everywhere inside the world,
> And watches over and makes good whatever is lacking in all that is
> done.[5]

No compliment is too extravagant to stimulate sales, not even the comparison between Blaise Pascal's genius and the soul of the world.

[4] *G.E.*, I, p. 314.   [5] *Ibid.*, p. 295.

And in order to be sure of marketing the machine, the Pascal family relied on the solidarity of the Academy. In 1644 Bourdelot, who presided over the Academy which met at the Prince de Conti's, wrote to Blaise to make an appointment for him:

Monsieur,
    I spoke yesterday to His Highness who expressed his impatience to see your Pascal wheel. If you would care to come tomorrow at ten o'clock in the morning, I think that this would be the most convenient time for him. . . .[6]

What was still more important was that through the intermediary of Bourdelot, Blaise managed to make contact with the greatest intellect of all, Queen Christina of Sweden, who was barely older than himself. When, in 1652, he sent her one of his machines it was accompanied by a letter of dedication bursting with a radiant pride in which the absolute of genius expresses itself without modesty. Under cover of the conventional expressions of respect, Pascal compared scientists to monarchs.

    Unless I am mistaken . . . [the scientists] could pass for sovereigns. The same degrees are to be found between men of genius as between the conditions of men; and the power of kings over their subjects, or so it seems to me, is only an image of the power of minds over inferior minds on whom they exercise the right of persuasion which to them is what the right of command is to a government in politics. This second empire, indeed, seems to me to belong to an order which is all the loftier because minds belong to a higher order than bodies, and all the more equitable because it can only be distributed and preserved through merit whereas the other form of power may be the result of birth or wealth. It must therefore be admitted that each of these empires is great in itself; but, Madame, I hope that Your Majesty will allow me to say without offence that one form of power seems to me to be defective without the other. However powerful a sovereign may be, something is lacking in his renown if he does not display intellectual pre-eminence. . . .[7]

The calculating machine was a small thing compared with the strength of these declarations which dazzled Bourdelot and were the prelude to the profounder pages of the *Pensées* on the orders of greatness.

      [6] *G.E.*, I., p. 283.   [7] *G.E.*, III, pp. 30-1.

When, at the same period, in 1652, Pascal was going round Paris as a fashionable lecturer in the salons of the Duchesse d'Aiguillon and the Marquise de Sablé, he did not omit to give a demonstration of the famous calculating machine before delivering his lecture on physics. The strange machine therefore impressed the young man's name on everybody's mind. Huyghens described it in minute detail, as Diderot was to do a hundred years later in the *Encyclopaedia*. But if the inquisitive flocked to Roberval's, if a few amateurs enriched their collections by the acquisition of a Pascaline, the bona-fide purchasers moved slowly. The inspectors of taxes, who would have found it a great comfort in their work, considered it too dear—a hundred *livres* was quite a sum—and preferred to go on doing their calculations with counters or on their fingers.

As regards mechanics, Pascal was born too soon. His ideas outstripped the technical resources of his day. The great shortcoming of his machine was the excessive friction of the gears.[8] After his death his invention was perfected. Leibnitz devised a machine which was capable of multiplying and dividing. Today computers perform miracles of swiftness and perfection. But like Pascal's machine the only things they do not possess are initiative and will power.

[8] Cf. P. Humbert, *op. cit.*, p. 62.

CHAPTER IV

God and a Problem of Physics

B LAISE PASCAL was twenty-two years old when he finished
work on his calculating machine.

Morally, he had inherited from his father the obstinacy
and tenacity of the Auvergnat, a vast and enquiring mind which
seemed to re-create everything to which it was applied; but as
has been well said of this mind, in order to give of its best it had
to take as its starting-point a problem propounded by somebody
else.[1] For the time being it was applied almost exclusively to the
exact sciences and to experiment. But the young man felt the
feverish, joyous restlessness of youth when confronted with life.
What may well have intensified his restlessness was the precarious
state of his health: for the gifted, subtle and penetrating brain
had to reckon with the frayed nerves of a very highly strung
person, with the feminine element in his make-up which was
visible in his features. Blaise Pascal, however, had not yet
experienced genuine physical suffering. His childhood and
adolescence had been happy and cosseted. The infant prodigy
had made one discovery after another. Life appeared to him to
spout upwards like a magic display of new and fresh ideas. He
was violently conscious of the joys of knowing and feeling.

God, who would one day become sole master of this splendid
life which had begun with salons, mathematics and triumphs to
the applause of the exponents of preciosity and the Academicians,
had remained up to this point almost silent. Now he intervened
suddenly in the turn taken by events which in themselves were
commonplace.

One day in the winter of 1645 Commissioner Pascal learnt that

[1] P. Humbert, *op. cit.*, p. 32.

two of his friends were about to fight a duel. He decided to go to the place of the duel in the hope of bringing about a reconciliation. His carriage was unusable owing to the frost. The coachmen had no frost shoes for the horses. The President wrapped himself up and left the house on foot. A few moments later people passing in the street saw him fall and brought him back home, supporting him, for he was unable to walk properly. The fall in the slippery street had caused intolerable pains in the thigh. M. Pascal gave as the names of the doctors who were to attend him two noblemen, the brothers Deslandes and de la Bouteillerie, who had studied surgery, were believed to be very gifted as bone-setters and had built a small hospital on their estate. As they were not at their Paris home, a carriage was sent to their country estate to fetch them. They arrived late; the fracture was serious, the patient an old man, and the treatment lasted three months.

The two doctors were ardent Christians. When they had become intimate acquaintances of the Pascal family, they told the family that there was in the neighbourhood a sort of Curé d'Ars, M. Guillebert, a former professor of philosophy. His reputation and preaching attracted large crowds to his little parish of Rouville where Blaise and Jacqueline probably went to hear him preach.

MM. Deslandes and de la Bouteillerie described the astonishing conversion of M. Guillebert under the influence of Duvergier de Hauranne, titular Abbot of Saint-Cyran, who had died two years earlier after being detained for many years in the Bastille on the orders of Richelieu.[2] The Abbé de Saint-Cyran, they said, was an extraordinary ascetic, a splendid spiritual director whose memory had profoundly coloured the minds of his disciples. In

[2] On Jean Duvergier de Hauranne, Abbé de Saint-Cyran (1581–1643), the only study until recently was the thesis of J. Laferrière, *Étude sur . . .* (Louvain, 1912). H. Bremond in his *Histoire littéraire du sentiment religieux . . .* appeared to throw fresh light on the subject. It was not in fact done until the publication of J. Orcibal, *Jean Duvergier de Hauranne, abbé de Saint-Cyran, et son temps* (Louvain-Paris, 1947). The same author has recently published a little book called *Saint-Cyran et le jansénisme* in the series "Maîtres Spirituels". Reference may also be made to the *Mémoires* of Lancelot and to the writings of Saint-Cyran of which there is unfortunately no critical edition. Orcibal has revealed the political aspects of the problem and the connection between Saint-Cyran and Bérulle. The most interesting is the Saint-Cyran of the first period who had a profound intuition amounting at times to genius of some of the deepest truths which the Catholic Church of our own day is in the process of rediscovering.

collaboration with his friend Jansen, Bishop of Ypres, he had brought the theology of St Augustine back to life in the Church and converted the celebrated barrister Antoine Lemaître. They spoke of Mme Angélique Arnauld, Abbess of Notre-Dame de Port-Royal du Saint Sacrement, of the recent book by her young brother, M. Antoine Arnauld, on *Frequent Communion*. The Pascals read Arnauld's book and also Duvergier de Hauranne's *Lettres chrétiennes et spirituelles*. They told one another that until then they had not really understood Christianity. They had paid too much attention to worldly cares; they were *bien pensants*, went regularly to Mass, did their Easter duties and listened to sermons with wandering attention, but left theological subtleties to the doctors of theology, and prayer to nuns. Now, when he read Saint-Cyran and Arnauld, Blaise realized that some men watched the movements of their soul with the same meticulous precision that he had applied to the regulation of the wheels of his calculating machine. He must read the Bible and the writings of the Fathers of the Church with the same care: St Augustine, St John Chrysostom, St Bernard. He borrowed their works and discussed them with his father. He may even at this time have looked through Jansen's *Augustinus*. What had Jansen done? he was asked. Nothing except systematize St Augustine's teaching on Grace. This *summa* of the central dogma of Christian life seen through the great authority of ecclesiastical tradition was destined to play the same role, or so Pascal's friends thought, as the *Summa* of St Thomas in the middle ages.

To these authors, Blaise and Jacqueline Pascal added the theologians of the mystical life: St Francis de Sales, Cardinal de Bérulle, founder of the French Congregation of the Oratorians, and Père de Condren, who enjoyed a great reputation. They came to know M. Vincent de Paul and the whole group of reformers who had had a profound impact on Catholic life in the France of Louis XIII. Never before had Blaise examined the mysteries of his faith with such care.

By the spring of 1646 something had already changed in the family of the Commissioner of Taxes. They went to fewer dances; they paid less attention to clothes and fine poetry. They discussed theology. Life took on the slightly solemn air that is found in so many provincial families in which the father, accompanied by his children, is a regular attendant at the offices at the parish church and goes to the meetings of some pious confraternity. At home Jacqueline began, with the fervour of a twenty-one-year-old, to lead the life of a religious. She who was so proud, so ardent, so sensitive, had found without realizing it the path that she was seeking: the surrender of self, sacrifice, humility. The girl with the heart of a Cornelian heroine found her heart mysteriously expanding in the life of prayer. She refused an offer of marriage.

But the family who had been converted to the somewhat rigid piety of the Curé of Rouville went on discussing mathematics and science more intensely than ever. During the summer they were visited by Petit, an old friend of the President's, who was passionately interested in astronomy and physics. He came from Paris and was going on to Dieppe. One Shrove Tuesday, some two years earlier, a warship called the *Sénégalais* had sunk in the entrance to the harbour after an explosion caused by a careless sailor who had lighted his pipe too near to the powder magazine. The submerged wreck of the *Sénégalais* contained 40,000 *écus*. Now a Marseillais, one Jean Pradine, had invented an "underwater vessel" with the aid of which it was possible "to stay for six hours under water with a lighted candle" and so to search wrecks. Pradine had begun work in the harbour of Dieppe. The new invention was discussed at the Pascals'. What prevented water from getting into the diving bell? Could you go down to any depth without the atmospheric pressure in the vessel increasing and upsetting the diver? M. Petit was dying to be present at the experiment.

He brought other news. In Italy a scientist, whose name he no longer remembered, he said, had performed a curious experiment. By turning a long tube filled with mercury upside down in a basin, he had seen the column of mercury move downwards. The space at the top appeared to be empty. Père Mersenne had been present at the experiment, but on his return to Paris had been unsuccessful when he tried to repeat it. He had therefore dropped the whole business without even bothering to let his friend Descartes know about the phenomenon, but Pierre Petit was anxious to try the experiment again. The Pascals, father and son, were highly intrigued. The President believed in the possibility of the vacuum. That in itself was an original view. It is difficult today to realize that the problem of the existence of the vacuum could have aroused such passionate argument in the seventeenth century, but metaphysics appeared to be involved, as it was to be again two hundred years later in the problem of spontaneous generation and in our own time in the splitting of the atom. In 1646 no philosopher would admit that the existence of empty space was even possible because they all confused the vacuum with the void. The learned went so far as to claim that rather than permit an interstitial vacuum in nature, the skies would fall.[3] Descartes himself shared this view.

The few original partisans of the possibility of a vacuum like Roberval, Petit, Mersenne and the two Pascals had only the vaguest notion of the amount of empty space that could be produced and were completely unaware of the effects of atmospheric pressure.

Petit had to leave for Dieppe. On his return the experiment was tried. Rouen possessed a large glass factory situated at the junction of the Rue des Prés and the Rue de la Pie-aux-Anglais. The party went to the factory to have a tube blown—it was called a blow-pipe—of the width of man's little finger, four feet long, and hermetically sealed at one end. When the tube was ready, the three friends obtained fifty pounds of mercury from the grocer at a cost of forty-five *sols* a pound. They then returned to the glass manufacturer. Petit made a funnel of cardboard and with infinite precaution filled his tube with mercury. He put the remainder of the metal into a large wooden vat, covered the mercury in the vat with water, then applied his middle finger to the opening of the mercury-filled tube and very slowly, with his cuffs rolled up while several assistants were holding the fragile tube by its middle and top to prevent it from breaking, he balanced it in the vat. When the opening of the tube came into contact with the mercury in the vat, Petit took away his finger and at once "we saw", he wrote, "the mercury move downwards and leave the top of the tube, not all at the same time or in a moment nor

[3] A statement reported by Gassendi, quoted by F. Strowski, *Pascal et son temps*, 7th ed. vol. II (Paris, 1921), p. 63, n. 1.

too slowly either, but like the water you pour from a ewer and, most admirable of all, it went down by more than eighteen inches, which is an extraordinary amount and something I would never have believed."[4]

Everyone began to discuss the experiment. Blaise, who was immensely intrigued, declared: "The simple-minded—we would call them imbeciles—might say that the space which appeared empty contained air that in order to avoid the vacuum had penetrated the glass, entering by means of the pores." "But," retorted Petit, "why does not more of it get in? Why has not all the mercury in the tube fallen into the vat if air could get into the blow-pipe through the pores of the glass?"

They decided to go on with the experiment. "After we had watched the apparent or genuine vacuum for a long time with astonishment and had measured and marked the blow-pipe, I lifted it gently by the top," wrote Petit, "and strange to relate the vacuum became larger still . . . ."[5]

Finally, Petit raised his tube so much that the opening came into contact with the layer of water lying on the mercury in the vat and the water rushed into the blow-pipe.

There was one thing which the gentlemen found particularly fascinating: the constancy of the height of the mercury in the tube. Étienne Pascal and Petit declared "that nature could not allow a greater vacuum". They realized almost at once that they had just said something silly because if you raised the tube the vacuum became larger though the level of the mercury remained the same.

The following day Pierre Petit was obliged to return to Paris, leaving Blaise Pascal in the grip of a problem which was more difficult than the problems of geometry because the solution did not depend on reason alone. The young man repeated the experiment on his own account in order to be sure that he was fully aware of the precise implications of the problem.

All through the winter he applied himself simultaneously to improvements in the calculating machine, lectures on the experiments with the tube, and theological works. For he was studying theology. More than that, at the end of the winter of 1646 he found an opportunity of testing his abilities in what was for him a

[4] *G.E.*, I, p. 334.   [5] *Ibid.*, p. 335.

new field. At Rouen there was talk of a former Capuchin named Forton, Sieur de Saint-Ange, who was advocating a somewhat novel form of theology. Saint-Ange was self-taught, intelligent, but inclined to take risks and rather woolly-minded. He claimed to prove the dogma of the Trinity and other Christian mysteries by reason alone. On 1st February there was a debate at the home of de Montflaines, a King's counsellor, to which Forton was invited. Pascal and his young friends were scandalized by some of his views. "He said that a mathematician was more or less able to estimate the number of men who would have lived in the world from the beginning to its end",[6] and could do so by estimating the amount of chemical substance that terrestrial matter would provide for the purpose of reconstructing their bodies at the Resurrection. On the idea of substance, he put forward certain philosophical views which in a sense anticipated those of Leibnitz. When asked about the probable duration of the world, his answers were very sensible and today seem shrewd and well thought out, but these fertile intuitions were submerged in an obscure jumble of words. As soon as he was back home, Pascal proceeded to make a rough calculation of the number of men according to the theories of Forton. He reached the conclusion that humanity would last about four billion years. Now, Forton had claimed that the birth of Christ had taken place half-way through time. In the course of a second debate the young men raised the objection that "it followed that the period between the creation of the world and the birth of Jesus Christ must have lasted two thousand million years."[7] To which Forton replied, very appositely and very sensibly, that the number of years of the creation was not clear and that on this point the Bible was obscure. But he put forward other views which were more shocking, so much so that the young men accused him of heresy to Mgr de Harlay, Archbishop of Rouen. Harlay's auxiliary was the famous Camus, an ecclesiastical novelist, a good fellow with a florid and Salesian cast of mind. When he found himself in charge of the case he tried to suppress it.[8] But Étienne Pascal refused to stand for that.

[6] G.E., I, p. 381. Cf. E. Jovy, Pascal et Saint-Ange (Paris, 1927).
[7] Ibid., p. 400.
[8] Documents in V. Cousin, Blaise Pascal (Paris, 1849), pp. 379–92.

He supported his son and in spite of the disapproval of a good many of the parish priests of Rouen, who thought that too much fuss was being made over nothing, he was unyielding. Forton had to sign a retraction which the archbishop transmitted to the people of his diocese. Camus wrote a letter to the archbishop of which the first sentence is a perfect portrait of the man: "My pen is a dove bringing an olive branch in its beak."[9]

This story, in which Pascal displayed the passion of an inquisitor, shows that he had inherited the aggressive, litigious attitude of his ancestors who had been jurists and judges; it is also a sign of the seriousness and the arrogance of his theological convictions as well as his ability to turn suggestions made by his opponents to good account. The debate with Forton taught him the importance of reconciling in theology truths which appear contradictory and of presenting the dogma of original sin in a way which would not shock the unbeliever. Later on, when he was with M. de Rebours, he too wanted to prove the truth of the mysteries by pure reason.

In the spring Pascal became ill. The nights that he had sat up working on the calculating machine, the mental concentration required by his experiments and researches in the field of physics, his theological studies, his religious practices and his social contacts had overstrained him. He suffered from intolerable stomach pains accompanied by violent migraines.[10] It was the beginning of a cancer or the first symptoms of a cerebral lesion whose origins were probably tubercular and hereditary. Blaise Pascal had started his apprenticeship in physical torture. The treatment he prescribed for himself was energetic: riding on horseback through the flowering orchards of Normandy, playing tennis and amusing himself. His migraines disappeared, then returned. It is amazing to see with what energy and drive the young man pressed on with his work despite his physical sufferings. He went to Paris with his sister Jacqueline who acted as nurse. When he was there he saw Roberval. They both heard that Père Magny, a Capuchin

---

[9] V. Cousin, *op. cit.*, p. 391.
[10] The best studies of Pascal's illnesses are those by Dr. P. Just-Navarre in the *Mémoires de l'Académie des Sciences, Belles-Lettres et Arts de Lyon*, 3rd series, vol. XI, 1911, pp. 295–405, and of R. de Sinéty, "La Maladie de Pascal," in *Études sur Pascal* (Paris, 1923), Archives de Philosophie, vol. I, cahier III.

who had taken refuge in Poland, had just published a pamphlet on the experiments with the vacuum, and Père Mersenne was able to tell them that the name of the Italian scientist mentioned by Petit who had carried out the first experiment was Torricelli. At the end of September Roberval published an account in Latin of Pascal's experiments at Rouen.[11]

A few days later, on Monday, 23rd September, at ten o'clock in the morning, Descartes paid a visit to Pascal who was still sick. Roberval was present. He showed the philosopher the calculating machine, and did some additions and subtractions with it. Descartes admired the invention, then went on to talk about the vacuum. "Monsieur Descartes, when asked what he thought had penetrated the tube, looked very serious and replied that it was some sort of subtle matter. . . ."[12] Pascal made a non-committal answer, but Roberval became heated and embarked on a vigorous defence of the possibility of the vacuum.

"I will talk to M. Pascal because he discusses things reasonably," answered Descartes, "but not with you because you are prejudiced".

Then, seeing from his watch that it was noon, he took his leave as he was dining in the Faubourg Saint-Germain. But Roberval refused to let go and Descartes had to take him with him in his carriage. "There", says Jacqueline, "they upbraided one another, but too heatedly for it to be treated as a game, or so I judged from what M. Roberval told us when he returned here after dinner where he found Monsieur Dalibray."[13]

The following morning Descartes, who was proud of his medical knowledge, paid another visit to Pascal which lasted three hours, so that he could examine him. He advised prolonged rest and soups. After the discussion Jacqueline made her brother have a hot bath:

He found that it gave him a slight headache, but that was because the water was too hot; and I think that having his foot bled on Sunday evening did him good because on Monday he talked vigor-

[11] G.E., II, pp. 21–35.
[12] Letter from Jacqueline Pascal, G.E., II, p. 43. (*Matière subtile* is a technical term of Cartesian philosophy.– *Trans.*)
[13] *Ibid.*, p. 44.

ously all day long, in the morning to Monsieur Descartes and after dinner to Monsieur Roberval with whom he argued for a long time about many matters relating as much to theology as to physics; and yet it had no ill-effect except to make him perspire a great deal during the night and prevented him from getting much sleep, but he did not have the headaches that I expected would follow the exertion.[14]

When Descartes called on him, Pascal already had the manuscript of his first work in his drawer, for we can hardly count the page he wrote on conic sections. The title of the work was a long one: *New Experiments relating to the Vacuum, carried out with tubes, syringes, bellows and siphons of several different lengths and shapes with different liquids such as quicksilver, water, wine, oil, air, etc. with a Treatise on the same subject in which it is shown that a Vessel as large as it can be made may be emptied of all the matters known to nature and the senses and what Power is necessary to produce the Vacuum. Dedicated to Monsieur Pascal, King's Counsellor in his Councils of State and in Private by Sieur B. P. his Son.* The little work was published in October by a publisher with this delightful imprint: "In Paris by Pierre Margat, Quai de Gèvres, at the Bird of Paradise".

Pascal describes Torricelli's experiment briefly, then the experiment at Rouen in company with Pierre Petit. He states that the philosophers were not convinced:

> The strength of their prejudices drove them to raise other objections which took away [from the experiment] the credence it deserved. Some said that the upper part of the blow-pipe was full of spirits of mercury; others of an imperceptible quantity of rarefied air; others, of a matter *which only existed in their imagination;* and all of them, conspiring to banish the vacuum, laid great stress on that power of the mind known in the Schools as subtlety which, when it comes to solving real difficulties, can only offer vain words without substance . . . .[15]

Le Tenneur, a lawyer who corresponded with Mersenne and a friend of Périer's, was rougher still and treated the vain words as "twaddle".

[14] G.E., II, pp. 45-6.   [15] Ibid., p. 59.

Pascal combined scientific prudence with a sense of humour. If he described his experiments in a clear style, he was careful not to exaggerate the results. He had proved the existence of the vacuum: that was all. In order to procure a vacuum it was necessary to overcome a power. Since it could not be more closely defined, he called it nature's abhorrence of the vacuum. But he made some important observations. The abhorrence was not "greater when it came to admitting a larger rather than a smaller vacuum". Moreover, it was strictly limited. Before Descartes, Pascal divined that atmospheric pressure caused the column of mercury to rise in Torricelli's "tube", but it still had to be proved. That was what he intended to do. It was a splendid undertaking for a twenty-four-year-old physicist.

CHAPTER V

The First Jesuit

AT A TIME when he was on the point of discovering the existence of atmospheric pressure and understanding why the level of the column of mercury remained constant in Torricelli's tube, Pascal met his first Jesuit.

The Jesuits played a large part in the intellectual life of France. Their schools had produced among others Pierre Corneille and René Descartes. One of their most eminent scholars and philosophers was Père Noël. He had been professor of philosophy at La Flèche and was now Rector of the College of Clermont, the present Lycée Louis-le-Grand. A man of advanced years, not a bad fellow and not entirely stupid, he was a characteristic example of a type of mind which is still with us, which wraps up its scholasticism in a learned jargon and claims that the findings of Einstein and Freud really support Aristotle. When he read Pascal's book on the vacuum, it never for a moment occurred to the good father to modify his own pronouncements. Without contesting the results of the experiments, he tried adroitly to interpret them in the light of his own philosophy. The Jesuit, however, was to discover that, unfortunately for him, he had stumbled on an exceptionally tough opponent.

Père Noël decided to write an open letter to Pascal. According to the Jesuit, it was the purified air of the igneous spirits which penetrated the top of Torricelli's tube. The pores of the tube served as a filter! And let us enjoy the reverend father's idea of a definition: "Light, or rather illumination, is a luminary movement of rays composed of transparent bodies which are only moved in luminary fashion by other transparent bodies."

Pascal was to immortalize this absurd statement. His reply was a marvel of clarity. It bore all the marks of his youthful genius which was faithful to the Cartesian method of reasoning: a refusal to indulge in verbiage, the art of drawing comparisons, the rigorous application of principles. In the clear, simple language of an educated man, he exposes the *petitio principii* of the Jesuit father. Père Noël replied. He thanked Pascal for his letter which was "truly learned, clear and courteous", but quite impenitently returned to his thesis on the mixture of elements which make up the composition of air. Never had an Aristotelian provided such entertaining examples of sheer lunacy. The Jesuit concluded, triumphantly, that what penetrated the top of Torricelli's tube was Descartes's "subtle matter". What is more, he went over to the offensive and poured ridicule on Pascal's vacuum. "It is a space", he said, "which is neither God, nor creature, nor body, nor mind, nor substance, nor accident. . . ." The good father was confusing the vacuum with non-being.

When Père Noël replied he was ill like Pascal himself and he asked his correspondent not to send a further reply, but to wait until they were both better so that they could meet and discuss the problem.

It was at this time that Pascal began to write a *Traité du vide*, which he never finished. All that we have is a draft preface which is a genuine masterpiece. In it he bestows on the infant experimental science its credentials. He distinguishes between those theories which depend on reason and experiment: "Geometry, arithmetic and music [i.e., acoustics], physics, medicine, architecture and all the sciences",[1] and those which depend on evidence: "History, geography [in so far as it is the science of place names], jurisprudence, languages and theology."[2] He settles his account with the physics of Aristotle and at the same time claims that he is true to the Aristotelian method: "What could be more unjust than to treat the ancients with more restraint than they displayed towards their predecessors, and to show them an inviolable respect which they only deserve from us because they did not show it to those who enjoyed the same advantage over them."[3] Against the old Jesuit and the entire Sorbonne he uses the argument of progress in the sciences:

[1] *G.E.*, II, p. 132.   [2] *Ibid.*, p. 130.   [3] *Ibid.*, pp. 135–6.

By reason of a special prerogative, not only each man advances from day to day in the sciences, but . . . all men collectively are constantly making progress as the universe grows older because precisely the same thing occurs when one generation succeeds another as at the different periods in the life of the individual. So that succeeding generations of men in the course of so many centuries should be regarded as though they were a single individual who goes on living and who is always learning, which explains how wrong it is for us to respect antiquity in the persons of its philosophers . . . . Those whom we call the ancients were truly original in everything and, properly speaking, represented the childhood of humanity; and since we have added to their knowledge the experience of the centuries which followed them, it is in us that will be found the antiquity which we revere in others.[4]

On his sickbed Pascal became the witness and one of the architects of what was to become the great Western myth: the myth of Progress. But he avoided the confusions of the nineteenth-century thinkers and was careful to distinguish between the positive sciences and traditional morality. He did not, for instance, fall into the crude errors of Auguste Comte, Taine and Renan. In 1848 Renan advanced this fatuous proposition: "In a hundred years humanity will know more or less everything that it can know about its past. Then it will be time to stop."[5] Taine compares man to bees and silkworms: "We may regard man as a superior animal who produces philosophies and poems in much the same way that silkworms produce cocoons and bees their hives."[6]

Pascal had already answered them in advance: "Bee-hives were just as well proportioned a thousand years ago as they are today. . . . Nature shows them the way to the extent that they are under pressure of necessity . . . . It provides the necessary knowledge, which is always the same, for fear that they [the animals] may fall into a decline, and does not allow them to add anything lest they exceed the limits that it has laid down for them. It is not the same with man who has only been *produced for infinity*."[7]

[4] *G.E.*, II, pp. 139–41.
[5] E. Renan, *L'Avenir de la science* (Paris, 1890), Preface, p. xiv.
[6] H. Taine, *La Fontaine et ses fables*, 23rd ed. (Paris, 1922), p. v.
[7] *G.E.*, II, p. 138.

Far from regarding progress as something predetermined, Pascal sees it as the beginning of a vocation for the infinite.

Six months later, in May 1648, the same infinite turns up on the lips of Roberval. Descartes had returned from the Hague. Under the aegis of Mersenne he made up his quarrel with Gassendi. In the course of meetings at the house of the Abbé d'Estrée, they discussed the problem of the vacuum. Torricelli's experiment was repeated in the presence of Descartes. Roberval was also present. The gentlemen proceeded to debate the composition of matter. Descartes showed himself a partisan of ether or "subtle matter". Gassendi preached the existence of indivisible atoms. Roberval, on the other hand, reflected the views of Pascal, attacked Descartes "not merely on the question of the vacuum . . . but also on the question of atoms, which he rejected, and matter which he took to be infinitely divisible."[8]

Pascal continued to wrestle with the problem of why the mercury remained suspended in Torricelli's tube. He became convinced that the cause of the phenomenon was atmospheric pressure. He wrote to his brother-in-law, Périer, to ask him to perform a definitive experiment which Mersenne and Roberval had advised him to carry out, declaring at the same time that in their view the results would be negative. What he proposed was that the height of the mercury should be measured simultaneously in a tube at Clermont and another on the heights at Puy de Dôme. If there were a difference in the level, it would be proof of the effect of atmospheric pressure. The preparations took ten months. During this time Descartes, who was in Holland, had installed a barometer containing mercury in his room and noted that the height of the column varied according to the weather.

While the debates about the vacuum were going on, Pascal did not forget God. On 26th January 1648, he wrote the strangest of letters to his sister Gilberte, reporting a conversation he had had earlier that day. He told her that he had been to see M. de Rebours, a penitent of Saint-Cyran's and spiritual director of the nuns of Port-Royal de Paris, a fine man of fifty of whom Besoigne said that "he underwent what the Abbé de Saint-Cyran called the

[8] Baillet according to *G.E.*, II, p. 204.

perfect novitiate in that he abandoned all secular studies and put aside everything that he had learnt earlier in the world".[9] M. de Rebours received Pascal with great courtesy and discussed apologetics with him. "I told him", Pascal wrote to his sister, "that I thought that by following the principles of common sense, it would be possible to prove many things which the opponents [of Jansen's theology] maintain are contrary to it and that careful reasoning led one to believe them though they must be believed without the aid of reason."[10] There is already something of the *Pensées* in this pronouncement. Pascal's idea was to go back to the method of Forton, Sieur de Saint-Ange. He saw the possibility of proving the dogma of original sin from the wretchedness of man. To his great surprise, M. de Rebours showed little enthusiasm for his views. He was afraid of any form of polemic because he belonged to the tranquil minds at Port-Royal who disliked controversy and the mass of printed paper which was at once the glory and the misfortune of the celebrated monastery. "Reasoning", he said to Pascal in effect, "is no more than a form of vanity. It leads to pride. You are too much of a geometer!"

Pascal protested and the priest interpreted his protestations as obstinacy. In short, "the entire conversation took place in this equivocal atmosphere and in a state of embarrassment which was the same at all the other [meetings] and which it proved impossible to remove."[11] M. de Rebours had doubts about Pascal's conversion. If Pascal were really converted, he thought, why did he not give up mathematics and physics, and why was he so interested in theology instead of humbling himself and praying? Now Pascal was conscious of his strength and was certain that he was right. He wanted to engage in controversy and thought himself capable of convincing other people. M. de Rebours probably quoted the Gospel parable of the two blind men to him. The young man was deeply distressed and disturbed by it. He admitted his confusion to his sister in a page filled with bitter disappointment:

[9] *Histoire de l'abbaye de Port-Royal, II, Histoire des Messieurs*, vol. IV (Cologne, 1752), pp. 206–7. It appears from a recent note by M. J. Mesnard that M. de Rebours had a very well stocked library.

[10] *G.E.*, II, p. 174.   [11] *Ibid.*, p. 175.

I have become still more conscious of my complete incapacity since the visits of which we have spoken, and far from finding ways of bringing light to others, I came from them in a state of trouble and confusion that God alone can cure and at which I will work conscientiously, but without worrying and without rushing into it, knowing that either of these things would take me further from my objective. . . .

What follows becomes still graver:

I tell you that God alone can give me calm and that I will apply myself to it because I find nothing but occasions for giving rise to this trouble and increasing it in those to whom I looked for reassurance in ridding myself of it; so that finding myself thrown back on my own resources, it only remained for me to pray to God to bless me with success.[12]

This was the first of Pascal's confidences about religion and it is tantamount to admitting that he was going through a spiritual crisis. He was reduced to a state of interior solitude and seemed to have no confidence in anyone except his elder sister who was living far away from him.

Why did he not turn to Jacqueline? It was because he realized that she was moving in a very different direction from his own. She had found that her path lay in pure and simple renunciation. She had decided to become a nun. For her everything was clear. Hers was a joyful soul; she sacrificed her poetic gift without a qualm.

Nevertheless, brother and sister sought one another out in order to read together Monsieur de Saint-Cyran's long letter to the Abbé du Hamel dealing with "the dispositions for the priesthood". It is an admirable treatise of three hundred pages which expresses the moving doctrine of the priesthood that was being preached at the time by Père de Bérulle, Condren, the Oratorians and the Sulpicians according to which every priest is an image of Jesus Christ whose perfection it is his duty to reproduce. The letter concludes with a moving comparison between the priest and the Blessed Virgin.

[12] G.E., II, p. 173.

But it needed more than this to take Pascal away from his scientific work. He wore himself out on the job. In February and March 1648 he prepared from a distance the Puy de Dôme experiment and wrote a treatise on conic sections. He learnt that the friends of Père Noël were claiming that he had come round to the Jesuit's views and that they had arranged the publication of a book by Père Noël entitled the *Plein du vide* ("The Fullness of the Vacuum"), a copy of which was sent to him. He began work·on his reply. The Jesuit could not be taken seriously. Pascal decided to put an end to the controversy by an open letter and chose Le Pailleur, the old family friend, as the correspondent to whom it would be addressed. He was busy sharpening a formidable weapon. The letter to Le Pailleur was the first of the *Provincial Letters* dealing not with "proximate power", but with the existence of the vacuum.

Père Noël, writes Pascal, has confused the *definition* of the vacuum with the statement that it exists. He is woolly-minded and unable to distinguish "dimensions from matter or non-being from the vacuum". He goes on to discuss in turn each of the views attributed to him by the Jesuit. Noël's account of the experiments is judged without indulgence. The Jesuit is writing about experiments that he has not seen. His account is inaccurate; he is guilty of blatant confusion; he makes himself ridiculous and what he says is in bad taste.

Blaise Pascal had treated Père Noël's pranks as a joke, but when the President got to hear the details of the controversy between the Jesuit and his son he was angry. He wrote a defence in the legal style of the seventeenth century — which reminds us that he was a former judge—upbraiding the Jesuit for attacking a young man and comparing his extravagance with the moderation displayed by his son. The Commissioner of Taxes was no stylist. Blaise's artistic gifts, his liveliness, his irony and subtlety, his sense of the ridiculous were inherited from his mother, Antoinette Begon. Yet compared with the Jesuit's gibberish, Étienne Pascal's prose is almost a model of clarity. Literary French was still unborn.

In May 1648 Étienne Pascal went to Paris. On the advice of Singlin, her spiritual director, Jacqueline persuaded Blaise to break the news to their father that she wished to become a religious. Étienne Pascal replied that he would think it over. He then announced that he did not approve of his daughter's wish, would not consent to her departure and reproached Blaise bitterly, accusing him of allowing his sister to take decisions without consulting him. He ordered Louise Delfault, the housekeeper, to stop Jacqueline from visiting Port-Royal and then returned to Clermont. At the end of June he received a letter from Jacqueline in which the girl asked permission to make a retreat at Port-Royal in order to test her vocation.

While Blaise Pascal was going on with his experiments and his mathematical work in Paris, while his brother-in-law Florin Périer was travelling in Poitou, while Jacqueline was at her prayers, a revolution broke out in Paris. After a long period of incubation the Fronde exploded. The Regent, Anne of Austria, and Cardinal Mazarin had to yield to Parliament. In July the posts of commissioner of taxes were abolished. Étienne Pascal was relieved of his appointment. The news from Paris reaching the provinces was alarming. There were musket shots in the streets during the night. It seemed as though France, following the example of England, was on the point of doing away with the monarchy.

At the end of August there were riots in the capital. The little streets in the centre were blocked by barricades. During this period Florin Périer, who was back at Clermont, was preparing under the distant but vigilant direction of his brother-in-law to carry out one of the most important experiments of the seventeenth century in physics. Even at the most tragic moments of her history France has always had men who continued their disinterested pursuit of truths which were unaffected by the vicissitudes of politics.

CHAPTER VI

Atmospheric Pressure

IN THE YEAR 1648, which was an unhappy one for a France in the throes of foreign invasion and ruined by civil war, summer was slow in coming. Florin Périer kept a fruitless watch at the summit of Puy de Dôme: the mountain remained covered with snow. Then political events came to distract his mind from scientific work. Until the middle of September it was impossible for him to perform the experiment whose results Pascal was awaiting impatiently in Paris. He wanted to know once and for all whether the rise in the level of the mercury was due to atmospheric pressure or not. If the pressure to which the mercury was subjected was lower on the top of a mountain the case would be proved; if not there must be some other explanation of the phenomenon.

On Saturday, 19th September, the weather at Clermont was of the kind that meteorologists today describe as "unsettled with bright intervals and some showers". Périer rose at dawn and at 5 a.m. saw that the summit of Puy de Dôme was clear of snow. He went to tell his friends, Père Bannier, who was a Franciscan, Canon Mosnier, two judges, MM. Laville and Begon, and lastly Dr La Porte. They all assembled at 8 a.m. in the garden of the Friars Minor at the lower end of the town. Périer had previously obtained sixteen pounds of mercury. He brought the mercury with him as well as two tubes and some basins. Torricelli's experiment was repeated with the two tubes which were placed side by side. In each of them the mercury had stopped at a height of "twenty-six fingers, three and a half lines". Périer left one of the tubes where it was in charge of one of the Friars Minor, Père Chastin, and with his other assistants climbed to the top of Puy de Dôme. When he reached the summit, he repeated the experiment with the tube he had brought with him. As Pascal had pre-

54

dicted, those present saw that the level of the mercury had gone down "by three fingers, one and a half lines". In order to eliminate any possibility of error, Périer repeated the experiment six times at the apex of the mountain. He confirmed his findings by doing it over again at several points on the way down. As the little troupe went lower down the mercury rose higher in the tube. Halfway down they observed that the mercury was halfway between what it had been at the summit and the level it reached again in the garden of the Friars Minor when the expedition had returned. The accuracy of Pascal's intuition had been proved. By its admirably rigorous method this model experiment recalls that of Pasteur on microbes.

The next day, Père de La Mare suggested to Florin Périer that they should repeat the experiment at the foot and the summit of the highest spire of the Cathedral of Clermont. The results confirmed those which they had obtained in the garden of the Friars Minor and at the summit of Puy de Dôme. Two days later Périer wrote to his brother-in-law giving him full particulars of the experiments.[1]

Pascal at once published the letter which was followed by a "Notice to the Reader" in which he set out the philosophical implications of the experiment. This widened the area of the debate. The philosophers had claimed that "nature abhors a vacuum". They were wrong. But, he said,

this is not the only instance in which, when the weakness of men has been unable to discover the true causes, their subtlety had substituted imaginary causes which they have expressed by the use of specious names that fill the ears but not the mind; it is thus that people say that the sympathy and antipathy of natural bodies are the efficient and declared causes of various effects, as though inanimate bodies were capable of sympathy or antipathy; it is the same with anti-peristasis [equilibrium by which nature remedies certain anomalies] and several other chemical causes which only offer an illusory satisfaction of man's avidity to know hidden truths and which far from revealing them, only serve to veil the ignorance of those who invent them and to nourish that of their followers.[2]

[1] Letter from Florin Périer to Blaise Pascal, G.E., II, pp. 351-8.
[2] G.E., II, pp. 370-1.

While these scientific activities were going on, the Pascal family were divided over Jacqueline's religious vocation. Gilberte and Blaise were on their sister's side, but Étienne objected to his daughter's departure. There were some painful arguments and violent clashes of personality. In the end, Étienne Pascal emphasized the state of his health and extracted a promise from Jacqueline not to enter the convent as long as he was alive. The girl obtained no more than permission to make a retreat from time to time at Port-Royal. She went there in January 1649 and found the monastery of Port-Royal des Champs in a state of alarm. The armies were plundering the surrounding country; the roads were infested with brigands. In Paris, where her brother was living, the food situation was difficult. We have to remember those terrible years if we are to understand Pascal's political views. For a period of several years he saw rioting in the streets and France given over to anarchy.

In the midst of these troubles—the opposition of her family, her brother's illness, the slow weakening of her father, civil war, an atmosphere of violence and slaughter—Jacqueline remained perfectly calm. Her letters to Gilberte were filled with the imperturbable confidence of a Christian soul. In May she went with her father and brother to stay with her sister at Clermont. She continued to correspond with Mère Agnès Arnauld. The kindly, witty religious was a mystic who was endowed with unshakable good sense and a lively intelligence, while her profound awareness of the presence of God never made her lose her sense of humour. She commiserated with Jacqueline over the way in which her entry into the convent had been delayed and on 4th February 1650 wrote her the following note: "There is nothing to fear for a person who claims nothing in the world except to seek too hard for the satisfactions of the mind."[3]

These encouragements reached her at a time when the girl sadly observed a cooling of her brother's religious fervour. We have no precise information about this barely perceptible detachment, but we may assume that the moment when brother and sister found themselves in such sharp opposition was the result of a

[3] *Lettres de la Mère Agnès Arnauld, abbesse de Port-Royal*, published by P. Faugère (Paris, 1858), I, p. 166.

slow evolution. Early in 1650 Jacqueline must have begun to feel disturbed by her brother's attitude.

She herself had returned for a time to poetry. Her talent had matured. She translated into French verse the hymn *Jesu nostra Redemptio*. True, she did not manage, as Huysmans and Claudel were to do later, to convey the mystical appeal of the lilting, naïve, popular Latin poetry of the middle ages, which the seventeenth century regarded with the same uncomprehending indifference as romanesque church windows. Santeuil wrote majestic hymns for the Gallican breviary in verse as puffed up as Bossuet's episcopal robes. Jacqueline clothed the Gothic, monkish poetry in seventeenth-century alexandrines, but thanks to its swelling rhythms and restrained emotion her translation sometimes achieves the classic beauty of the canticles of Corneille and Racine. This is how she addresses Jesus:

> *Jusqu'au fond des enfers tu fis voir ta splendeur,*
> *Rachetant tes captifs de leur longue misère . . .*
> *Que la même bonté t'oblige maintenant*
> *A surmonter les maux dont ton peuple est coupable,*
> *Remplis ses justes voeux en les lui pardonnant,*
> *Et qu'il jouisse en paix de ta vue ineffable.* [4]

In the very depths of hell you showed your magnificence,
Redeeming your prisoners from their long misery . . .
May the same bounty now force you
To overcome the evils of which your people are guilty,
Fulfil your fair promises by forgiving them
And let them enjoy in peace your ineffable vision.

On the advice of Singlin, Mère Agnès persuaded her not to continue but rather to hide her talent. "You should hate your genius", she wrote to her.[5] Jacqueline gave up poetry.

She returned to Paris with her father and brother in November 1650, lived there like a religious in the world, seldom left her half-cloistered room, always wore a black dress and went often to church. One of her meditations on *The Mystery of the Death of*

---

[4] *G.E.*, II, p. 421.   [5] *Lettres*, Ed. Faugère, I, p. 173.

Our Lord Jesus Christ, written a year later, has been preserved.[6] As we read the long prayer we are disappointed by the absence of poetic feeling, by the moralizing, didactic, impersonal tone, by a sort of arid intellectualism. The chilly, neutral, abstract style has no room for any hint of emotion or poetic imagery. Unlike her brother the youthful poetess finds no place in her prayer for her heart or her imagination.

But at this period Blaise Pascal seemed remote indeed from ever being able to write *The Mystery of Jesus*. He was busily engaged in defending the copyright in his work on the experiments at Puy de Dôme against a young doctor of philosophy at the University of Clermont. He obtained a royal licence for the commercial exploitation of the calculating machine, looked after his health, was visited by scholars and friends, did the social rounds and was seen at Court. He greatly enjoyed social life and was out of sympathy with his sister. His Christian faith remained intact, but it was no longer anything more than an intellectual conviction which imposed no obligation on him to renounce the world.

On 24th September 1651 Étienne Pascal died in Paris in the presence of Jacqueline and his son Blaise. Gilberte was prevented from leaving Clermont by the birth of her son. In any case, travel had been made almost impossible by the war which was then at its height. The Prince de Condé was in open rebellion; northern France was occupied by the Spaniards; mutinous regiments were approaching Verdun; Burgundy, Anjou, Provence and Vendée were among the dissident provinces.

On the death of their father Blaise wrote a short treatise on "The death of a Christian" in the form of a letter to his sister and brother-in-law. The work shows that at this period his theological convictions were unimpaired and that he fully subscribed to the rigorous "theocentrism" which Henri Bremond described as the hallmark of the school of spirituality of the Oratory and Saint-Sulpice. That the Christian should pay less attention to moral values than to the worship of God was also the view of the follow-

[6] On the circumstances in which the meditation was written, see Mère Agnès' letter of 20th May 1651 (I, p. 186): "I have chosen for you the mystery of the death of Our Lord Jesus Christ. . . . Try, therefore, my dear sister, to grasp the virtue of our mystery." The text of Jacqueline's meditation is in *G.E.*, II, pp. 447–73.

ers of Saint-Cyran. Pascal's letter follows almost word for word some pages of Père Condren, unpublished at that time, which Père Quesnel included in *L'Idée du sacerdoce et du sacrifice de Jésus-Christ*. It is a pity that Bremond did not make use of it to enrich his *Histoire Littéraire du sentiment religieux*.[7]

We know that life and the life of Christians is a perpetual sacrifice which can only be completed by death; we know that when he entered the world, Jesus Christ considered himself and offered himself to God as a sacrifice and a true victim; that his birth, his life, his death, his resurrection, his ascension, his presence in the Eucharist, his eternal seat at the right hand of God are only a single and unique sacrifice. . . .[8] The completion [of the sacrifice] is death in which through the annihilation of life, the creature pays to God the fullest homage of which he is capable by annihilating himself before God and by worshipping the sovereign existence of him who alone can truly be said to exist. . . .[9] It is one of the great principles of Christianity that everything that happened to Jesus Christ must happen in the body and soul of every Christian; that as Jesus Christ suffered in his earthly life, died to this earthly life, was raised with a new life, ascended into heaven and sits at the right hand of the Father; so the body and soul must suffer, die, rise again, ascend into heaven and sit at the right hand.[10]

The letter emanates peace and confidence in the salvation of Étienne Pascal. There is nothing in it of the Jansenist terror of hell. It is a call to joy, confidence and hope supported by the teachings of Pauline mysticism which were triumphant in the seventeenth century.

At the end of his letter to Gilberte, Pascal prayed to God "to have for you and for my sister more tenderness than ever".[11] Now, in the course of the week that followed Blaise and Jacqueline appeared at the Châtelet before two notaries, Jean de Monhenault and André Guyon, to deal with the disposal of their father's estate, which was to lead to a long and painful dispute between them.

In order to live in a manner which he regarded as suitable to his position as a scientist and a man of the world, pay the cost of

[7] 11 vols., 1915–33. Only the first three have been translated into English.—*Trans.*
[8] G.E., II, pp. 541–2.   [9] *Ibid.*, p. 544.
[10] *Ibid.*, pp. 553–4.   [11] *Ibid.*, p. 559.

his experiments in physics, his servants and the upkeep of his carriages, Pascal needed the whole of his father's estate, which was to a considerable degree compromised by political events. He decided to pay Jacqueline an annuity with the proviso that if she took the veil he would be under no obligation to pay her anything more, which was in conformity with the law. Not long afterwards, in the morning of 4th January 1652, having told Gilberte, who had come to Paris to settle their family business, of her intention, Jacqueline abruptly left the house in the Rue Beauregard without saying goodbye to her brother. She entered the Abbey of Port-Royal de Paris, which at that time stood at the corner of the Rue du Faubourg Saint-Jacques and the Boulevard du Port-Royal on the site occupied today by the Maternity Hospital.

The previous day [wrote Gilberte] she asked me to speak to her brother in the evening so that he would not be unduly surprised. I did it as discreetly as I could, but though I told him it was only a retreat so that she could learn a little about the life, he was extremely upset. He went sadly up to his room without seeing my sister who was in the small room where she used to go to pray. She did not come out until my brother had left the room because she was afraid that the sight of her would distress him. I passed on the affectionate remarks he had made and afterwards we both went to bed. But though I approved with my whole heart of what she was doing because I believed it was the greatest thing that could happen to her, the greatness of this resolution nevertheless astonished me to such a degree and so occupied my mind that I did not sleep all night. When I saw that my sister did not get up at seven o'clock, I thought that she had not slept either and as I was afraid that she might not be well I went over to her bed where I found her fast asleep. The noise that I made woke her and she asked me the time. I told her and when I enquired how she felt and whether she had slept well, she replied that she felt well and had had a good night's sleep. She got up, dressed and left, performing these actions like any others with a tranquillity and calm of mind which were extraordinary. We did not say goodbye, fearing that it would upset us, and I moved out of her way when I saw that she was ready to leave.[12]

Jacqueline Pascal was twenty-six and three months.

[12] G.E., I, pp. 163-4.

CHAPTER VII

Man of the World, Gambler and Courtier

WITH his father dead, his sister in a convent and Gilberte at Clermont with her husband, Blaise Pascal found himself alone in the house in the Rue Beaubourg where he had moved after leaving the Rue de Touraine. He was looked after by Louise Delfault who had brought him up.[1] Although his health was not entirely restored, he was able to lead a normal life. He worked, wanted to buy himself an official appointment, to continue his study of mathematics, to exploit his calculating machine commercially, to give fashionable lectures, to have friends and to lead a brilliant and luxurious life. He felt himself capable of startling his age and was terribly conscious of his own worth. Although he remained a sincere Christian, he did not feel that he had a religious vocation and decided to follow the example of his father who had never believed for a moment that he was denying the Gospels by trying to make a career for himself in this world.

He was aware of the difficulties, the first of which was his modest financial position. In order to keep his four or five servants, his carriage, his horses, and hold a few receptions, his income of 2,500 *livres* was hardly sufficient at a time when his father had enjoyed an income of 12,000 *livres* and when a bishop was paid 100,000. He therefore found himself in financial difficulties. On two occasions in her *Life* of her brother, Gilberte insists on the fact that he had a "small income". And Mère Angélique pointed out to Jacqueline that her brother's income did not permit him

---

[1] On Louise Delfault, see a little book by A. Féron (Rouen, 1926). She died in 1659 and Blaise Pascal was her executor.

"to live like other people in his position".[2] He set to work to do so none the less.

He was twenty-nine. It was the end of youth. His personality was about to undergo a complete transformation. As a result, he was to earn a brilliant reputation as a scientist and a writer. The *Provincial Letters* and the *Pensées*, which germinated during these decisive years, were no more than the chance exercises of a universal genius.

At this period Pascal's life was dominated by two very different people: his sister, who was a nun, and a duke and peer.

Jacqueline was a postulant at Port-Royal. In spite of the rages that the tenacious resistance of the sensitive, delicate but indomitable little sister aroused in the great neurasthenic, her brother remained deeply attached to her. The place where they often met and inflicted such painful wounds on one another still exists. It was the parlour of Port-Royal which today has become a network of deserted rooms lying on the right-hand side as one enters the ancient building of the Maternity Hospital. The little chapel is also intact with its grille (recently excavated) through which Jacqueline in the nuns' choir could see the silhouette of her brother at religious ceremonies. The remains of Mère Angélique still rest beneath the floor.

Jacqueline was indeed tortured by her brother. On 7th March 1652, two months after her entry, she wrote him an endless, pathetic letter inviting him to her clothing. She expressed herself in the usual manner of the Pascals, certain of being right, stating it so proudly, almost haughtily, but with deep, even tearful, emotion. She mixed the formal *vous* with the familiar *tu:* "Do not set yourself up against the divine light; do not hinder those who do good and do good yourself; or if you do not possess the strength to follow me, at least do not hold me back. Do not show yourself ungrateful to God for the grace he has given to a person whom you love. . . .[3] Do out of virtue what you will have to do from necessity. Give to God what he asks of you by taking it. . . . It was only my fear of upsetting those whom I loved which has postponed my happiness until now. It is not reasonable for me to prefer others to myself any longer, and it is right that they

[2] *G.E.*, III, p. 74.   [3] *Ibid.*, p. 15.

should do violence to their own inclinations in order to repay me for the violence I have done to mine these last four years. I look principally to you for this sign of affection, and I am inviting you to my betrothal which with God's help will take place on Trinity Sunday."[4]

She also invited Gilberte and Louise Delfault, the housekeeper, but her proud soul asserted itself: "I am writing to my faithful [Louise Delfault]: please comfort her if she needs it, and encourage her. I am telling her that if she feels so disposed and thinks that I can fortify her still more, I shall be delighted to see her, but that if she is coming with the idea of opposing me, I am warning her that she will be wasting her time. I must say the same to you and to everyone who would like to do it in order to spare you all useless trouble. I have been patient for too long. . . ."

Then came the threat delivered in the blistering style of a true Pascal: "I have only invited you to the ceremony as a matter of form because I do not believe that you would ever have dreamt of missing it. You can be assured that I shall have nothing more to do with you if you do."[5]

When he received this letter Blaise went into one of his violent rages which brought on a migraine. The next day he went to the parlour of the monastery, saw Jacqueline, was "filled with pity, at the pain he caused her", and after the intervention of the astute Arnauld d'Andilly, made up his mind to give his consent.

The ceremony took place on Trinity Sunday in the Abbey chapel. Gilberte and Blaise represented their dead parents and played an active part. Gilberte escorted her sister when she went to light a candle at the offertory. Then, in accordance with the ritual, she held her hand to guide her to the altar rails for interrogation by the celebrant. They walked in procession to the monastery door. Pascal saw his sister bow to the abbess who cut off a lock of her hair.[6] The door closed behind her; a moment later she reappeared wearing the habit and the white veil of the novices of

---

[4] G.E., III, p. 17.   [5] Ibid., p. 18.

[6] These details are taken from the chapter called "The Manner of giving the Novice's Habit at the Monastery of Port-Royal of the Blessed Sacrament", pp. 286 et seq. of the Constitutions du monastère de Port-Royal du Saint-Sacrement (Paris, Desprez et Desessartz, 1721), in which will also be found the rules for children written by Soeur Sainte-Euphémie.

Port-Royal of the Blessed Sacrament. Jacqueline was to be known henceforth as Soeur Sainte-Euphémie. Pascal attended the ceremony silent, respectful, and cross.

At the beginning of June, the following year, Soeur Sainte-Euphémie made her profession, that is to say, took her final vows which attached her once and for all to the monastery. She then wrote to her brother asking him to pay over to Port-Royal her share of their parents' estate, which would have been illegal. This time Blaise and Gilberte were united in protesting and refusing.[7] They were strictly within their rights in doing so. Anyone who entered religion under the Ancien Régime was regarded as legally dead. Deeply wounded in her affections, in her sense of fairness and in her pride, Jacqueline fell ill. "I could not be more astonished at not succumbing", she wrote.[8] She had a series of pathetic talks with Mère Agnès, the novice mistress, and with the abbess, Mère Angélique. They both did their best to comfort her. How motherly and affectionate these pious, aristocratic women appear! How well they knew how to guide the proud and touchy girl, sometimes with humour, always with indulgence and perfect good sense! How far they are from resembling the ridiculous caricatures of their enemies!

Threatened with the deprivation of her dowry, Jacqueline suggested that she should make her profession as a lay sister in charge of the kitchen and the heavy work. The abbess refused with a smile. They must negotiate. Once again Jacqueline was visited by her brother in the parlour. She could not hide her distress from him. In his usual manner he began by flying into a rage; then, when faced by Jacqueline's silent suffering, the tears may have run down his own cheeks. "He was embarrassed and decided of his own accord to put matters right."[9] Three or four more talks in the parlour were necessary because Pascal tried to reduce the dowry. But at last, on 4th June 1653 in the afternoon, at the large grille in the parlour in the presence of Mère Angélique, Mère Agnès and three other religious, the gift to Jacqueline of an income of 1,500 *livres* and the promise to make over to her a

[7] See "Relation de Jacqueline Pascal" in *G.E.*, III, p. 55. M. Mesnard has published a study of the whole question in the *Revue du XVIIe Siècle*, No. 15. He has disposed of the stupid accusation sometimes brought against Pascal.
[8] *G.E.*, III, p. 56.   [9] *Ibid.*, p. 84.

capital of 5,000 *livres* was signed by the lawyers.[10] Pascal behaved with perfect courtesy towards the abbess.[11]

The next day he was present at her profession. In a letter to his brother-in-law he expressed his annoyance: "My sister made her profession yesterday, Thursday, 5th June, 1653. It was impossible to delay it. The gentlemen of Port-Royal were afraid that a short delay might lead to a long one. . . . That is how they have repaid me. . . ."[12]

But in future, in spite of his coolness towards his sister, he could not prevent her from being there praying in the choir of the little chapel, praying to God for the beloved brother, offering up her life so that grace might make a saint of the brilliant, restless, touchy genius. Mauriac calls her a "little Jansenist". "Little Cornelian" would be nearer the mark: martyr to her sensibility and her love.

The visible place that Jacqueline had occupied in Pascal's life was filled by a new, enthusiastic and lifelong friendship for Arthus Gouffier de Boissy, Duc de Roannez. Pascal may possibly have met the twenty-two-year-old aristocrat after one of his fashionable lectures in which he had spoken brilliantly and eloquently about the calculating machine or Torricelli's experiment. At any rate, the two young men were dazzled by one another. Pascal was impressed by the elegance of the young duke, his refined upbringing, his manners, his attractive personality, his considerable wealth. Arthus de Roannez admired his friend's extraordinary intelligence, the charm of his conversation, his reputation as a scientist. They soon became inseparable. Pascal had his room at the duke's house and accompanied him on his travels. He literally bewitched him.

The Duc de Roannez had a younger sister, Charlotte, who was nineteen. Pascal exercised the same irresistible ascendancy over her as over her brother without there being the least substance in the absurd story of a romantic friendship that some people have imagined. No one who has any idea what the spiritual direction of the priests of Port-Royal was like will feel disposed to admit

[10] Deed executed and authenticated by notary, *G.E.*, III, pp. 41–2.
[11] "Relation de Jacqueline Pascal" in *G.E.*, III, p. 89.
[12] *Ibid.*, pp. 46–7.

that Singlin would have allowed Pascal after his retreat to have had frequent meetings with Mlle de Roannez if he had previously been in love with her. And if he had ventured to declare himself, Pascal's own delicacy of feeling would certainly have driven him to break off all relations with her at that time.

Through the intermediary of the young duke, Pascal made the acquaintance of Antoine Gombaud, Chevalier de Méré. He was an enigmatic figure, forty-five years old, a friend of Balzac and of the painter du Fresnoy. He was a guest at the Hôtel de Rambouillet and enjoyed the respect of the Duc de La Rochefoucauld. He was regarded by the high society of the day as a specialist in the art of pleasing, the mentor of pretty women in matters of taste, finesse and conversation. Méré was a snob who called himself the philosopher of snobbery and claimed to be a faithful adherent of a tradition which went back to the Greeks. He disdained mathematics on the ground that they blunted people's wit and flattered himself that he could divine people's feelings by a science which was as exact as geometry, but infinitely more subtle.

Méré, who indulged in romantic friendships with the Duchesse de Lesdiguières and the Maréchale de Clérambault, who enjoyed the favours of Ninon de Lenclos, talked about nothing so willingly as love. He admired Cleopatra whom he considered the perfect example of the coquette. He himself was regarded as a master in the art of flirtation. He played for high stakes and his luck was such that people sometimes suspected it of being guided.[13]

It was probably in September 1653 that Pascal decided to go to Poitou with the Duc de Roannez, Méré and Miton. He was induced to do so by his friendship with the duke, who was governor of the province, and by his own interests. "Some unpublished papers", says J. Mesnard, "prove that Pascal was a shareholder in a company for draining the marshes of Poitou".[14] In his treatise De l'Esprit, Méré boasts that he took advantage of this journey of the four young people to teach Pascal something about the ways of the world.

I went on a journey with the D[uc] D[e] R[oannez] whose

[13] Chevalier de Méré, vol. I, Les Conversations. (Texte établi et présenté par C. H. Boudhors, Paris, 1930.) Introduction, pp. xxviii–xxxii.
[14] Op. cit., p. 51.

opinions are well balanced and deeply pondered and whom I find good company. M. M[iton], whom you know and who is popular with the entire Court, was one of the party; and because it was an outing rather than a journey, we did not bother about anything except enjoying ourselves and gossiping about everything on earth. L.D.D.R. is mathematically minded and to prevent boredom while we were on the road he had invited a man who was neither young nor elderly, but between the two, who was little known at the time, but who since then has been much discussed.[15] He was a great mathematician who knew nothing about anything else. These forms of learning do not confer social graces and the man possessed neither taste nor sensibility, but had something to say about every subject we discussed. What he said nearly always surprised us and often made us laugh. He admired the wit and eloquence of M. du Vair and repeated the jokes of the Lieutenant of Police of O.[16] The last thing we wanted to do was to disabuse him, but we spoke to him in good faith. When two or three days had passed in this wise, he began to have doubts about his own views and thereafter simply listened or asked questions in order to inform himself about the subjects that came up for discussion; he had some writing tablets which he took out of his pocket from time to time and made notes. It is very remarkable that before we reached P[oitou] he said practically nothing which was not right and which we would not have wanted to say ourselves: it is no exaggeration to say that he had come a long way. To tell the truth, the pleasure he showed us for adopting a different tone was so visible that I do not believe that it would be possible to experience a greater. . . .[17]

Méré goes on to quote some verse which the unknown traveller had written to celebrate his pleasure and claims that henceforth he abjured mathematics.

There is a good deal of fabrication in the story. The verse put

[15] According to Boudhors, an age of man was equivalent to thirty years. This means that Pascal was exactly between two spans of thirty years. Boudhors goes as far as to think that the journey took place somewhere about his thirtieth birthday, 19th June, 1653. This is impossible. Pascal received and signed the receipt for the contract giving effect to his donation to Port-Royal on 5th September.

[16] For Boudhors this was the first letter from Orléans where the travellers made a stay.

[17] Chevalier de Méré, vol. II, Les Discours. (Texte établi et présenté par C. H. Boudhors, Paris, 1930), pp. 86–7.

into Pascal's mouth was probably written by Méré himself. As for abjuring mathematics, Méré knew perfectly well that it was pure invention. The chevalier always adopted a high line with his new friend and had such a fascination for him at this time that Pascal failed to see what a marked strain of pedantry and fatuity there was in him. Until then, Pascal's acquaintances, like those of his father, had been mainly among the bourgeoisie, scholars and lawyers. His family, to be sure, had known Corneille and through the family he had come into contact with the world of the poets and the *précieuses*, but he was unaware that there existed a philosophy of worldliness. In a brilliant series of conversations Méré taught him psychological insight. Until he met him, Pascal knew little about himself and had never been taught to put himself out to please. He was too sure of himself, too wrapped up in his naïve mathematical pride. He realized that he had made a mistake and discovered with delight the art of pleasing whose aims and methods were completely different from those of the art of convincing.

Méré did still more. Since he was unfitted by his own "mongrel style", as Mme de Sévigné called it, to offer himself as a model for Pascal in the art of writing, he had the sense to draw the young man's attention to the great Master of French Literature. He made Pascal re-read Montaigne's *Essays*. Pascal had previously regarded it as a book like another, perhaps even a dangerous and a superficial one. Méré convinced him that he should look on it less as a compendium of religious indifference and free-thought than as a breviary of self-analysis, as an antidote to the rationalism of scientists and as a model of the art of writing.

Pascal certainly wrote well, as we can see from his letter to Père Noël. He used a clear, vigorous language, but his syntax had too many subordinate clauses. A careful reading of Montaigne under Méré's guidance taught him the things in which he was deficient: lightness, vivacity, pungency; the kick in the tail of a sentence; the swift playful images; the art of understatement, of avoiding wearisomeness by an unexpected sally; all the Gascon impishness of the *Essays*. As a disciple of genius, he attended a school for masters. "Montaigne taught him to write", he admitted.[18]

18 According to MS. 4.333 in the Bibliothèque Nationale published by Boudhors (*Revue d'Histoire Littéraire de la France*, January 1913).

For two years he read and re-read Montaigne, pen in hand, soaked himself in the substance of the *Essays*, learnt to discover in himself what the Archimedes of psychology had revealed of his own mind and mood. Montaigne had been endowed with a very large share of what Méré lacked: ideas and genius.

In Paris Pascal made appearances in the salons of the Duchesse de Longueville, the Marquise de Sablé and the Duchesse d'Aiguillon; he went to Court, as we know from his sister's *Life*.[19] At this time he was much given to gallantry, gambling, hunting and dancing. The anonymous witness who recorded his observations on Montaigne wrote: "He liked entertaining books, Scarron, his novel. . . ."[20] In Poitou he must have enjoyed Rabelais. He was certainly a very gay fellow and for once Sainte-Beuve was wrong when he claimed that "Pascal was not perhaps much given to laughter".[21] On the contrary, the future author of the *Provincial Letters*, who roared with laughter in his hotel room at the *King David*, was a friend of the theatre. The *Pensées* mention Scaramouche, the Italian actor Fiorelli, who played in the Commedia dell'Arte.[22] Pascal may even have applauded Molière on the boards.

It would be pleasant to be able to attribute to him the authorship of the famous *Discours sur les passions de l'amour*, but it seems very unlikely that he wrote it.[23] We know nothing about his sentimental life apart from Marguerite Périer's dubious statement that he had decided to marry a wealthy woman.[24]

If he was enjoying a brilliant social life, Pascal had in no sense given up physics and mathematics. It was at this period that he wrote the two treatises on the *Équilibre des liqueurs* and the

[19] Lafuma, p. 38. Eng. tr. p. 41.
[20] According to MS. 4.333 in the Bibliothèque Nationale. See Z. Tourneur, *Beauté poétique* (Melun, 1933), p. 128.
[21] *Port-Royal*, ed. Doyon, III, p. 3.
[22] Brunschvicg, No. 12. Lafuma No. 964.
[23] On the authenticity of the treatise, see Lafuma, *Controverses pascaliennes* (Paris, 1952), pp. 145–52, and the earlier works of the same writer which should be completed by his article, "Post-scriptum au *Discours sur les passions de l'amour*" in *Revue des Sciences Humaines*, July–September 1953, p. 275, where he proves that the author of the *Discours* was replying to questions formulated by Bussy-Rabutin.
[24] Lafuma, III, p. 61.

Pesanteur de la masse d'air which were not to be published until 1663 when he had been dead a year.

In these two short treatises physics is not wrapped up in barbarous jargon. Pascal records with delight his recent discovery of one of the secrets of nature. He does not carry his reader off into the laboratory; he leaves him in the drawing-room. His style is that of cultivated people. The explanatory engravings are decorated with little landscapes and in the diagrams the hands holding the test tubes (known in those days as vessels) emerge from cuffs with lace frills.

Stigmatizing the conclusions of his earlier works, Pascal demonstrates the first principles of hydrostatics: atmospheric pressure is responsible for effects once attributed to nature's abhorrence of a vacuum. He has scarcely explained the diagrams in his treatise when he embarks on the interesting consequences of his discoveries about the behaviour of fish:

"Why the weight of water does not compress them visibly. . . . Why we do not feel the weight of water."[25] He takes concrete examples: "If we put a worm in paste, even if we squeezed it between our hands we should never be able to crush it or even wound or compress it because the pressure is exercised on all its parts."[26]

The *Traité de la pesanteur de la masse d'air* is still more pungent and concrete. It exudes sprightliness and irony. Pascal was thinking of the Jesuits who were disciples of Père Noël and opponents of the existence of the vacuum. Each application of his principle of atmospheric pressure is stated with a little chuckle of defiance. The weight of air becomes the magician who plays the tricks recently attributed to the abhorrence of the vacuum. But Pascal has stolen his secret from him. It is that which "creates the difficulty of opening a pair of sealed bellows . . . of separating two polished bodies placed together"[27] and which causes "water to rise in syringes and pumps".[28] More than that, it causes flesh to swell when leeches are applied to it, and explains the attraction of milk when children are fed at the breast by their nurses.

As a final shaft, Pascal allows himself the pleasure of calculating

[25] *G.E.*, III, pp. 186–7.   [26] *Ibid.*, p. 189.
[27] *Ibid.*, pp. 206, 209.   [28] *Ibid.*, p. 211.

the total weight of the atmosphere, when limited and not extended in space, and gives the figure of "eight million million millions, two hundred and eighty-three thousand, eight hundred and eighty-nine million millions, four hundred and forty thousand million pounds."[29]

In the conclusion at the end of the two treatises he describes the method that should be applied to physics. It is experiment. Perhaps this example will open the eyes of those who dare not cast doubt on an opinion which has always been universally accepted: for simple workmen have been able to prove in this instance that the great men whom we call philosophers were wrong.[30] Pascal makes fun of the learned. Malherbe used the porters at the Hay Market as arbiters of the language of poetry; later Molière was to use his housekeeper as judge of his comic dialogue. Pascal proclaims that in matters governed by experience a workman can discover things of which the philosophers are ignorant and, better still, he can discover things that, owing to an ingrained obstinacy, the philosophers refuse even to consider.

As a scientist Pascal combined the experimental qualities of the workman with the critical intelligence and gift of generalization of the philosopher. With the experiments at Puy de Dôme he proved that Galileo was mistaken in believing that water in pumps could never exceed the level reached at Florence. And he closes with a page in which the eloquence and the poetry of the scholar are linked to the irony of the man of the world:

This experiment demonstrated that water rises in Pumps to very different heights according to variations of altitude and weather, but is always in proportion to the weight of the Air. It perfected our knowledge of these effects: it put an end to all doubts; it proved that the abhorrence of the vacuum was nothing of the sort; it shed on the subject all the light that we could wish.

Let anyone explain, if it is possible, otherwise than by the weight of Air, why suction pumps do not raise water at Puy de Dôme in Auvergne so high by one quarter as at Dieppe.

Why the same siphon raises the water and exercises an attraction over it at Dieppe and not in Paris.

[29] *G.E.*, III, p. 253.   [30] *Ibid.*, p. 263.

Why two polished bodies in close contact are easier to separate on a church tower than at ground level.

Why a completely sealed bellows is easier to open on the roof of a house than in the yard below.

Why, when the air is more heavily charged with vapours, the Piston of a sealed syringe is more difficult to draw.

Lastly, why all these effects are always proportionate to the weight of Air like an effect and its cause.

Is it because nature abhors a vacuum more on mountain tops than in valleys, in damp weather than in fine? Is its abhorrence not the same on a Church Steeple, in an attic and in the Yard?

Let all the disciples of Aristotle collect all that is most profound in the writings of their Master and his commentators in order to explain these things by the Abhorrence of the vacuum if they can; if not, let them recognize that experiment is the true Master who must be followed in Physics; that the experiments performed on mountains have demolished the universally held view that nature abhors a vacuum and have established this fact which should never be forgotten: that nature has no abhorrence of a vacuum, that it does nothing to avoid it, and that the weight of air is the real cause of all the effects which have hitherto been ascribed to an imaginary cause.[31]

Although he did not know it at the time, this was Pascal's farewell to physics, because having disposed of the problem of the existence of the vacuum and contrary to the incautious assertion of Méré, he returned in 1654 with delight to mathematics, the light of his youth, his joy and his form of relaxation. He re-established contact by way of arithmetic. He invented a new and complicated method of division by a process which was independent of the decimal system and which had the advantage, according to the specialists of our own time, of providing evidence of "the very clear idea that there exist different methods of counting which are equally legitimate and that our own is a *pure convention*".[32]

During the same period Pascal wrote a *Traité de la sommation des puissances numériques* ("Treatise on the summation of numerical powers") in which he taught how to "calculate the sum of any

[31] G.E., III, pp. 265–6.
[32] Introduction to *De numeris multiplicibus*, G.E., III, p. 313.

power of the terms of an arithmetical progression" and deduced the principle of integral calculus. His conclusions go beyond mathematics and have human and philosophical implications.

I shall not linger over the other cases [he wrote at the end of the treatise] because this is not the place to examine them. It is sufficient for me to have stated in passing the foregoing rules. The remainder will be discovered without difficulty by adopting as a basis the principle that *it is impossible to increase a series of quantities by adding to it, in any number one pleases, quantities belonging to a lower order of infinitude.* Thus points add nothing to lines, lines to surfaces, surfaces to solids; or—to speak in figures as one should do in a mathematical treatise—roots do not count in relation to square roots, square roots in relation to cube roots and cube roots in relation to quadro roots. So that quantities of an inferior order can be disregarded.

I was anxious [Pascal goes on] to add these few commonplace remarks for the benefit of those dealing with indivisibles in order to bring out the connection, always admirable, that nature, which is in love with unity, establishes between things that in appearance are far removed from one another.[33]

By a stroke of genius when making notes ten years later for his *Apology for Christianity*, he discovered that there existed between the order of human greatness and that of supernatural greatness the same discontinuity as between the two orders of numerical powers.

Pascal's scientific work was not confined to these treatises. In the company of Méré and Roannez and like everyone belonging to high society in the seventeenth century Pascal gambled in the drawing-rooms. At Court you played "a hell of a game", said an historian, and Louis XIV himself once lost six hundred thousand *livres* in six months. Now, Pascal's attention was drawn by his partner Méré to problems where play had a connection with mathematics. It was the problem of deciding how, when a game was broken off, the players should be repaid their stakes and therefore how to calculate the chances of loss and gain which remained to each of them. Méré thought that he could solve the

---

[33] G.E., III, p. 367. The original is in Latin.

problem without calling on mathematics. With his friends Carcavi and Roberval, Pascal tried to discover the exact solution of the problem and corresponded with Fermat about it. He sent him the results of his own calculations which were identical with those of the scholar from Toulouse. Pascal was delighted to find that they were at one: "I would like in future to open my heart to you if it were possible, so delighted am I to find that we are in agreement. I observe that truth is the same at Toulouse as in Paris."[34] It is the reply to the aphorism inspired by Montaigne which is to be found in the *Pensées*: "Truth on this side of the Pyrenees, error on the other side."

The problem of the repayment of stakes gave Pascal the idea of using very simple data to draw up a table of proportionate wins and chances which led to the invention of the famous arithmetical triangle. To tell the truth, the triangle existed before him. Specialists sometimes quote some of the sixteenth-century mathematicians, Stiefel, a German; Tartaglia, an Italian; Stevin, a Belgian; Hérigone, a Frenchman, who in a textbook published in 1634 had already sketched the path that Pascal followed. But it is a fact that in this, as in the course of his experiments on the vacuum, Pascal displays his genius by the breadth of his views and the number of the deductions he makes from the data. With Carcavi, Fermat and Roberval he laid the foundations of the calculation of probabilities which in a letter to the Academy of Sciences of Montmor, the friend of Gassendi's, he calls by this title which he himself regards as staggering: "the geometry of chance."[35]

Fermat, who was very fully occupied by the appointment he held and who encountered insuperable difficulties in putting his calculations and demonstrations down on paper, showed a desire to attach Carcavi and Pascal to himself as secretaries. Pascal dodged the honour though he continued to correspond with the learned judge: "Sir, if I have collaborated with you in this [the rule of the parties], seek elsewhere for someone who will follow you in your numerical discoveries of which you were good enough to send me particulars. I must confess that it is far beyond me; I am only capable of admiring them and beg you very humbly to

[34] *G.E.*, III, p. 382.   [35] *Ibid.*, p. 308.

complete them at the very first opportunity that you have the leisure to do so."[36]

The letter is dated 27th October 1654. The courteous refusal, which may have concealed a touch of irony, to go on interesting himself in Fermat's discoveries is easier to explain when we know that Pascal was passing through a spiritual crisis and was in a state of great confusion.

[36] *G.E.*, III, p. 431.

CHAPTER VIII

Night of 23rd November

TOWARDS the middle of September 1654, a month before writing the letter to Fermat quoted in the last chapter, Pascal paid one of his usual visits to Jacqueline in the parlour of the Abbey of Port-Royal. When visited by close relatives, the nuns were allowed to open the grille which enabled them to talk more intimately.[1] On that day, as on other occasions, Pascal gave his sister the family news and told her about his work. Then the tone changed.

> During the visit [Jacqueline wrote later], he opened his heart to me in a way which filled me with pity. He admitted that, in the midst of his many occupations and the pleasures of the fashionable world *by which he seemed to set great store*, he was conscious of an urge to abandon everything; that owing to an extreme aversion for the follies and distractions of society and a continual sense of guilt, he felt detached from all these things in a manner quite unlike anything he had ever experienced before; but that he felt himself so abandoned that he was not conscious of any inclination to turn to God; that he tried with all his strength, but was aware that it was much more his own reason and his own mind which forced him in what he knew was the right direction and not the action of God; that if, in his present state of detachment, he had the same sense of God's presence as in the past when he felt capable of undertaking anything, he must have been terribly attached to worldly things *to resist the graces that God sent him* and to turn a deaf ear to his appeal.[2]

[1] See *Constitutions du monastère de Port-Royal*, p. 144: "The sisters may speak with the grille open to their father, mother, brothers, sisters, sisters-in-law, uncles, nephews, aunts, nieces, and first cousins. . . . They must speak to all other relatives who are less close with the grille closed."

[2] Letter from Jacqueline to Mme Périer dated 25th January 1655 (*G.E.*, IV, pp. 61–2). It will be apparent how far the formula is from being Jansenist.

The talk came to an end. Brother and sister attended vespers: one under the small, visitors' cupola, the other behind the grille (still there today, though rust-covered), uniting her ardent responses to the arid, mechanical and bitter prayer of that troubled heart.

From that autumn day onwards—autumn is the mildest of all the seasons in the Île-de-France—Pascal returned often, almost daily, to see his sister. Their talks became longer and longer. "If I were to describe them all", wrote Jacqueline, "it would fill a book".[3] Every time he went Blaise confessed his discouragement and his pride. He was repelled by the idea of placing himself under the direction of a priest and making a proper confession— a complete baring of his soul—instead of the mechanical Easter confession to which he was accustomed. With his sister he had put aside all false modesty, but he experienced the sort of fright which is well known to all those who take their religion seriously. To expose oneself to another person completely, to say that one is not Blaise Pascal, the young and brilliant scientist, the celebrated physicist who is always right, the friend of the wealthy Duc de Roannez, the person to whom the most distinguished salons opened their doors, but the poor sinner whose inglorious portrait is to be found in all the manuals of piety; to be made to recite decades of the rosary, to come into collision with the sourness, the narrowness, the rustic simplicity of the clergy and their naïve belief in their own infallibility; to be lost among the crowd of churchwardens, to make oneself ridiculous among the muttering herd who have renounced everything because they have nothing to renounce.

Jacqueline showed a marvellous understanding of her great, proud, wounded brother. She saw "grace growing in him visibly", as she tells us in her touching account. She obtained a promise from him that he would contact Monsieur Singlin, the nuns' confessor.

Singlin, a man of humble origins—he was the son of a wine merchant—was about fifty years old at this time.[4] His brown, dry face breathed austerity. He had been Monsieur de Saint-Cyran's favourite disciple. He was not very intelligent or very

[3] *G.E.*, IV, p. 62.   [4] See Besoigne, *op. cit.*, IV, pp. 160–206.

cultivated, but had acquired from his master a lofty and inflexible conception of the rights and duties of the priesthood. He demanded an absolute submission from his penitents.

In accordance with his usual practice, he began by putting Pascal off and making himself unavailable, advising him to read the Bible, to pray, to meditate and, if possible, to make a residential retreat. Then he left Paris for Port-Royal des Champs. It was during his absence, on the night of 23rd–24th November, that the most moving event in the whole of Blaise Pascal's life took place.

On that evening Pascal had gone to his bedroom at his home in the Rue des Francs-Bourgeois-Saint-Michel. He had opened his Bible in the translation of the theologians of Louvain which had almost certainly belonged to his father, and was reading the account of the Passion of Christ in the tense, majestic language of the seventeenth century:

Jesus said these things: then lifting his eyes to heaven said: Father, the hour is come, glorify thy Son so that thy Son may glorify thee. As thou hast given him power over all flesh that he may bring eternal life to all those whom thou hast given him. And this is eternal life that they may know that thou art true God and that he whom thou hast sent is Jesus Christ. I have glorified thee on earth. I have completed the work that thou gavest me to do. . . . I have borne witness to thy name before the men whom thou gavest me from the world: they were thine and thou gavest them to me and kept thy word. . . . And now I come to thee and say these things to the world so that my joy shall be accomplished in them. . . . Father, I would that those whom thou hast given me, here where I am, should also be with me that they may see my glory, which thou hast given me because thou hast loved me before the creation of the world. Righteous Father, the world has not known thee, but I have known thee and thus have known that thou hast sent me. And I have taught them to know thy Name and will make it known to them that the love with which thou hast loved me may be in them and I in them . . .

Pascal read on:

Now the maid at the gate said to Peter: Wert thou not also one of the disciples of this man? And he said: I am not one of them. . . .

Again he read:

Pilate led Jesus forth and sat on the judgment seat in the place
called Lithostrotos and in Hebrew, Gabbatha. Now it was the eve of
the Passover about six o'clock: and he said to the Jews: Here is your
King. But they cried out: Away with him, away with him, crucify
him . . . And he bearing his cross came to the place known as
Calvary and in Hebrew Golgotha, where they crucified him with
two others, on each side and Jesus in the middle. . . .

As he read, Pascal saw the scene unfold before his eyes as he was
so often to see it again: Judas left the room to go and betray
Jesus, and Pascal knew very well that he, too, had betrayed him.
It was in his own room that he heard Peter deny Jesus. It was not
Peter: it was he himself, Blaise Pascal. The pitiful procession of the
Crucified crossed the Rue des Francs-Bourgeois-Saint-Michel in
the winter night. Jesus was being dragged by a rope. He collapsed
under the weight of the cross; the crowd spat and yelled. "It is
there", thought Pascal, "and I am outside; I am laughing with the
crowd; I deny; I am amused. I play dice like the soldiers." Then
the cross was laid on the ground and the body of Jesus was placed
on it. A soldier lifted the hammer to drive the nail into the
shuddering flesh. No, it was not the soldier; Blaise Pascal had
recognized his own hand. And the hammer fell. He heard a
feeble cry. All at once tears poured from his eyes; he wept
silently. The door was locked. He was alone. No one could hear
him. He wept, but if he wept it was because he resembled Peter:

The cock crowed for the second time and Peter remembered the
word that Jesus had said: Before the cock crows thou shalt deny me
thrice. And he began to weep. . . .

If Pascal wept it was because he was forgiven. Jesus was sorry
for him; he gave him the grace of repentance and tears. Pascal
was near to him. He was aware of the grace. It broke his heart and
at the same time filled it with the joy that Jesus promises to his
disciples in St John's Gospel. Pascal saw everything in a new light.
Up to then he had sought God by means of the thought of the
scholar and the philosopher. That only brought him to the ideal
God: the God of Cartesian idealism. He now discovered Jesus

Christ and the living God of Jesus Christ who reveals himself by
charity in the heart. He wept for joy.

He looked at his watch.[5] It was 10.30. Overcome with emotion,
burning with love and feverish, he drew a tiny cross on a sheet of
paper which had fallen out of his folio Bible; then he wrote the
date of the Christian martyrology:[6] "Monday 23rd November,
Feast of St Clement, Pope and martyr, And others belonging to
the martyrology. Vigil of St Chrysogonos, martyr and others,
From about half past ten in the evening until . . ."

He thought of the revelation of the God of the heart and of love
which he had just received. Was not the first revelation the
appearance to the Moses of the Burning Bush in the Old
Testament: the fire which was to appear so often in the Bible
until Pentecost and which fills the liturgy of the Holy Spirit?
In eis ignem accende. It was at once the fire of Sinai and the Paraclete
promised to the Apostles. Pascal wrote: "Fire. 'God of Abraham,
God of Isaac, God of Jacob, not of the philosophers and the
scholars. Certainty, Certainty, emotion, joy, peace. God of Jesus
Christ *Deum meum et Deum vestrum* Thy God shall be my God'
Oblivion of the world and of everything, except God."

How was he to seal the union with the God of Jesus Christ and
forget the world except by seeking help from the thick volume
which lay open in front of him and which he was reading when
grace descended on him. "He can only be found by the ways
taught in the Gospel. Greatness of the human soul. 'Righteous
Father, the world has not known thee, but I have known thee.'
Joy, Joy, Joy, tears of joy."

Pascal turned to the Gospel in order to copy the sentence which
condemned the world in which he had been living. Jesus Christ
himself had told him that he did not know God, but now he did

[5] "Mlle [Marguerite] Périer told me that her uncle always wore a watch attached
to his left wrist", Lafuma, III, p. 66.
[6] The *Memorial* was published for the first time in the *Recueil de plusieurs
pièces pour servir à l'histoire de Port-Royal* (Utrecht, 1740), pp. 259–60. It is there
said that God "sent a vision [to Pascal] who never spoke to anyone about it
except his confessor. It was only known after his death by a short note written in
his hand which was found on him, etc." (p. 258). It will be seen that the tradition
according to which Pascal had a vision is without solid foundation except a misinterpretation of the *Memorial* based on emblems in the form of a flaming cross
which precede and follow the text.

know him. His emotion and his joy grew greater. It is of joy that Jesus Christ speaks so often in the homily after the Last Supper: "I have told you these things that my joy may be in you and your joy may be full. . . . Therefore you are sad now, but I shall see you anon and your hearts shall rejoice and no one shall take your joy from you."

But suddenly there was a cry which troubled Pascal's joy: "I have separated myself from him."

At this point begins the second stanza of the prayer in which joy and the torments of remorse mingle. Pascal had cut himself off from Jesus Christ. He had belonged to the world. He was shattered at the very thought of it.

All those who have taken the "fire" as the centre of Pascal's experience were wrong. "If there is no longer fire, there is no longer certainty", wrote Bremond; "and if there is no longer certainty, there is no longer joy."[7] This statement is contradicted by the evidence of the autograph manuscript. The word "certainty" was written in later; the "fire" is obviously no more than a reference to the biblical text in Exodus written by a wise hand. It is only from the mention of "separation" from Jesus Christ that Pascal's handwriting begins to show signs of intense emotion, to betray a trembling of his whole body: the hand crabs the letters, which thicken; words remain formless, incomplete, a sort of shorthand; the syllables fuse into a point; the sentences which Pascal could no longer manage to form sprawl across the page in thick characters or are replaced by a series of feverish hooks. The hand regains control of itself, clutches the paper like a drowning man. Up to that point it had been no more than pious notes: now it became the written proof of an ecstasy. The text expresses an anxious rhythmical appeal in the form of a tragic litany similar in style to the prayers of Charles Péguy:

I have separated myself from him.
Dereliquerunt me fontem aquae vivae.
Lord, wilt thou forsake me?
Let me not be separated from him eternally.

[7] Bremond, *op. cit.*, vol. IV, *L'École de Port-Royal* (Paris, 1925), p. 367.

"This is eternal life, that they should know that
thou are the only true God and him whom thou hast sent, J.C."
    Jesus Christ, Jesus Christ,
I have cut myself off from him . . .
Let me never be separated from him.

After the event Pascal added: "I fled him (like the apostles),
denied him (like Peter), crucified him (like the Jews)."

Pascal was not inspired, as Bremond thought, by a sort of
Jansenist certainty about his own salvation. On the contrary, he
was anxious to preserve a grace which had bowled him over, but
which might prove transitory. He was not the recipient of some
revelation about the future; but his uneasiness was soothed; he
had under his hand the great folio volume which contained the
secret of perseverance. At the beginning of his meditation he had
written of God:

He can only be found by the ways taught in the Gospel.

He went on to conclude in a mood of serenity:

We can only keep him by the ways taught in the Gospel.

Having discovered the pledge of Jesus Christ, he was able to
finish the meditation with a steady hand: "Total and delicious
renunciation."

Then, at midnight, he finished writing, added a reference to the
martyrology and the time at which the ecstasy ended: "about
half past twelve midnight". He completed a quotation from the
Gospels. After "Righteous Father, the world has not known
thee", he added: "but I have known thee". After "God of
Abraham . . . not of the philosophers", he added, in a hand which
was different from the rest of what he had written, this little
sentence which is plainly an addition: "Certainty, Certainty,
emotion, joy, peace." Certainty not of his own salvation, but
of the presence of God like Moses on Sinai and the apostles after
the Last Supper; certainty that he had been chosen for a special
grace, that he had won joy and peace of soul.[8]

[8] Thus the careful study of the original manuscript enables us to assert three
things:
    1. That the account was written between ten o'clock and midnight, Pascal
having simply added at the end "about half past twelve midnight";

It is of great importance to realize that it was only a very long time afterwards, when the manuscript account of Pascal's nocturnal passion was worn out and reduced to scraps because he carried it about with him like a treasure in his pocket, that it was re-copied on to parchment. There is no doubt that Pascal carried the original on him, because it was found sewn to his clothing and was stuck, worn and torn along the folds though it was, at the beginning of the manuscript of the *Pensées*. Pascal was in the habit of carrying papers about with him and the manuscript of the Wager remained for a long time in his pockets. As for the mystical writings, he made a practice of sewing them to his clothing. This was common practice at the time: Richelieu, St Vincent de Paul and St Jeanne Chantal all did it.[9]

The interval which separates the two versions of the Memorial —the original manuscript on paper and the copy on parchment of which only a facsimile survives—is most important. It completely disposes of the thesis of those who attempt to use the strange hieroglyphics of the parchment copy to make certain inferences about the nature of the experience of 23rd November. The parchment copy is a later work, a new work of Pascal's, which may perhaps provide evidence about his later development. In the copy the cross at the head of the page is surrounded with rays. The word "fire" is now written in large, heavy capitals. Why these capitals which encourage conflicting interpretations? It was because for Pascal FIRE was synonymous with GOD which was also written in capitals. In line 10, Périer, who made a copy of the parchment version, misread the word *joye* and wrote *veue* which he later corrected by inserting the right word above.

In his new version Pascal gave the biblical reference. The short strokes which end seven of the sentences in the original manuscript, and are signs of a powerful emotion, are regularized in the

---

2. That the hallucination exists simply in the minds of the commentators who were bowled over by the *Recueil d'Utrecht* and the copy with marginal decorations which was the only one reproduced by Bremond;

3. That Bremond's argument will not stand up to the examination of the original manuscript because it is based on the sentences that are most alien to the religious feeling which is only to be found at the end of the original.

[9] On Richelieu, see *G.E.*, IV, p. 3, note 1. For the others, see F. Droz, *Études sur le scepticisme de Pascal* (Paris, 1886), p. 16, n. 1.

copy. Their number is increased; there are a dozen of them. They appear round the word "fire" and in the last line of the original version, but have no real significance. Finally, Pascal added three fresh lines in which Périer admitted that he had been unable to read certain words clearly. This tends to prove that the addition, far from being carefully written like the rest, had been made, later still, in haste. And that is the version which Henri Bremond substituted for the original in order to judge the nature of Pascal's ecstasy!

An interesting parallel could be drawn between the night of Pascal and that of Descartes. In his *Olympica* Descartes wrote the following sentence which is reported by his biographer, Adrien Baillet: "[10th November 1619] *Cum plenus forem enthousiasmo et mirabili scientiae fundamenta reperirem. . . .*" And Baillet goes on to describe in detail three dreams which Descartes had on the night of the Feast of St Martin. He felt himself driven by the wind against the wall of a church, heard a clap of thunder "and opening his eyes, he saw many sparks flying all over the room". Lastly, in a third dream, he found himself reading an anthology of poetry:

> This last dream, in which there was nothing that was not gentle and agreeable, pointed to his own future. . . . But he took the two earlier dreams for warnings relating to his past life, which might not have been so innocent in the sight of God as in the eyes of men. The impression which remained with him of these disturbances led him on the following day to reflect on the path he was to follow. In his perplexity, he turned to God and besought him to make his will known to him, to enlighten him and guide him in his search for truth.[10]

How clearly we perceive in this account all the resemblances and all the differences between Pascal and Descartes, between the two great geniuses who were at once so close and so far from one another.

They were both Christians, both enlightened by God in the course of a November night, but with a light which has neither the same origin nor illuminates the same truths. Descartes

[10] Adam-Tannery, *Oeuvres de Descartes*, vol. X, pp. 182–6.

1. DESCARTES. Portrait by Frans Hals.

2. LE DUC DE ROANNEZ. Portrait by Philippe de Champaigne.

3. GILBERTE PÉRIER (née Pascal).

4. The original autograph text of the Mémorial.

dreamt; Pascal was awake. When he woke Descartes reflected,
while Pascal, who had not slept, read the Bible. If Descartes felt
remorse it was before God, whereas Pascal was conscious of
having denied and crucified Jesus Christ. Descartes was seeking
truth and wanted to discover it on his own. Pascal possessed
truth; it was enough for him to remain faithful to it. Descartes
left on one side the dogmas of faith; Pascal flung himself into them
completely. The two Catholics were separated by the Bible and
the Mediator.

For the heart of Pascal, that heart which felt God, perceived
during the night of 23rd November the totality of the truths
which were to nourish his religious life for the eight years that
followed. He had the contemplative's overwhelming perception
of the identity of the God of Moses and the God of Jesus Christ
which is the central truth of the Passion in the Gospels. He
experienced, in the depths of his being, the opposition between
the living God and the God of the philosophers. But since God is
a living God he must be loved, and all love brings with it the risk
of infidelity on both sides. God could abandon Pascal and Pascal
could turn his back on God. For Descartes's pursuit of an abstract
intellectual truth Pascal substituted a personal drama.

The night of 23rd November did not produce any marked
change in Pascal's outward life. He did not leave his middle-
class house in the Rue Monsieur-le-Prince; he did not break with
the Duc de Roannez, with Méré or with Miton; he seemed,
indeed, closer to them. Nevertheless, he wished to consult
Singlin. Since Singlin was at Port-Royal des Champs, Pascal
made up his mind to go there, "but", Jacqueline tells us, "he had a
marvellous intuition that it was known that he was in contact
with someone besides myself at the monastery."[11] He therefore
worked out a neat little stratagem. He could say that he was
obliged to absent himself on business, use an assumed name, leave
his servants and his carriage at a village close by and go on foot to
visit Singlin, with the result that "nobody would have any knowledge of their meetings".[12] Singlin, who had been told about the
plan, refused to see Pascal incognito and wrote him a letter in

[11] G.E., IV, p. 65.   [12] Ibid., p. 65.

which he appointed Jacqueline his spiritual directress. Jacqueline gave this piece of news to her sister Gilberte in a letter written on 8th December. "It is not right that you should remain any longer in ignorance of the change wrought by God in the person who is so dear to us. . . . He has put himself completely in the hands of M. S[inglin] and I think that it has been done in a spirit of childlike submission. . . . I have observed in him a humility and a submission even towards me which are surprising. . . ."[13]

At the end of December, Singlin returned from Port-Royal des Champs. He had a meeting with Pascal. It is probable that Pascal told him about his spiritual state. The Duc de Roannez had returned to Paris. Pascal ran the risk of succumbing again to the usual round of amusements and entertainments. Singlin advised him to make a retreat at Port-Royal des Champs. Pascal told his friend of his plan. "He let him into his *secret* and with his consent, which was not forthcoming without tears, he left on the day after the Feast of the Epiphany", that is to say, 7th January 1655.[14] As we can see, Pascal was still anxious to keep what he was doing a secret. He wanted to be diplomatic with his friends in high places. He had not given up everything. His connection with the Duc de Roannez was so close that he needed his consent.

He went to stay at the Château de Vaumurier which was close to the abbey and belonged to the Duc de Luynes. But finding that he was not left sufficiently to himself, he asked for a cell in the Granges of Port-Royal and spent the whole of the month of January there.

[13] *G.E.*, IV, pp. 15–16.   [14] *Ibid.*, p. 66.

CHAPTER IX

The Visit to Port-Royal des Champs

THE building at Port-Royal known as the Granges where Pascal went to stay is still standing. It escaped the destruction of the abbey ordered by Louis XIV and carried out with such vandalism between 1709 and 1712. It is a rural building of two storeys with long windows and a tiled roof on to which the skylights of the attics open. Today you can see, not far from the book-lined rooms of Arnauld and Nicole, the narrow cell with whitewashed walls and red brick floor that Pascal is supposed to have occupied. Was it really where he stayed? It is not a matter of great importance. Since a series of strange accidents conspired to destroy his birthplace, the Château de Bien-Assis, and all the other houses where in turn he made his home and even his grave, the cell at Port-Royal is one of those places, all too few in number, where after the lapse of three hundred years we can still find his memory present and intact.[1]

At Port-Royal des Champs Pascal made the acquaintance of the Solitaries, our "hermits", as Mère Angélique called them. They consisted of a group of clergy and laity who had been converted either by Saint-Cyran or his immediate disciples. The "Gentlemen" were drawn from different walks of life: noblemen, ex-judges, a doctor, priests who had surrendered their livings and in some instances had given up the exercise of their priestly functions, bootmakers and farm labourers.[2] This group differed from the other religious communities, of which there were so many in

[1] With the exception of the house which is still standing, No. 54, Rue Monsieur-le-Prince. See p. 6 above.
[2] On the Solitaries, see the memoirs of Lancelot, du Fossé, Besoigne's history, Sainte-Beuve's *Port-Royal* and A. Hallays' short but charming book *Les Solitaires de Port-Royal* (Paris, n.d.).

87

the seventeenth century, in its attachment to a somewhat rigid form of Christianity that found its charter in Antoine Arnauld's book on *Frequent Communion*. Apart from this, their life was very much that of lay Carthusians without habit or vows.[3] They got up at 3 a.m. to sing matins and lauds together, then returned to their cells for meditation. About 6 a.m. they sang prime and terce, attended mass at which all received Communion at least once a fortnight and some several times a week. At the end of the morning they recited sext and none, in the evening vespers and compline, and went to bed at seven o'clock. During the day, in addition to saying the office, some of them did manual work while others, following the example of the Benedictines, devoted themselves to works of scholarship. A number of them went in for gardening. Arnauld d'Andilly, for example, cultivated espaliers and translated St Teresa and St Augustine. Antoine Arnauld wrote lengthy theological treatises. Later on his nephew, Lemaistre de Sacy, translated the Bible. The result was that in the space of a few years they turned out several hundred volumes of theology, meditations and saints' lives, written in a slightly colourless style and far removed in form and substance from the lofty speculations of Cardinal de Bérulle, Père de Condren, Saint-Cyran and Monsieur Olier. Serious, devoid of either poetry or humour, a trifle dull, their style not only became characteristic of the books produced by Port-Royal, but served as a model of style for the average devotional work during the classic period. The best example is the *Essais de morale* of Nicole, that Boileau of the things of the spirit. On a very much higher level were the treatises of the Oratorian, Duguet, who was the Newman of the *ancien régime*, and the works of Père Quesnel, a great writer.

The core of this ascetic little world, so utterly different from the salons where Méré propounded his aphorisms with their preciosity, was a family of Auvergnats, the Arnaulds, who thanks to their parliamentary and provincial background, their moral solidity, resembled the Pascals but without their poetry, their panache and their brio, their imaginative gifts; without, in short, their flash of genius.

---

[3] The account that follows is taken from the "Récit de la conduite et des exercices spirituels des pénitents de Port-Royal des Champs", 23 Novembre 1644 in Fontaine, *Mémoires pour servir à l'histoire de Port-Royal*.

As soon as he was converted, Blaise found himself very much in his element at the Granges of Port-Royal. He admired the simple life, for which he had a yearning. Far from missing the salons, he enjoyed a happy sense of relaxation. Jacqueline learnt that his gaiety bubbled over on the slightest pretext. He did not strike a discordant note. Nobody at the Granges was a prey to melancholy any more than they were in monasteries or seminaries. They sang all day long. They made jokes; they laughed during recreation. Their jollity was encouraged by the presence of children. For the Solitaries, following the example of monks, had added to their Thebaid a sort of school which was the equivalent of the girls' school run by the nuns at Port-Royal in Paris of which Soeur Sainte-Euphémie had become headmistress and drawn up the rules. The "little schools" of the Granges became a centre of pedagogic research and one of the finest centres of Hellenistic studies of the seventeenth century. Lancelot taught there and compiled his celebrated *Jardin des racines grecques*. For the same children Arnauld, with the assistance of Nicole and Pascal, wrote a *Logic*. In between doing their Latin translations and attending religious services the pupils often amused themselves with catapults, cards and backgammon. It may have been his contact with them that gave Pascal a marked fondness for children which remained with him for the rest of his life.

What is more, Port-Royal left an indelible impress on the whole of Pascal's religious life. He based his outer life on that of the Solitaries and made a habit of reciting the breviary in Latin like priests. If he never considered taking Holy Orders or made any move in that direction, it was probably because of the influence of his confessors at Port-Royal. His piety and his meditations under the direction of the Gentlemen remained quite different from those of the disciples of Monsieur Olier, the Jesuits or the Lazarists. First and foremost his life was dominated by the theological pre-occupations and discussions of Port-Royal. But if he sometimes stayed at the Granges, he never took up residence there, always kept his Paris home, his servants, his carriage and, until the end of the year 1660, his magnificent library, and generally maintained the standard of life of a person of quality.

During his first retreat Pascal was directed and confessed by

Lemaistre de Sacy, nephew of Mère Angélique and Antoine Arnauld. Lemaistre de Sacy was the younger brother of Antoine Lemaistre, the first of the Solitaries and the founder of the group. Pascal was introduced to Arnauld d'Andilly, the patriarch and friend of Anne of Austria; to Monsieur Hamon, the doctor, a naïvely charming Franciscan soul with an intense feeling for nature: the man whom Sainte-Beuve described as "one of the Magi in rags". He did not meet Dr Antoine Arnauld, the sun of the Solitaries, who was away at the time of the first retreat.

It seems clear that Pascal's meditation on the agony of Jesus Christ, known as the *Mystère de Jésus*, must have been written at the beginning of his visit to Port-Royal during the period immediately following his conversion.[4] The occasion was very probably one of the notes distributed periodically to the nuns and the Solitaries which contained a reference to the mysteries of the rosary.[5] In this connection Jacqueline had already composed a long prayer on the death of Jesus. Mme Périer tells us that Pascal used to receive these notes.

The nuns were also encouraged to meditate on the mysteries of the Passion of Jesus during the recital of the canonical hours. In *La Religieuse parfaite*, a little book containing treatises by Mère Agnès and Soeur Sainte-Euphémie, meditation on the agony of Jesus is recommended every night during matins:

> At this time we must worship Our Lord in the sorrow and agony that he went through in the Garden of Olives, beseeching the eternal Father to take away from him the cup of his sufferings and consider that if the Fathers of the Church teach us that all the actions of his life were at the same time the works and sayings by which he taught his followers even better than by word of mouth, there is no doubt that the prayer in the garden with all the attendant circumstances has great things to teach those who hear and understand it. . . .[6]

[4] This is the very pertinent view of L. Lafuma, II, p. 178, and M. Raymond. See Lafuma, *Controverses* . . . p. 98.
[5] The rule of the Solitaries appended to the *Mémoires* of Fontaine states explicitly that one of the methods of prayer was the recitation of the rosary and meditation.
[6] "Exercice de dévotion sur la Passion de Notre-Seigneur" in *L'Image d'une religieuse parfaite et d'une imparfaite* (Paris, 1666), p. 379.

We possess a minute autograph copy of Pascal's meditation on the agony of Jesus on two large sheets of paper and written apparently at a sitting without the deletions and pieces stuck on to the manuscript that we find in the *Pensées*.[7] These extraordinary pages are the finest that he has left us. They enable us to penetrate the depths of his inner life, to overhear his dialogue with Jesus Christ. They are a sequel to the *Memorial*, make explicit its brief notations, elaborate and explain them. In the *Mystery* Pascal resumes the prayer on the Passion of Jesus which he had begun on the night of 23rd November, but this time he concentrates his attention on the moment that best fits his own state of mind, which was that of a sick man recently converted who was still worried over his ability to persevere. For the agony presented him with the spectacle of "Jesus alone and abandoned to the wrath of God", that is to say, in the same state as he himself when he went, in great distress, to confide in his sister that he had never felt so abandoned by God. Jesus also suffered from the feeling of complete moral isolation which Pascal had experienced during those two or three months of spiritual aridity. Jesus suffered the torment of "ennui": his uncertainty about the divine will. But Christ, once he knew it, obeyed. He taught Pascal that conversion can only operate through prayer, vigils, suffering, the betrayal of friends, by being "torn away from one's nearest and dearest", and the acceptance of death. As in his meditation on the night of 23rd November, in the course of which Pascal saw that he had abandoned, fled from, denied and crucified Jesus Christ, so once again he saw himself in the guise of the sleeping apostles whose salvation was wrought by Jesus without their suspecting it.

The entire meditation consists of very short versicles[8] and in the first part the same themes recur, insistently, in the manner of refrains: the sleep of the apostles; the abandonment of Jesus Christ; his goodness; the loneliness of his suffering. There are no images. There are simply two or three words which are used to evoke the setting: the garden of torment; the horror of night;

[7] The actual title of the *Mystère de Jésus* "could well have been added by Marguerite Périer", Lafuma, II, p. 177. The same writer adds: "We believe (the regular handwriting suggests it) that the *Mystère* was written during the first quarter of 1655, perhaps at the Granges . . . " (p. 178).

[8] In French *verset* which means a verse of the Bible.—*Trans*.

Judas. There is no symbolism except the dark night in the shadow of which it is impossible to make out anyone's features. Everything is centred on the inner drama, on Jesus whose name is repeated at the beginning of each versicle like a litany in order to create the obsessive sense of his presence and to concentrate on him the whole of the emotion of his disciple in prayer. There is no attempt at fine writing or "style", yet the brief observations are bathed in an intense poetry. The use of the same tense for the verbs, the chance assonances of a language which is naturally musical, contribute to the effect. The present indicatives: "Jesus suffers . . . Jesus seeks . . . Jesus is alone . . ." accentuate the vividness and immediacy of the *Mystery*. In the manner of Bérulle, Pascal "multiplies and declines the participles". "He does not know", Bremond wrote of the cardinal, "how to get rid of the idea of the ephemeral, how to enable us to perceive, beneath actions which vanish almost as soon as the gesture has begun, states of mind which do not pass away or, at any rate, which last for some time."[9] Pascal writes: "Jesus *finding them sleeping . . . finding them still sleeping . . . seeing* all his friends asleep . . . Jesus, *being* in agony." The emotion becomes still more powerful when the present extends into the future: "Jesus will be in agony until the end of the world." And Pascal sometimes returns to a past which is irreparable in order to suffer from it: "Jesus prayed to man and his prayer was not answered."

Pascal only thinks of himself once or twice when applying the moral conclusions of the drama with which he feels that the whole of his destiny is bound up. He is carried away in ecstasy and participates in the suffering, the more so because he is conscious within himself of the moral suffering of Jesus. And he feels it alone. The sleep of the apostles gives to Pascal's wakefulness, to the tête-à-tête of the disciple and the Master at the moment of his supreme moral suffering, its exceptional character. The *Memorial* had produced tears of joy. In the first part of the *Mystery*, on the other hand, we are aware of Pascal's anxiety. He is afraid for himself; he is not sure of his moral recovery. He seeks God uneasily. And when he reaches a state of perfect conformity with the suffer-

[9] H. Bremond, *op. cit.*, vol. III, *L'École française*, Paris, 1921, p. 68. Eng. tr. (London, 1936), p. 57.

ings of Jesus Christ, the atmosphere is created which is necessary for the perception of the full resonance of the tender and tragic words that the Lord addresses to his disciples by raising his voice himself: "Be comforted", says Jesus. Pascal is completely occupied with Jesus Christ. Jesus is occupied solely with Pascal's interior agony and advises calm, abandonment and trust. To Pascal's uneasiness Jesus replies: "Thou wouldst not seek me unless thou hadst already found me"—a saying which was already to be found in St Augustine and which expresses marvellously the Catholic dogma that there is no other certain sign of the presence of grace except human effort and the perpetual search for God. If Pascal seeks God with such anxiety, it is a sign that Jesus thought of him at Gethsemane and that he shed those drops of blood for him; let him preserve his trust, but an active, moving trust in Jesus Christ; let him shed tears as he had done on the night of 23rd November. Let him put his trust in the Church. Jesus teaches Pascal a form of spirituality which is wholly Catholic and in which the intuitions of the *Memorial* are elaborated and developed. "He [Jesus Christ] can only be found by the ways taught in the Gospel," Pascal had noted down on the night of his conversion. Jesus now confirms it for him:

"Be guided by my precepts: see how well I led the Virgin and the saints who allowed me to act on them . . ."

"Thy conversion is my business . . ."

"I am present to thee by my word in Scripture, by my spirit in the Church and by inspiration, by my power in the priests . . ."

"Thou must bear physical bonds and servitude . . ."

Jesus used the second person singular to confess the most painful love for Pascal:

"I am more of a friend to thee than this man or that . . . they would not bear what I have borne from thee, and would not die for thee at the time of thine infidelity and cruelty. . . ."

"I love thee more fervently than thou lovest thy depravity. . . ."

No Christian mystic has put into the mouth of Jesus words so commensurate with the supernatural simplicity of the Gospels or expressed the naked, bleeding love of the infinite when reproducing the gentle authority and the inimitable tone of the most marvellous of human voices.[10]

The sob in the night, the prayer riddled with personal references to the recent conversion of the sick man, is full of the theological riches of the Christian past. It is related to St Augustine by the experience of grace to which it bears witness, to St Bernard and to mystics like Suso and the author of the *Imitation* by its moving love of Jesus Christ's suffering humanity, by its allusions to those drops of divine blood which fall to the ground, to the tears which furrow Pascal's cheeks, to the groups of apostles sleeping like the figures carved on the portals of cathedrals. It takes up again the theme of the prayers of Saint-Cyran and Bérulle by its assertion of the eternal nature of the states and mysteries of Jesus Christ and its insistence on complete abandonment to God whose will is manifest in all the events of life. In this respect Pascal anticipates the admirable spiritual teaching of Père de Caussade. His prayer belongs to the seventeenth century by virtue of the majesty that the Lord preserves in his sufferings, by the modesty of the manner in which love is expressed that constitutes the originality of French devotion in the *grand siècle*.

There is no exaggeration, no romanticism, nothing of the Gongorism of the Spanish or of the bad taste of Lacordaire. For the true character of Pascal's religious genius lies in this: that through the restraint, the dignity, the classic austerity, which gives to the prayer of his contemporaries an impression of being a little too correct and too stilted, he was able, while using the simplest words, to avoid leaving out anything of the most poignant of human dramas: tears, blood, weariness, the calamities of that dark night in which two agonies met: the agony of the Saviour and his own.

Why did the Gentlemen of Port-Royal, who published so many mediocre works of piety, omit to publish *The Mystery of Jesus* after Pascal's death, with the result that it remained un-

[10] See the autograph manuscript of the *Mystère de Jésus* in the photographic reproduction of Brunschvicg (folios 87–88 and 99 at the bottom) taking account of Z. Tourneur's important emendation (Edition paléographique des *Pensées*, p. 23. Cf. Lafuma, I, p. 489). In place of "Ask thy director when my words are an occasion of evil in thee, and of vanity or curiosity . . . " read: "Confess to thy director. . . . "

published until the middle of the nineteenth century? Had they failed to realize that these two pages were one of the summits of Christian prayer and that, without intending it, Pascal had shown himself the equal, if not the superior, of St Augustine and St Teresa of Avila? The tragic cry of that voice was too intimate and must have offended their modesty.

There are other highly personal meditations of Pascal's in the manuscript of the *Pensées*. In folio 107, for example, of which it has been said that "like the Memorial of 23rd November 1654 the sheet of paper was folded into eight and carried for a long time in a pocket."[11] In it we find the following dialogue with Jesus dating from 1656:[12]

Do not compare thyself to others, but to me. If thou dost not find me in those with whom thou comparest thyself, thou art comparing thyself to someone who is hateful. If thou findest me, compare thyself with me. But with whom shalt thou compare thyself? With thyself, or with me in thee? If with thyself, it is with someone hateful. If it is with me, thou comparest me with myself. Now I am God in all things.

I often speak to thee and give thee advice because thine own guide cannot speak to thee, and I do not want thee to be without a guide.

And perhaps I do it in answer to his prayers, and so he guides thee without thy noticing it.

Thou wouldst not seek me if thou hadst not already found me. Therefore, be not troubled.[13]

In this passage we are conscious of the reappearance of an anxiety which underlies the whole of this particular entry. The absent guide is Singlin whose name was deciphered by Tourneur.

There are also meditations by Pascal on the tomb of Jesus Christ and on that other mystery of the rosary, the Resurrection.[14]

From the time of his stay at Port-Royal Pascal never ceased to pray.

It was probably at the end of Pascal's stay at the Granges that

[11] Z. Tourneur, *Pensées de Blaise Pascal* (Edition paléographique), p. 27, note 3.
[12] L. Lafuma, *Controverses pascaliennes*, p. 98.
[13] Laf. 751: Br. 555.
[14] Laf. 752 and 742: Br. 552 and 554. (Brunschvicg made the mistake of dislocating the meditation in his numbers 554, 250 and 661.)

Lemaistre de Sacy, who acted as superior of the community, invited the young man to give the Solitaries a sort of spiritual conference. In seminaries and monasteries it is still common practice today to ask a person of standing who is making a retreat there to address the whole community.

It provides an opportunity for groups who are somewhat isolated from the world to learn what the century is thinking without disturbing the isolation that is necessary to them. Pascal may well have begun by declining on the ground that he was incapable of speaking of spiritual things to the Gentlemen who were more advanced than himself in the way of sanctity and whose religious knowledge was wider than his own. But Monsieur de Sacy and the other Solitaries had had an opportunity during recreation times of appreciating the neophyte's brilliant conversation. And if they had no inkling of his genius, they were aware of his great reputation as a scientist and lecturer. They therefore asked him to talk to them about the favourite reading of polite society, the books that were in fashion at the moment.

As it was January the meeting was held in one of the rooms of the Granges.[15] Pascal was very probably armed with notes[16] to which he added the works of Epictetus translated by Jean Goulu, known in religion as Dom Jean de Saint-François, in 1609, and the folio edition of Montaigne's *Essays* of 1652.[17]

At his side was the superior, Monsieur de Sacy, wearing a soutane, with his frank, open countenance which revealed his calm, thoughtful temperament. He was an enemy of Cartesianism which he found insufficiently religious and sought in the works of St Augustine "not the things which would provide fresh

[15] The conversation between Pascal and Lemaistre de Sacy, which forms part of Fontaine's *Mémoires*, was published before the *Mémoires* by Père Desmolets in 1728. "The conversation between M. Pascal and M. de Sacy must have been written down on the spot by M. Fontaine", said Père Guerrier in a letter to Marguerite Périer (*G.E.*, IV, p. 23). A critical edition of the text, based on seven manuscripts which had survived, was published by J. Bédier. An edition with a commentary has recently been published by J. Guitton: *Pascal: Entretien avec M. de Sacy sur Epictète et Montaigne* (Aix, 1946). M. Lafuma has published a critical edition of Desmolets in *Opuscules et lettres de Pascal* (Paris, 1955).
[16] According to the perfectly tenable hypothesis of Brunschvicg, *G.E.*, IV, p. 21.
[17] This was the discovery of F. Strowski. See *Pascal et son temps*, II, pp. 232 *et seq.*

material for controversial purposes, but those which would provide his piety with fresh nourishment".[18] Sitting round them were M. Lemaistre, the former barrister; M. d'Andilly, his grave countenance framed with white hair, the lover of gardens and mystics, whose pears were as highly praised as his translation of St Teresa; possibly M. Hamon who had returned from a consultation in the country; M. de Pontchâteau; the worthy Fontaine, M. de Sacy's young secretary, and others who were less well known.

Has anyone pointed out the extent to which the group was composed of young men? With the exception of d'Andilly, who was a little over sixty, the others were all between the ages of thirty-five and forty-five. Pascal was thirty-two and Fontaine thirty.

Pascal began with a broad exposition of the philosophy of Epictetus which was very fashionable at that time. Epictetus preached detachment from everything, taught all the human virtues and duties: "I venture to say", declared Pascal, "that he would deserve to be worshipped if he had been equally conscious of his powerlessness."[19] For Stoicism was founded on pride which ended with a eulogy of suicide.

Turning from Epictetus to Montaigne, Pascal, who for the occasion put on the spectacles of the *libertins*, saw in the author of the *Essays* the model of the sceptics. Montaigne "casts a universal doubt over everything and his doubt is so general that it ends by undermining itself, that is to say, if he doubts and even doubts the last supposition, his uncertainty recoils upon itself in a perpetual circle."[20] In order to make his exposition more convincing, the lecturer may perhaps have held up for his audience to see the frontispiece of his own copy of the *Essays* where beneath the portrait of the author was drawn a pair of scales with the rubric: "What do I know?" Then he explained to his hearers how Montaigne had demolished the claims of the jurists to arrive at absolute truth and underlined "the vanity of the most firmly accepted opinions".[21] Next, he assembled in a vigorous synthesis

---

[18] *G.E.*, IV, p. 27. Fontaine gives a detailed account of the Solitaries' discussion on Descartes.

[19] *Ibid.*, p. 35.   [20] *Ibid.*, p. 37.   [21] *Ibid.*, p. 40.

the arguments of the *Apology for Raymond de Sebonde* with which he associated himself. Finally, he made his own the heavy blows that Montaigne delivered against the philosophers and, in a tone of triumph, proceeded to attack Descartes without actually mentioning his name.

Who knows, therefore [he said], whether common sense which we take to be judge of the true possesses the being of him who created it? What is more, who knows what truth is and how we can be sure of possessing it without knowing it? Who even knows what being is, which is impossible to define because there is nothing that is more general so that in order to explain it, it would be necessary to start by using the word we are trying to define and say: It is etc.? And since we do not know what soul, body, time, space, movement, truth, good or even being are, and are unable to explain the idea that we have formed of them, how can we be sure that it is the same in all men, considering that we have no means of recognizing it except the uniformity of consequences, which is not invariably a sign of the uniformity of the principles underlying it? For the principles may well be different and yet lead to the same conclusions, each knowing that the true may often be deduced from the false?[22]

The Cartesians in the audience must have pulled long faces. Pascal made an ingenious use of Montaigne in order to demolish the principles of the master. He did not stop there. He showed that Montaigne also attacked the sciences. "In short, he analysed all the sciences with great profundity, demonstrated the uncertainty of the axioms of geometry and the terms which it did not define, like space, movement, etc., and physics in a good many other ways, and medicine in an infinity of ways, and politics and morality and jurisprudence and the rest."[23] What eloquence in the summary itself!

Pascal's exposition appeared to be complete. M. de Sacy then addressed the audience. With great discernment he praised the lecturer in a sentence which tells us many things and shows that he was by no means so ignorant of Montaigne as he boasted of being. "I certainly think that the man possessed intelligence, but

[22] *G.E.*, IV, p. 43.   [23] *Ibid.*, p. 44.

I am not sure that you do not attribute to him rather more than he had by the connections that you rightly establish between his principles."[24] Then he went on to praise St Augustine. The lecturer immediately joined issue with him. Pascal, who was inexhaustible, replied magnificently in the purest style of the *Pensées* with their vigour and richness of imagery. He praised Montaigne in a voice warm with admiration: "I confess, Monsieur, that in this writer I cannot see without delight proud reason so overwhelmingly defeated with its own arms, and *the bloody rebellion of man against man*, which hurls him from the society of God, where he had raised himself by the aphorisms of his feeble reason, into the nature of animals. . . ."[25] To be sure, Pascal added a strong criticism of Montaigne's Epicureanism. His conception of virtue was "naïve, homely, amusing, entertaining, and so to speak, capricious; it followed what attracted it and bantered lightheartedly about the strokes of good or ill fortune; sprawling voluptuously in the bosom of untroubled idleness. . . ."[26]

Pascal ended by showing that in his opinion the study of Epictetus and Montaigne combined to throw into relief the failure of man's attempt to come to grips with the mystery which he presents for himself and bears witness to the contradictions of human nature. The two philosophies "smash" against one another in order to make way for the truth of the Gospel which reconciles them.

A little fearfully de Sacy expressed his admiration for Pascal's verve and his skill in administering a cunning dosage of two conflicting poisons, but he warned his listeners against the indiscreet reading of these dangerous books. In his opinion it was a moot point whether one should not attach to the *Essays* a label representing a skull and crossbones. Pascal agreed at once: "If", he said, "Epictetus attacks sloth, his work leads to pride . . . and Montaigne is absolutely pernicious for those who are in any way prone to impiety and vice. That is why the study of them needs to be very carefully regulated . . . . It seems to me that it is only by bringing them together that they could fail to do damage because the evil of one provides an antidote to the evil of the other."[27]

[24] G.E., IV, pp. 45-6.   [25] *Ibid.*, p. 48.   [26] *Ibid.*, pp. 50-1.   [27] *Ibid.*, p. 56.

We owe it to Fontaine, the delightful historian of the Solitaries, that the text of Pascal's lecture has been preserved together with those of similar talks between Saint-Cyran, Lemaistre and Singlin. Fontaine had either made notes or had access to those of Pascal himself. It may be that another member of the audience wrote up the lecture from his notes.

The lecture on Epictetus and Montaigne, which aroused the admiration of Maurice Barrès, owes something of its fame to the fact that it anticipates the dialectic of the *Pensées* and serves as an introduction to them. Pascal might have spoken to his audience at Port-Royal about the metaphysics of Descartes over which they were greatly concerned, of the findings of physics or the application of calculation to the laws of chance. If he preferred to speak about "the search for decency" (*honnêteté*) which provided Méré with the subject-matter of his discourses, and if he deepened the meaning of the search, if he transformed it into the anxious quest by man for the secret of his nature and destiny, he reveals the meaning of his own restlessness.

The charm of his talk lies in the fact that in it we meet Pascal the lecturer, analyst and literary critic. And what a critic he is! He goes straight to the heart of a work, unravels its message and presents a striking summary of it. He opens up the path to a constructive and synthetic criticism.

It is easy to imagine him in the eighteenth century undertaking a similar analysis of Jean-Jacques Rousseau and Voltaire; in the nineteenth century, of Chateaubriand and Stendhal; or in our own time of Gide and Maurras, plotting the paths by which man endeavours to escape his destiny: pride and pleasure, reason and emotion, morality and poetry, and reconciling them in his own work.

And even if he had not yet embarked on the final synthesis, what a treat to attend a reading of the *Essays* by their greatest reader! It is the reading of the work of one genius by another genius; it is Racine annotating Euripides and Tacitus; Péguy commenting on Bergson; Claudel introducing Rimbaud.

While Pascal was meditating at Port-Royal, an event occurred at the Church of Saint-Sulpice in Paris on 31st January 1655 which was to have far-reaching consequences. One of the assistant priests, the Abbé Picoté, refused the Duc de Liancourt absolution because he had sent his little daughter as a boarder to the nuns of Port-Royal and because he had staying with him two priests who were suspected of Jansenism. The priest exceeded his powers in the most extraordinary way. The duke protested in vain that he submitted completely to the decision of the Church. Monsieur Olier, the parish priest, supported the Abbé Picoté and went as far as to threaten to refuse the duke Communion if he came to the altar rails.

In fact, two years previously Pope Innocent X had issued a bull condemning five propositions extracted from Jansen's *Augustinus*.[28] The five propositions were not actually to be found in the book, but their equivalents, or something almost identical, were there. The bishops had supported the Pope's condemnation; Arnauld and his friends maintained that the contentious propositions were not contained in the *Augustinus*, that the sentences which were similar to the propositions could, when read in their proper context, be given a perfectly orthodox interpretation which was in fact Jansen's own. Another possible interpretation was close to Calvinism, and it was this, they thought, that the Pope and the bishops had in mind when they condemned the five propositions.[29]

What was described as the distinction between "law" and "fact" was not scholastic hair splitting or a subterfuge to prevent Jansen's book from being condemned as heretical. It was necessary to discover precisely what doctrine the Pope had condemned.

But the French bishops censured Arnauld's interpretation. The Jansenists promised to remain silent about the matter when, unfortunately for everybody, Picoté reopened the case. For in both camps there were well-balanced minds and hotheads. On Port-Royal's side wisdom was represented by du Barcos, a nephew of Saint-Cyran's, Singlin and Lemaistre de Sacy who counselled

[28] Official translation of the Bull dated 31st May 1653 in *G.E.*, IV, pp. 85 *et seq.*
[29] The unanimity of the bishops in associating themselves with the Pope prevented the supporters of Jansen from even thinking of refusing to accept the bull. It will be apparent that A. Bayet was guilty of an anachronism when he said: "On the question of law, the popes are infallible, etc." (*Les Provinciales de Pascal*, Paris, 1929, p. 45). Papal infallibility (defined in 1870) was not in question at this time.

silence. But others were tugging at the bit. Antoine Arnauld, seizing the opportunity provided by the Sulpician, set to work on a pamphlet against Picoté.

When Pascal was staying at the Granges he little suspected that in a short time he, too, would find himself carried a long way from Epictetus and Montaigne, that he would play a brilliant part in one of the controversies which was to rend the Church in France for more than a century to come. For the moment he gave himself up to prayer and rejoicing. At the end of January, in a long letter to Gilberte, Jacqueline described the outcome of their brother's religious evolution and his ardour.

> He has been given a room or cell among the Solitaries of Port-Royal and has written to me expressing his great delight at finding himself treated and lodged like a prince, but a prince according to the judgment of St Bernard in a solitary place where you promise to practise the virtue of poverty in every way that discretion permits. He attends the whole of the office from Prime to Compline without experiencing the slightest hardship in rising at five in the morning; and as though God wished him to unite fasting with keeping late hours in defiance of all the precepts of medicine, which have forbidden him to do either, supper is beginning to bring on stomach troubles and I think that he will give it up.[30]

She recounts the rumours circulating about Pascal since he had left Paris: "Some say that he has become a monk; others that he is a hermit, and others still that he is at Port-Royal. He knows and is not allowing it to worry him."[31] She announces that, at the end of January, her brother returned to Paris "where he is detained by business", but that he is in a hurry to return to Solitude.

In fact, by October he was back again at Port-Royal des Champs, living under the pseudonym of Monsieur de Mons, his grandmother's name. Jacqueline wrote to him from Paris on 26th October to ask for information about a new method of reading: "Our Mothers have instructed me to write to you so that you can let me have full details of your method of teaching people to read by *be, ce, de,* etc., in which it is not necessary for children to know the names of the letters."[32] Pascal had begun to

[30] *G.E.,* IV, pp. 66–7.   [31] *Ibid.,* p. 67.   [32] *Ibid.,* p. 77.

take an interest in educational problems which was to prove lasting in a milieu which was brightened by the presence of children. He had already anticipated the method of reading that is used today by which instead of teaching children the letters one by one, they are grouped in syllables. In this field, too, Pascal was a precursor. During the same month of October a young orphan of sixteen, the nephew of a religious, became one of the pupils. He appeared to be extremely intelligent, delicate and sensitive. Lancelot, who congratulated himself on finding that he showed such brilliance in Greek and poetry, had been told to supervise his reading with particular care. Pascal had an opportunity of seeing him, possibly about Plutarch and Euripides. He soon became the favourite pupil of Monsieur Lemaistre, who called him his son. His name was Jean Racine.

In December Pascal was back in the Rue des Francs-Bourgeois-Saint-Michel. Jacqueline wrote to him, jokingly:

> People congratulate me on the great fervour which lifts you so far above common practice that you have relegated the broom among the unnecessary household utensils. . . . It is necessary that, for a month at least, you should be as clean as you are dirty so that it can be seen that you are as successful in showing a humble diligence and vigilance towards the person who serves you as in the humble neglect of what affects you; and after that, it will be glorious and edifying for others to see you covered with filth if it is really true that this is the sign of a greater degree of perfection, which I doubt because St Bernard did not hold this view.[33]

In fact, the biography of the saint who had founded the Cistercian Order, to which the Abbey of Port-Royal was attached, relates "that it pleased him always to be clad poorly, but never in a squalid manner."

In the meantime Arnauld was busy trying to extricate himself in the Picoté affair. He had attempted to rouse public opinion by writing his *Lettre d'un Docteur de Sorbonne à une personne de condition* ("Letter from a Doctor of the Sorbonne to a Person of Quality") which was published on 24th February 1655. The letter had pro-

[33] *G.E.*, IV, p. 81.

voked some sharp rejoinders, in particular one by Père Annat, a
Jesuit and the confessor of Louis XIV. Arnauld replied with a
Seconde lettre de M. Arnauld, Docteur en Sorbonne, à un Duc et Pair
("Second Letter from Mr. Arnauld, Doctor of the Sorbonne, to
a Duke and Peer") in July 1655. The letter was denounced at the
Sorbonne: Arnauld felt that he was heading for a condemnation
and would lose the battle. He was being asked by people on all
sides to put his case before the public. In December he wrote a
further note defending his position and one January evening, when
Pascal was at the Granges, someone read the note to Arnauld's
friends who had gathered at the time fixed for spiritual reading.[34] Everybody listened attentively. Arnauld's style was clear,
but ponderous and academic; his arguments remained abstract,
theological and boring. When the reading came to an end
everyone was silent. "I'm sure", somebody said, "that you think
it's a bad piece of work and I think you're right." Then someone
said to M. Pascal: "But you're young. You ought to do something."[35]

Pascal replied "that in fact he saw how the case could be presented, but that all he could promise to do was to draft a plan
provided that there was somebody to polish it up and put it into
a state in which it could be published".[36]

And when he was back in his cell he set to work on Arnauld's
notes.

[34] This emerges from Marguerite Périer's account (*G.E.*, VII, p. 60). But a
letter from Mère Angélique (*G.E.*, IV, p. 107) proves that Arnauld was in
hiding. In Paris, says Pontchâteau (*Recueil d'Utrecht*, p. 229). It was therefore
somebody else who read his note.

[35] *G.E.*, VII, pp. 60–1. I have amended the account which attributes the
remark to Arnauld himself.

[36] This is also included in the information due to Nicole in *Les Provinciales ou
Lettres écrites par Louis de Montalte* . . . with notes by Guillaume Wendrock, new
edition, Amsterdam, published at the expense of the Society, 1767 (vol. I, p. 8).
Cf. *G.E.*, VII, p. 67.

Part II

THE PROVINCIAL LETTERS
(1656–1658)

"It was the old French argument . . . about the *honnête homme*, life against the domination of the Schools; it was the old saying of Montaigne and Rabelais, of Descartes and Molière, of Pascal and Rousseau against our enemies—the learned."

Charles Péguy

CHAPTER I

Clandestine Journalism

PASCAL was under the impression that he had done no more than provide a draft for the defence of Arnauld; but when he read it, the entire company cried out: "It's fine! It will go down splendidly! We must get it printed!"[1] The Gentlemen were dazzled, mesmerized by the nonchalant manner in which the newcomer treated the doctors. And those sly winks at the reader! The mocking, bantering tone! The air of respect which puffed up the Sorbonne out of all proportion in order to be in a better position to deflate it like a balloon by a series of pinpricks! Everyone agreed that the cunning pages must be given to the public. The letter was printed on large sheets and dated 23rd January 1656. It exploded immediately like a powder magazine: one of the most staggering publishing successes of the Ancien Régime. It was greeted with roars of laughter all over Paris and the Picoté case took an entirely unforeseen turn.

Pascal was naturally persuaded to write a sequel to the First Letter. For a whole year, in letters which were published either once or twice a month, he continued his luminous defence of Port-Royal.

We know how he worked. In the course of a conversation in 1674, when he was being asked questions by Boileau about the assistance given to Pascal, Arnauld replied "that they helped him, but in this way: when he had written a letter he came and read it to them [Nicole, Arnauld, Dubois, Saint-Gilles, etc.] and if they found that a single one of the company was unmoved and remained unsmiling when all the others acclaimed it, Pascal re-

[1] Words put into Arnauld's mouth by Marguerite Périer, Lafuma, III, p. 67. We have seen that it was impossible for him to have been at Port-Royal des Champs.

wrote it and kept on revising it until it satisfied everybody; that the Sixteenth Letter was not written entirely by him; that others had worked on it, that it was a little obsequious and did not stand up as well as the remainder."[2]

In the *Histoire des Provinciales*, which he wrote for the sixth Latin edition of the *Letters* translated by Mlle de Joncoux, Nicole confirmed a statement by Dr Vaillant. Montalte, he said, "often took a whole three weeks to write a single letter. He even re-wrote several of them as many as seven or eight times in order to bring them to the state of perfection in which we have them."[3]

The number of copies printed was enormous for the age: between six thousand and ten thousand copies.[4] According to Dom Clémencet, Père d'Avrigny put the number of readers of the "Little Letters" at a million.[5]

These broadsheets, which were sold for two *sols*, six *deniers*, found their way into every corner: the alcoves and salons of the marquises; the homes of magistrates and judges; the cells of monks; the desk of the chancellor and the office of Mazarin, the prime minister.[6] Some people jumped for joy. From the provinces, Mme de Sévigné begged her friends to send them to her. Guy Patin collected them.[7] But others, particularly the Jesuits, were furious. The doctors had to bleed Chancellor Séguier who was on the verge of apoplexy.[8] During a meal in the refectory at the Sorbonne, Dr Meusnier, after approving of the Second Letter with a smile, found himself publicly accused of heresy by Dr Morel.[9]

Although they laughed over it the magistrates, on the orders of the central government, tried to proceed against these clandestine publications. The printers risked imprisonment and had a taste of the Châtelet. At half past eleven on 2nd February Savreux, his wife and two messenger boys were arrested.[10] His shop was closed. There were searches at Desprez's and at Petit's whose wife went

---

[2] *G.E.*, VII, p. 63.   [3] *Les Provinciales*, 1767 ed., vol. I, p. 12.
[4] E. Jovy, *Études pascaliennes*, IX: "Le Journal de M. de Saint-Gilles" (Paris, 1936), p. 181.
[5] Jovy, *op. cit.*, VI, p. 32.   [6] "Le Journal de M. de Saint-Gilles", p. 181.
[7] *G.E.*, VI, pp. 305–6.   [8] *G.E.*, IV, p. 227.
[9] "Le Journal de M. de Saint-Gilles", p. 118. The charge is reproduced in *G.E.*, IV, p. 190.
[10] "Le Journal de M. de Saint-Gilles", pp. 119–20.

up to the first floor when the police arrived. She piled the type into her apron and took it round to a friend's where three hundred copies of the Second Letter were printed at nightfall and twelve hundred the following day.[11] Two months later, on 30th March, the police seized some type at the printing works of Langlois and the lieutenant of police at Aubray searched the Abbey of Port-Royal des Champs without finding anything.[12] Informers were placed in all printing works, with the result that from the Third Letter onwards printing presses had to be hidden in the homes of private persons or in hotel rooms.[13] With the connivance of the registrar, they were actually hidden for a time at the Collège d'Harcourt, today the Lycée Saint-Louis.

A year after the beginning of the campaign the tone changed; Pascal delivered an attack on Père Annat and the government became angry. On 23rd January 1657, a regulation by the lieutenant of police—today we would say the Prefect of Police—was posted in the streets of Paris which forbade the publication of books and pamphlets without the King's licence, that is to say, without the censors' certificate.[14] It became necessary to redouble precautions and distribute the type after the eight pages of the Seventeenth Letter had been printed. As the lines at the end were not straight because the letters had slipped, Pascal added this ironical postscript: "We go the rounds of the printers. . . . It is too much of a bother to be reduced to printing at Osnabrück."[15]

In June, three months after the publication of the last of the Letters, the records of interrogations at the Châtelet prove that the printer Langlois was in prison.[16] He remained there for four months and about October Desprez was arrested. "With great difficulty he escaped the penalty of whipping and was condemned to five years' banishment."[17] A year later, in 1658, Préveray, too, found himself in the Châtelet for publishing a second Latin edition of the Letters.[18]

It will be apparent therefore that we are concerned with a form

[11] G.E., IV, pp. 161–4. Cf. the account by Dom Clémencet, Histoire générale de Port-Royal, III, pp. 347–57.
[12] Ibid., p. 127.   [13] Marguerite Périer, Lafuma, II, p. 67.
[14] G.E., VI, p. 305.   [15] Ibid., p. 373.
[16] Interrogation of Langlois, G.E., VII, pp. 70–4.   [17] Ibid., p. 221.
[18] Ibid., p. 81, quoting Hermant, Mémoires, IV, p. 156.

of literature which owed part of its success to the fact that it was clandestine.

Needless to say, the author of the *Letters* remained strictly anonymous. If he had revealed his identity, he would have risked imprisonment in the Bastille. A spokesman of the Jesuits said, charmingly, that he would go to the stake "if the full rigour of the law were applied". The fact that his name was a secret heightened the general curiosity in the same way as with Vercors during the Occupation. Some people attributed the "Little Letters" to Antoine Arnauld, which shows that they could scarcely have been familiar with the leaden prose of the doctor of Port-Royal. Others whispered the name of Gomberville, a decrepit academician, or that of the Abbé Le Roy de Haute-Fontaine. The magistrates and lawyers favoured M. Lemaistre, which was a great compliment to his tortuous and inflated style. They indulged, in fact, in the wildest speculations. Pascal was highly amused. He had signed the Third Letter with some enigmatic initials: "Your very humble and very obedient servant, E.A.A.B.P.A.F.D.E.P."[19]

You did not think that anyone would be interested to know who we are [he wrote at the beginning of the Eighth Letter]. There are, however, people who try to guess, but make a poor showing. Some take me for a Doctor of the Sorbonne; others attribute my letters to four or five persons who like me are neither Priests nor Ecclesiastics. All this misguided suspicion makes me realize that I have not succeeded too badly in my idea of only being known to you. . . .[20]

He could sleep in peace and ran little risk of discovery. To the great majority of his readers his name would have meant nothing even if they had been told it. Pascal's reputation was confined to the closed and worldly circles of the Duc de Roannez and the Marquise de Sablé. He was, to be sure, known at Court. He had become celebrated in the learned world owing to his work in mathematics and physics, but the inhabitants of that world were a thousand miles from suspecting him of being

[19] Meaning: *Et ancient ami, Blaise Pascal, Auvergnat, fils d'Étienne Pascal* ("An erstwhile friend, Blaise Pascal, Auvergnat, son of Étienne Pascal").

[20] *G.E.*, V, p. 135.

the author of a series of satirical pamphlets on theological subjects.

The Jesuits, who were not devoid of shrewdness, had divined almost at once from the style of the *Provincial Letters* that the author was not to be sought among the clergy, the people of the Sorbonne or the lawyers. The very offhand tone suggested the man of the world. Their police were very competent. They guessed that it was Pascal. Now, in May Pascal was living—under the name of M. de Mons with his servant who was called Picard—at an inn "whose sign was King David in the Rue des Poirées", right under the very noses of the good fathers, close to their citadel, the Collège de Clermont (today Lycée Louis-le-Grand). Périer, who had joined him there, was visited by Père de Frétat, a Jesuit whose brother had married Pascal's first cousin.[21] The priest was sent as an ambassador of the Society to inform Périer that the Jesuits were convinced that "his brother-in-law, Monsieur Pascal, was the author of the 'little letters' against them". Père de Frétat was so certain of it that he came, not to advise Pascal and Périer to declare their innocence, but to invite Pascal "not to continue, because if he did he might get into trouble". It was a threat. Périer was embarrassed and replied, without telling a lie: "Monsieur Pascal cannot prevent you from suspecting him. If he were to say that it is not he, you would not believe him. There is therefore nothing to be done." "Take care", answered the Jesuit as he took his leave. The most amusing thing about the story is that Périer's bed was covered with about twenty copies of the Seventh or Eighth Letter which were fresh from the press and had been laid out to dry. A Jesuit lay brother had even sat by the bed without noticing anything. When the two religious left, Périer breathed a sigh of relief and rushed into the next room where Pascal was. And the two of them burst out laughing like a couple of schoolboys on holiday.

It was not until two years after the publication of the first of the *Provincial Letters* that Nicole indirectly brought Pascal into the picture in a note in his Latin translation of the *Letters*.[22] A year

[21] On this incident, see the study by E. Jovy, "Pascal et le P. de Frétat", in *Études pascaliennes*, III, pp. 88–126.

[22] The note, which is on page 448 of Ludovici Montaltii, *Literae Provinciales,*

later another Jesuit, Père Fabri, which was probably the pseudonym
of Père Vavassor, revealed, it might be said officially, the name of
the author to those who were still unaware of it.[23] But for a century
and a half the *Provincial Letters* continued to appear under the
name of Louis de Montalte, a pseudonym borrowed by Pascal
from a work on law which he may have chosen because he saw
in it an allusion both to the name of his maternal grandmother
and to his native town of Clermont. In theory they retained their
clandestine character and were supposedly printed, without
the King's licence and without any risk, at Cologne, in Holland
or in England. In fact they were simply printed in Paris like many
other Jansenist works which purported to come from Utrecht and
like the novels of Diderot which purported to be printed at
Pekin or in the Monomotapa.

Abroad it took people longer to discover the identity of the
author of the *Provincial Letters* and the English translation was
preceded by a portrait of Montalte which, to put it mildly, was
fanciful.

With the *Provincial Letters* Pascal inaugurated what is known
today as "the press campaign". It is true that the *Gazette*,
launched on 30th May 1631 by Théophraste Renaudot, the
"inventor" of journalism, had preceded him. Its founder had
written: "The *Gazette* differs from history: history is the story
of things that have happened; the *Gazette* is simply a report of
the rumours circulating about them."[24] But the *Gazette* did not

etc. Coloniae, Apud N. Schouten, 1658, is reproduced in *G.E.*, IV, p. 351: "At
that time I was in Paris", wrote Nicole, "and as I sometimes applied myself to
mathematics as a rest from other more serious studies, I had formed a close
acquaintanceship with M. Pascal, whose great abilities in this field are known to
all the mathematicians in Europe. He was the uncle of the young lady and the
unimpeachable witness to the miracle, etc. . . . " In fact, contrary to the view
expressed by the editors of the *Grands Écrivains*, there was nothing rash in mentioning Pascal's name in connection with a miracle of which, as was well known,
his niece was the beneficiary.

[23] In his *Notae in notas W. Wendrockii*, 1659. Cf. *G.E.*, VII, p. 78, n. 1. In the
foreword to the edition of the *Provincial Letters* of 1767 we read: "There are few
people who are unaware that 'Wendrock' is the famous M. Nicole who concealed his identity under this name as M. Pascal had concealed his identity under
the name of Montalte" (p. xi).

[24] See P. Bouesseau, "Théophraste Renaudot", in *Petites-Affiches*, 24–26th
October 1953.

become involved in reporting great events. Now, the very title of Pascal's pamphlets: "Letters to the Provincial", which he did not devise himself, undoubtedly anticipates an article by a regular correspondent in Paris or by a special correspondent. And when he describes his interviews with a Jansenist, a Dominican and a Jesuit he behaves quite simply like a reporter of genius. He invents all the tricks of the trade: a sketch of one of the speakers knocked off in a couple of lines; the assumption of the detached and falsely naïve attitude of an impartial witness; the résumé of obscure controversies in a few simplified formulas. If he had been able to use the format and huge headlines of our daily papers, the result would have been stunning. Imagine this in banner headlines:

TO BE A CATHOLIC, YOU MUST BELIEVE THAT ALL RIGHTEOUS MEN POSSESS PROXIMATE POWER REGARDLESS OF MEANING.

And for the Second Letter:

WHY WE ARE ALL ECCENTRICS, HERETICS OR JANSENISTS.

And the Third:

IT'S EASIER TO CENSURE THAN TO JUDGE BECAUSE IT IS FAR EASIER TO FIND MONKS THAN REASONS.

For the Fourth:

FATHER BAUNY AND THE NEW REDEMPTION.

When Pascal had exhausted all the resources of reporting, he resorted to scandal-mongering. In religious and spiritual terms the case of the Casuist corresponds to a vast criminal bankruptcy, to a crack-up on the stock exchange of moral values, to a sort of theological Panama Scandal. And Pascal exploited this particular line to the full. He goes from one sensational revelation to another. He wants to shock. His technique is very much that of the crime pages of the dailies with the big circulations. His successor was not the worthy Nicole with his *Lettres sur les hérésies imaginaires*

("Letters on Imaginary Heresies"), but the Zola of the Dreyfus
Case, the Barrès of the Panama Scandal. Pascal himself might very
well have called the greatest of the *Provincial Letters*, beginning
with the Fifth, *J'accuse* or *Guilty Faces*.

But there is something more in the "Little Letters" than the
start of a brilliant career in journalism, or a press campaign, or
the rather noisy denunciation of a scandal; something which
makes them greater than Juvenal's *Satires*, the *Lettres persanes* or the
pamphlets of Voltaire and Paul-Louis Courier, and which relates
them closely to Cardinal Newman's *Apologia pro vita sua* or
Péguy's *Cahiers* against the Sorbonne: it is the presence of the
spirit. Anyone who feels and appreciates the things of the spirit
will discover beneath Pascal's surface laughter the profound
indignation and sometimes the tragic cry of wounded moral
delicacy of which we are conscious in Newman's opening pages,
trembling under the accusations of lying and hypocrisy brought
against him by Kingsley. Laughter is close to anger and comedy
verges on tragedy. For Pascal everything that he held sacred was
at stake. He defends his heart and his love, his purity of soul, the
grace which had opened his eyes; in short, God himself, in
exactly the same way that Péguy defends himself by defending
Joan of Arc and by pursuing with his passionate sarcasm Langlois,
Lanson, Lavisse and their like. And in the last *Provincial Letters*
the battle rises to a higher plane, becomes truly a conflict between
two souls, two adversaries who are invisible to one another: on
one side, Père Annat, the all-powerful confessor of Louis XIV;
on the other Soeur Sainte-Euphémie, who is silently praying in
her monastic cell and who, as Pascal somehow senses, will die
as a result of signing the formulary.

Begun in the light, bantering style of a theological argument
taking place amid laughter in a salon, the battle was destined to
end with death and bloodshed. And then God himself intervened
through the miracle of the Holy Thorn which burst on the world
in the middle of the row over the *Provincial Letters*. Pascal abandoned the shallow world of journalism in order to penetrate into
the kingdom of the Prophet.

If we risked a decidedly profane comparison—in the last
analysis death consecrates all the characters of a drama—we might

say that the *Provincial Letters* remind us of the last performance of the *Malade imaginaire*. It began with laughter, grease paint and crystal candelabra. It ended with coughing and spitting blood disguised as farce and, after the curtain had fallen, with Molière's agony, death and final appearance at the tribunal of the Sovereign Judge evoked by Bossuet. It is in this respect that the *Provincial Letters* are superior to *Tartuffe* and the *Lettres persanes*. Pascal was committed in the strongest sense of the term to three conflicts to which he brought the same pugnacity, but in which he used different methods: three eternal struggles: a battle fought with humour and ridicule against the academic attitude of the Sorbonne; a more serious battle against the abolition of sin by casuistry, and lastly an angry and sometimes almost desperate war on behalf of the "mystics" against the "politicians".[25] Three phases of the *Provincial Letters*, three aspects which after three centuries, so far from being out of date, make them appear just as topical, just as youthful, just as alive, as aggressive and as necessary as when they were written.

[25] The allusion is to a formula of Péguy's.—*Trans.*

CHAPTER II

The Comedy of the Sorbonne

THE *Provincial Letters* were a declaration of war against the Sorbonne and a pure product of the Latin Quarter. They could only have been written in the area circumscribed by the Seine, the Boulevard Saint-Michel, the Rue Soufflot, the Rue d'Ulm and the École Polytechnique, on the summit of the hill where today Pascal's remains lie buried and on the edge of which he made his home.

These few acres, where in the seventeenth century steep, dark, tortuous lanes interlaced, were dominated by the massive buildings of the Collège de Clermont, the stronghold of the Jesuits, by those of the Dominican priory of Saint-Jacques, the Collège de France and the Sorbonne. All through the middle ages the acropolis of the hill of Sainte-Geneviève had played the part of the intellectual agora of Europe, a clearing house for Western ideas. Pascal could find in it a vast population of learned and argumentative ghosts: the ghosts of Abélard, Albert the Great, St Thomas Aquinas, St Bonaventure and Dante—all the saints and apologists whose ink and saliva had helped to build medieval Christendom.

In the first *Provincial Letter*, fearing police intervention, Pascal had felt the need to live in the very heart of the quarter so that he could breathe in the theological aroma of the celebrated hill.[1] When he leant out of his hotel window "at the sign of King David", he could see the professors whom he caricatured passing by and enjoy the luxury of knocking off his portraits from life. He wanted to be as up-to-date as possible with the latest gossip

---

[1] I suspect that this was the real reason why he went to live at the King David inn.

and to be able, within a few hours of leaving the study of some learned doctor, to reach the Collège d'Harcourt where the printing presses were in action, making a détour by way of Desprez's bookshop in the Rue Saint-Jacques and returning home past the Dominican priory. In short, he wished like Péguy to be within easy range of the Sorbonne which he attacked without ever having been one of its pupils.

The beginning of the *Provincial Letters*, as Racine pointed out, was simply a series of comedies. When one comes to think of it, it was no mean feat to make people laugh until the tears ran down their cheeks when defending the cause of Antoine Arnauld in a purely theological controversy! In the first place, it was essential to state the case with exceptional clarity, make the subject as transparently plain as the theme of the *Bourgeois gentilhomme* and easily accessible if not to the porters of the Place de Grève, at any rate to women and students. Then, going back to the doctors of theology, show them bogged down by their jargon, their subtle, abstruse and sophisticated formulas. Nothing is more absurd than a pedant who no longer knows what he is talking about and finds himself caught in the middle of some spluttering, unintelligible speech. He is like the clown who trips himself up.

What is the substance of Pascal's complaints about the professors of the Sorbonne? Their verbosity. They were in agreement about the words they used without being able to agree on their meaning. They admitted that everybody possessed "proximate power" to do good, but they were very hard put to it to define the nature of the power. Some spoke of a "sufficient grace" which did not in fact suffice. For the complex and difficult reality of analysing a free action they substituted a meaningless vocabulary. Now, what was Molière's complaint against the doctors of medicine? Their blather, which purported to achieve victory over sickness and death with a stream of Latin words. Just as Pascal, in a parable, compares the Church to a man wounded by thieves before whom the doctors engage in verbal quibbles, so Molière shows us Macroton, Tomès and Diafoirus squabbling and gesticulating at the sick man's bedside.

Next, Pascal accuses the theologians of splitting hairs. In the very first act of the comedy, he observes that the quarrel is purely

one of words and tells the Thomist doctor of the discovery.
"Gently, he said to me, you have to be a Theologian to understand
the outcome. The difference between us is such a subtle one that
we can scarcely grasp it ourselves. . . ."[2]

The impossibility of knowing what they are talking about
which afflicts nearly all the doctors is already entertaining. In the
Third Letter Pascal returns to the charge: "There is only an
imperceptible difference between the proposition [of Arnauld]
and the faith. The distance is so minute that I might find myself
in opposition to the Doctors of the Church through having tried
too hard to bring myself into conformity with the Doctors of the
Sorbonne."[3]

It must be confessed that on this occasion Pascal's doctors of
theology outdo Molière's doctors of medicine. Nevertheless, the
motto which is common to both sections of the Faculty is
Béralde's retort: "You only have to put on a doctor's cap and
gown for every form of twaddle to become learned and every
folly sound reason."

The arguments and subtleties of the doctors are only amusing
and ridiculous in the mouths of the living. When we read
Arnauld's pleas we are smothered under the mass of abstractions.
Pascal, the inheritor of the verve of the great comic writers,
makes them behave like a collection of puppets. Six Turks'
heads in the first of the *Provincial Letters* and a dozen in the next
four. Since he was unable to make them perform on the boards,
the writer caricatures them with large strokes of the brush,
compelling them to argue and gesticulate in the most fantastic
manner. The Molinist's visit to the Dominicans is a scene of pure
burlesque. Pascal himself flits about like a butterfly, dives in and
out among his doctors of theology, passes from one to the other
and on the way prepares the big scene: his entry into the Jesuit
theologian's room in the Fourth Letter. And the Jesuit soon
gives place to the casuist in the Sixth Letter. After making steady
progress, Pascal finally has the feeling that he has scored a bull's-
eye. He drops the other supporting characters. The comedy loses
something of its breadth, but the shafts are concentrated in order,
in future, to riddle this one old boy. We are aware of the presence

[2] *G.E.*, IV, p. 130.   [3] *Ibid.*, pp. 215-6.

in the background of "the four animals: Suarez, Vasquez, Molina, Valentia . . ." and above all of Escobar.[4]

If Pascal has changed the subject, if he has abandoned the professors of the Sorbonne, it is because he had made them look sufficiently ridiculous. As early as Febuary 1656, after the appearance of the Third Letter, Méré is supposed to have advised a change of target. "Do not become involved in theological dissertations," he said to him. "Why not attack the casuists? The field is vast and might keep you busy for a long time to come. The subject-matter can be grasped by anybody, and instead of babbling about you and Jansenism, they will find themselves in a very awkward position; they will have to defend themselves."[5] Pascal and Arnauld had also received a warning from Rome that their defence of the famous five propositions was regarded with disfavour, but that nobody was likely to worry over much if they drew attention to the excesses of the moralists.[6]

In the case of the casuists Pascal returned to the method which had served him so well against the Sorbonne. In the first place the casuists must be made to look ridiculous. What we have now is a comedy of character with only two characters. The first of them, the visitor, is Pascal himself. He plays with his casuist as a cat plays with a mouse. He allows himself to be wheedled, appears naïve, pathetic, suffering, acquiescent, shrewd in appreciating distinctions. Then he smiles, grumbles from time to time, pins down his opponent, teases him with questions which are at once innocent and barbed, makes him angry and draws in his claws the moment that the other is on the point of discovering the double game of which he is the victim. In the end he has to restrain himself from bursting out laughing, retreats sometimes in order to have a better laugh, but it seems that he has to swallow his laughter. Pascal has leaned over the abyss of human folly and there are moments when he is seized with fear and giddiness.

The other, the person visited, is a good fellow though a trifle unctuous. A veritable glutton for casuistry, he loves his trade as though it were an art, a vocation, and pushes his passion for prob-

---

[4] *G.E.*, IV, p. 306.   [5] *Ibid.*, p. 230.
[6] See the comments of Cardinal Barberini on the Jesuits: "Le Journal de M. de Saint-Gilles", p. 148. Reference to Hermant, *G.E.*, IV, p. 231.

lems of conscience to the point of lunacy of the "connoisseur of plums". He is a collector of baroque decisions. He has replaced the Gospels by Escobar. "There's a *man* for you," I said to him, "that Escobar." "Everyone is fond of him," replied the Father. "He asks such nice questions. . . . You can't get out of them. . . . I spend days and nights reading him; I do practically nothing else."[7]

The good Jesuit, who suffers from a moral myopia, like all eccentrics is already absurd in himself. He is out of touch with life and has lost his common sense. His mania leads him, although he does not realize it, to make the most idiotic suggestions. Thus like Molière's avaricious and blathering fathers of families he is ready to make himself a laughing stock. If, as Bergson has maintained, the comic lies in the artificial, the mechanical grafted on to the living, the good Jesuit who does not realize that Pascal is laughing at him, who continues to pursue his obsession, is really the perfect example of the comic character. It has been said that in his caricature of the casuistical Jesuit, Pascal took pleasure in laughing at the absurdities of a person who was nothing but his own invention. It is perfectly true that the worthy Jesuit is an invention, but Pascal's genius enabled him to bring together a wealth of genuine characteristics for the purpose of creating a fictitious being and so to form his character by copying what he had observed. In many respects his old boy is drawn from life. His little gestures, his intonation and his style make us cry out: "They're just like that!" "It's they to the life!"

Except in one thing: their naïveté. In general, the Jesuits are not considered particularly naïve. Now naïveté is in fact the best feature of Pascal's Jesuit. He is not horrible; there is nothing of the rogue or of a Tartuffe about him. He is a good fellow who is decent and upright in his personal life and who retains enough of the reader's sympathy to prevent him from growing angry and to make him laugh. Now Pascal's laughter in the first letters is frank and open: it is without that appalling after-taste that we sometimes sense in Molière's.

In order to arouse the reader's interest, the presentation had to be in dramatic form. Pascal discovered the trick in the develop-

[7] G.E., IV, p. 307.

ment of the rhythm in each of his miniature comedies. Suppose, for example, we re-read the Fifth Letter, taking care to note the development. After a general exposition of the subject we come to the description of the casuist's entry: the inimitable presentation of Escobar, the explanation of the theory of probabilism, the enumeration of the doctors in casuistry with the broad comic effect of their Flemish, Spanish and Italian names. "What an argument," someone may say. But it is the rhythm of farce. The technique goes back to Rabelais. We laugh for the sake of laughing. We might have laughed just the same at such names as Akakia, Singlin and Petitpied, the doctors of Port-Royal. Let us look at them more closely: the enumeration of the foreign sources of casuistry is at bottom a reproach for not being French, for finding material in exotic countries like Spain and Italy where people behave extravagantly. With Pascal the French Catholicism of the classic period becomes aware of its originality which is expressed in its seriousness, its taste for moderation, its contempt for anything that is fanciful or exaggerated. It rejects the excesses of the Counter-Reformation. Later on, in the Ninth Letter, attacking Pères Le Moine, Binet and Garasse, Pascal will laugh at their lack of discretion and taste. He will collect a bouquet of ridiculous, inflated expressions whose extravagant verbiage betrays their sixteenth-century origin. We always find ourselves returning to Molière. Among the Jesuits of his own time Pascal discovered the "*Précieuses ridicules*" of the devout life.

The pace of his comedy must never be allowed to flag. Pascal made it a rule to excel himself. Re-read the Seventh Letter, the one that Boileau placed on the same level as the works of the Ancients, that is to say, higher than anything owing to the perfection of its style. It is controlled like a superb rapier duel which comes to life, grows more and more brilliant, rises to a dizzy crescendo. We feel like shouting: "Touché! Touché!"

Such was the comedy of the Sorbonne and the casuists. Almost half a century later they were the delight of Mme de Sévigné, who at that time was over seventy: "Sometimes in order to amuse ourselves," she wrote to her daughter, "we read the *Little Letters*. Lord! What charm! And how my son laps them up! . . . Is it possible to possess a more perfect style, a more subtle gift of mockery—more natural, more delicate, a worthier child of the Dialogues of Plato which are so magnificent?"[8]

To those who asked him which books he would like to have written if he had not written his own, Bossuet used to answer: the *Provincial Letters*.[9]

And a hundred years later Besoigne, writing the history of Port-Royal, enjoyed himself hugely when he came to the *Provincial Letters*. The comedy was a favourite with the Court and the man in the street.

But not everybody laughed so goodnaturedly, even among the Solitaries. Many people secretly blamed Pascal for his mockery. They felt vaguely that Catholicism had nothing to gain from these squabbles which were grist to the mill of the Reformers and the *libertins*. Mère Angélique, Singlin, du Barcos, Hamon and Lemaistre de Sacy were embarrassed by this war dance round the Jesuits.[10] They were not the only ones. And if Pascal, who was accused by his enemies of making fun of sacred things, replied bluntly in a passage of extraordinary eloquence, it was nevertheless true that the *Provincial Letters*, by holding priests up to ridicule in public, seemed to foreshadow the gibes of the philosophers of the eighteenth century who showed less respect for sacred things. Certain words were slipped in which went further than Pascal intended and anticipated Voltaire: "In truth, people are growing suspicious and only believe what they see. . . . Let us leave them to their differences. They are the quarrels of theologians and not of theology."

Stripped, as they are today, of these tiresome incidentals and of their anti-Christian posterity, the first *Provincial Letters* in their primal freshness remain a model of the way in which the battle against the academic mind should be conducted.

Péguy saw in them a couplet from the war song against pedants: "It was the old French argument . . . about the *honnête homme*,

---

[8] *Recueil des lettres de Mme la marquise de Sévigné à Mme la comtesse de Grignan, sa fille*, vol. VII (Paris, 1737), p. 456 (letter of 11th December, 1689). See Boileau's opinion, *op. cit.*, pp. 502–3.

[9] Voltaire, *Le Siècle de Louis XIV*, Ch. 32.

[10] *Vie de Pascal par Dom Clémencet*, pp. 27–8, who reports Arnauld's view: "You cannot imagine how M. Singlin nagged us about them."

life against the domination of the Schools; it was the old saying of Montaigne and Rabelais, of Descartes and Molière, of Pascal and Rousseau against our enemies—the learned."[11] He recognized in the *Provincial Letters* the prototypes of his *Cahiers*. For theology in no way enjoys the monopoly, as people sometimes try to make out, of becoming ridiculous by falling into minds infected with parrotry. It is not for the science of sacred things alone that twaddle lies in wait. The "intellectuals' party" belongs to all time. Deism, eclecticism, Kantism, sociology, Marxism, existentialism have in turn taken the place, at the Sorbonne, of Molinism and probabilism, revealing the same quirks under the same hats. They have either given birth or will give birth to their own scholasticism. Replace "proximate power" or "sufficient grace" by "morality without obligations", "scientific morality", "totems", "mana", "dialectical materialism", and you will see that there is nothing new under the sun. In short, the problem for Pascal was the divorce between genius and the professors, between the spontaneity of youth and the wrinkles of old age, between invention and repetition, intuition and subtlety, between life and the card index: the eternal conflict which plunged Socrates into the battle against the sophists.

[11] Quoted in *La République,notre Royaume de France* (Paris, 1946), p. 118.

CHAPTER III

The Scandal of the Casuists

CASUISTRY was not a novelty in the middle of the seventeenth century. As a form of jurisprudence it has always existed in the sphere of morality, but since the Renaissance it had acquired a special importance. The intellectual and social élites had become pagan. Now in France, at the end of the Wars of Religion, a victorious Catholicism had emerged as the state religion. The King—and Louis XIV was intransigent on the subject—insisted on the official practice of religion. It was a condition of society which we find difficult to imagine today, but it provided the confessors of the King, princes and courtiers with some very thorny problems. Since the reception of the sacraments was not entirely free and since His Majesty wished to keep his mistresses and go to Communion at Easter, how was his confessor to find a way of not refusing him absolution? In a period when duelling was still rife, was the Church to use the weapon of excommunication as she had done in the middle ages? The casuists tried to help everybody out of an embarrassing situation by the subtlety of their interpretations. The importance of the part they played was due to the virtual necessity of preventing everyone being banned from the practice of religion which was the supreme sign of civic loyalty.

The concern of the casuists does not in itself deserve blame. Laws have to be adapted; they must remain living and flexible. If they are too rigid, they cease to have any practical value. "A rigid system of morality", wrote Péguy, "may overlook the ramifications of sin, while a flexible system of morality would grasp, reveal and pursue its devious ways of escape. . . . It is in a flexible moral system that everything can be seen, exposed and followed up."[1] But in order to produce this moral flexibility and bring it into closer contact with life, the casuists had to return to the sources and seek their inspiration in the Gospels. Since the Renaissance they had accentuated the medieval tendency to turn morality into a superior form of law and to look for its principles in the works of the philosophers. They were more familiar with Aristotle than with the New Testament. So much so that their main concern was less to follow the winding path of life than to discover all the instances in which morality ceases to adapt itself and so to manipulate it. Far from making morality more flexible in Péguy's sense, they came near to making it ineffectual by reducing the extent to which it could be applied. They transformed it into a series of rigid maxims and definitions, then made a list of those cases in which the rigid definitions ceased to have any bearing on reality. Some of them became collectors of exemptions, exceptions, possible cases of flight and evasion which carried them outside the domain of morality; they finished by codifying the rules of abdication and drawing up the balance sheet of bankruptcy.[2]

The results of their labours in jurisprudence were reasonable or comic or monstrous according to the circumstances. In order to be fair to them, it must not be forgotten that the *Provincial Letters* were a *sottisier* and that apart from the blunders and follies denounced by Pascal, the great majority of the casuists' decisions were dictated by right judgment and by the determination to translate into precise terms the intentions of a moral or an ecclesiastical law. Is a man who is seriously ill subject to the law of fasting? Is a soldier in time of war subject to the rule of abstinence? Ought a starving man to die of hunger in front of a piece of bread which does not belong to him? If a bandit attacks me, have I the right to retaliate? In a thousand similar cases the decisions of the casuists expressed the findings of good sense and Pascal was the last person to think of protesting against such reasonable views. But side by side with an enormous number of unassailable decisions, there were others which were often more

[1] C. Péguy, *Note sur M. Bergson et la philosophie bergsonienne* (Paris, 1935), p. 52.
[2] F. Strowski has provided the best comment on this aspect of the problem: "Escobar", he wrote, "was neither a psychologist, a moralist nor a theologian: he was a jurist" (*Pascal et son temps*, III, p. 116).

ridiculous than wicked and were sometimes even dangerous. The Gospel orders us to give away our superfluous goods as alms. If like Vasquez we define superfluous goods in such a manner "that even kings would have hardly any", we are making a mockery of the Gospel. Escobar allows the ambush as a result of a terrifying definition of treachery according to which there would never have been a single traitor in the world. The same Escobar manages to remove sloth from among the deadly sins by asserting: "Sloth is a form of sadness which comes from the fact that spiritual things are spiritual, such as worrying over the fact that the sacraments are the source of grace".

Why, instead of simply laughing at these eccentricities, did Pascal grow angry? Why did he accuse the casuists not merely of falling into the absurd hair-splitting of the doctors of the Sorbonne, but of harbouring a definite plan to corrupt Christianity? For the violence of the tone of the final letters could not be explained if Pascal were only concerned with the foolishness of the professors of moral theology. He smelled a conspiracy, a scandal. He denounced it and his denunciation became more and more violent. He pursued the casuists with a personal hatred. He wanted to have them condemned by the Assembly of Clergy and to the very end persevered with this aim. He not only refused to repudiate the *Provincial Letters* when he was dying: in the year of his death he admitted to intimate friends that if he had to rewrite the letters, he would make them "stronger", by which we should understand less amusing, more tragic, more violent.[3] Why, if not because in his eyes the casuists obeyed the wish to restrict, in the world in which they worked as confessors, the area of sin and in so doing diminished to the same extent the kingdom of grace.

Sin and grace are geared to one another. It is uneasiness, remorse, sin, wounds which produce the remedy, forgiveness, cure. If human actions lost their evil qualities, the effectiveness of the Redemption would be diminished. God only has a hold over those beings who, whatever the cost, remain in the right relation

---

[3] See the testimony of Beurrier in Lafuma, III, p. 54. Corroborated by Marguerite Périer's direct statement in *Recueil d'Utrecht*, pp. 279–80. "I am asked whether I regret having written the *Provincial Letters*. I reply that far from regretting them, if I had to write them now (1662) I should make them even stronger" (Lafuma, I, p. 55).

with him and preserve intact their armour of decency, as Péguy would have said. Pascal exposed in casuistry a method of fabricating decent people by artificial means in order to annihilate or reduce the freedom to offend God. He regarded it as the opium of the soul. The battle against the casuists was no longer a matter of vocabulary, but of salvation. The whole of the Christian therapeutic against sin was at stake.

Two hundred and fifty years later Péguy denounced in the same way the pharisaism of Christians which enabled them to dodge the question of Redemption and salvation because they were on the right side of the moral law. Casuistry and middle-class morality are two ways of closing our eyes to our own inner turmoil and therefore of being unaware of the wretchedness and sinfulness of the world.

> The *honnêtes gens* [wrote Péguy] have no conception of the entry into a state of grace which sin essentially is. Because they are not wounded, they are no longer vulnerable. Because they lack nothing, no one gives them anything. Because they lack nothing no one gives them the thing which is everything. . . . Even the charity of God does not heal those who have no wounds. . . . It was because the face of Jesus was dirty that Veronica wiped it with a handkerchief. Now the man who has never fallen will never be picked up, and the man who is not dirty will not be wiped clean.[4]

Thus Péguy provides the key to Pascal's violence, his bitter tone and his rage against the casuists. In his view casuistry is the means of removing from souls their anguish and their sense of evil. We surreptitiously open the closed door of the lost paradise. But it is a false door and a false paradise. We forget the true one which was opened by the Redemption and by charity. The farce ceases to be a farce and becomes a tragedy. Pascal's cry breaks through at the end of his talks with the Jesuit father, the cry that he can no longer hold back:

> Men violate *the great commandment which contains the law and the prophets.* They attack piety in the heart; they take away the spirit which gives life; they say that the love of God is not necessary to

[4] C. Péguy, *Note conjointe sur M. Descartes* (Paris, 1935), p. 101.

salvation; they even go so far as to claim *that the dispensation from loving God is JESUS CHRIST'S gift to the world*. It is the height of impiety. The price of the blood of JESUS CHRIST is to obtain for us a dispensation from loving him. Before the Incarnation we were bound to love God; but since *God so loved the world that he gave his only begotten son*, the world redeemed by him will be discharged from the obligation of loving him. Ours is a strange theology. We dare to lift the *anathema* that St Paul pronounced *against those who do not love the Lord JESUS*. We ruin what was said by St John: *that whoever does not love remains in death;* and what Jesus Christ himself said: that *he who does not love him does not keep his commandments.* Thus we make those worthy to enjoy God in eternity who have never loved God in all their lives. That is the accomplishment of the mystery of iniquity.[5]

The Jesuits naturally protested vigorously against this interpretation of the work of the casuists. In one sense they were right. No one wanted to push matters to that point. But Pascal deduced extreme conclusions from certain dangerous premises of the theology of the moralists. He denounced "a soft, accommodating religion". He saw the eighteenth century dawning. He wanted Catholicism to preserve its integral character: scandalous, austere and decidedly harsh. Nothing was to be gained by diluting it. Pascal, who made such efforts to shake up those who were indifferent to religion, to arouse some spark of uneasiness in them, deplored the fact that the priests helped to send some of them to sleep, to pacify them; that they toned down dogma and blunted moral teaching.

As soon as the *Provincial Letters* appeared, some of Pascal's enemies cast doubts on the accuracy of his quotations.

The complaint that Pascal misquoted the casuists still turns up periodically. Every time this happens the *Provincial Letters* emerge vindicated from the detailed scrutiny, their reputation for accuracy enhanced. As Brunetière observed: "Pascal has been convicted of inadvertence or serious oversight in only two or three cases at most, but never of *fraud*."[6]

---

[5] "Deuxième Provinciale" in *G.E.*, V, pp. 273–5.
[6] *Études critiques*, 4ᵉ série (Paris, 1894), p. 85.

Moreover, it was an *a priori* assumption that, in such a vigorous attack, Pascal would never risk a misquotation which would have brought his enemies too easy a triumph. He left to Arnauld and Nicole, who were experts at the job, the responsibility of providing him with the material and the quotations necessary for the undertaking.

One day the question was put to him and he replied with his customary frankness. "People ask me whether I myself have read all the books I quote. I answer that I have not: I should have to have spent the whole of my life reading very bad books; but I have read Escobar twice from beginning to end; I had the other books read to me by friends; but I have never used a single passage without reading it myself in the book in which it appears and without examining the content or without reading what precedes and what follows it so that I should not run the risk of quoting an objection as though it were an answer, for this would have been wrong and unjust."[7]

The vigour of the campaign mounted in the *Provincial Letters* had a salutary effect on the Jesuits themselves. Bourdaloue was a witness to their moral inflexibility. And Rome by condemning the excesses of certain of the casuists demonstrated the fact that the protests of Pascal, who maintained with such eloquence that sin remains sin and that the Redemption should retain its dramatic character, were well founded.

[7] Lafuma, I, pp. 553–4.

CHAPTER IV

God Intervenes

THE Ninth Letter marks a turning-point in the polemic of the *Provincial Letters*. Pascal ceases to treat the casuists as his only target. He delivers a frontal attack on the Society of Jesus as an organized body. A recent event had encouraged him to adopt this new line: the miracle of the Holy Thorn which brought the struggle to its peak. Pascal was convinced by this supernatural sign that he had been entrusted by God with a sort of prophetic mission. He embarked on a crusade for purity in the ranks of Christendom. It was not done out of pride. It was possibly an exaggeration in the eyes of those who see Pascal's victory much more in the outcome of the battle of the *Pensées* than in the conclusion of the campaign fought in the *Provincial Letters*.

The Fifth Letter had been published on 20th March 1656. Three days later the Solitaries had left Port-Royal des Champs. On the Tuesday of the third week in Lent a young lady went to Port-Royal in Paris to warn the nuns that a certain M. de la Potherie, an eccentric priest and a great collector of relics, which were housed in his private chapel in the Faubourg Saint-Jacques, had offered to lend the community for a day or two a thorn from the Crown of Christ. The Abbess of Port-Royal, the Révérende Mère Marie-des-Anges Suireau, spent the day in prayer before the Blessed Sacrament. At first she declined the offer, "saying that it was not a time for amusing ourselves by looking at a holy relic, that we should think only of prayer and lamentation before God".[1] But one of the sisters pressed her and it was decided that they would venerate the relic on the Friday, during the prayer commemorating the Passion of Christ.

[1] "Relation sur la vie de la Révérende Mère Marie-des-Anges", in *G.E.*, IV, p. 328.

On 24th March "a very beautiful reliquary, in which a fragment of a thorn from the Holy Crown was encased in a little gilded enamel sun" was brought to the monastery.[2] In the choir the nuns sang the antiphon, then went to kiss the reliquary in the same way that on Good Friday the faithful kiss the crucifix. After the sisters came the little girls who were being educated at the convent, among them Marguerite Périer, daughter of Gilberte and niece and goddaughter of Pascal.

For the past two years the child had been suffering from a lacrymal fistula. An abscess had formed between the eye and the nose, suppurating into her mouth and throat. The doctors had considered trying to cure her by cauterizing it. When Marguerite came to kiss the relic, Soeur Flavie, her form mistress, touched her eye with the reliquary. No one thought any more about it and the relic was returned to its owner.

That evening the little girl, who was ten, said to one of her friends: "My eye's cured: it doesn't hurt me any more." The sister was told and found that there had indeed been a cure. She gave the news to Mère Agnès. The following day, in spite of the special silence that the nuns observed in Lent, she told Jacqueline Pascal and four days later Jacqueline passed the news on to her sister Gilberte, Margot's mother. The child was not only cured of her fistula, but also of the migraines which prevented her from sleeping and doing her hair. At the end of the week it was decided to show her to the surgeon d'Alançay. It will be apparent that Port-Royal was not at all disposed to proclaim a miracle and in her first letter Jacqueline Pascal was circumspect.

As soon as he heard the news, Florin Périer left Clermont by coach in order to get to Paris as quickly as possible. For two years he had entrusted his two eldest daughters to the nuns of Port-Royal. He was worried about Margot's health and up to that time Gilberte had refused to allow the brutal treatment by cauterization recommended by the surgeons. He arrived on Wednesday, 5th April, and in the parlour they presented him with the child who was completely cured. They told him what had happened. D'Alançay had come on 31st March. He had not seen the young patient for two months. When he arrived he had said to the sister:

[2] Letter from Jacqueline Pascal, *G.E.*, IV, p. 328.

"What do you expect me to do? Haven't I told you that it's incurable?" Nevertheless, he was asked to examine the child. He pressed her eye, put his spatula into her nose and was greatly astonished to find nothing at all. He began to laugh out of surprise. "There's no longer anything wrong with her," he said. Soeur Flavie told him what had happened. "It's a miracle", he said. However, he advised them to wait and see whether the fistula returned. And running into the convent doctor as he was leaving, he counselled prudence. "Let us not make a fuss, because you know the state of the house."[3]

The Mother Prioress asked to have the relic back. Reports of the miracle slowly began to circulate. On Good Friday the doctors and surgeons met to sign an attestation. The most famous doctors of the day put themselves out to come: Guy Patin, the Duc d'Orléans's doctor, and Félix, first surgeon to the King, who was sent officially by the Court, which was greatly interested, saw the little girl twice.[4]

At the beginning of May, Mère Angélique Arnauld gave an account of the event to her friend the Queen of Poland.[5] Crowds swarmed to the monastery. Early in June an ecclesiastical enquiry was instituted by the diocesan authorities in Paris with the intention of confirming the miracle officially. A member of the commission of enquiry interrogated all the witnesses. At the end of August Père Annat, who was furious, published his *Rabat-joie des Jansénistes*. Since he was unable to deny the miracle, he declared that it had happened to convert the Jansenists.

At the end of October the ecclesiastical enquiry was concluded. The vicar-general, A. de Hodencq, who was not in other respects a wholly admirable figure, recognized officially the miraculous nature of the little Marguerite Périer's cure.[6] On 27th October elaborate ceremonies were held at the monastery to celebrate the event.

By the time that it was fully daylight [wrote Jacqueline Pascal to her sister], there were a great many people in the church though it was raining heavily. A little altar was set up in the choir by the grille which was left open; it was decorated in white and covered

[3] Documents in *G.E.*, IV, pp. 332–53.   [4] *Ibid.*, p. 342.
[5] *Ibid.*, p. 348.   [6] *Ibid.*, VI, pp. 63–74.

with a fine chalice veil on which our Mother [the Abbess] placed the
reliquary with the Holy Thorn surrounded by a great many candles,
where M. le Grand Vicaire, who was the celebrant, came with the
cross and took the reliquary, accompanied by sixteen deacons who
were holding candles; and he carried it ceremoniously under a
canopy like a procession of the Blessed Sacrament until he came to the
altar with two deacons incensing all the time, and placed it in a little
tabernacle splendidly decorated, which had been specially prepared.
Then, kneeling in front of the grille with their long veils lowered,
and holding lighted candles, all the sisters sang the hymn, *Exite
filiae Sion*, and the antiphon, *O Corona*. With them in front of our
choir, right opposite the grille, wearing, very correctly but very
modestly, lay clothes, a grey dress and a coif, was the little one who
had been cured, kneeling on two big flagstones so that she was high
enough to be seen by the congregation who climbed up to where
they could get a view of her. After that, the altar was removed and
M. le Grand Vicaire celebrated Holy Mass, the Mass of the Holy
Crown which was sung with great solemnity: during it the grille
remained open so that the people had the consolation of seeing the
little one who was close by on a prie-Dieu covered with a rug, a
lighted candle in front of her and a chair so that she could sit down
when she felt tired. She stayed there with as much assurance as if it
had been her normal place, standing up and kneeling down at the
proper places . . . with as much modesty as if she had been very
devout, and with as much grace as if she had been coached in
advance. At the Preface she was moved to make way for the communion of the sisters which lasted a long time because all those whose
health and occupations permitted had kept themselves for this Mass
which was very solemn, the celebrant being accompanied by his two
deacons and six acolytes with lighted candles. . . . The *Te Deum*
was sung during which the celebrant, after incensing the Holy
Thorn, venerated it first of all, then gave it to all the ministrants at
the altar to kiss; then one of the priests took it to be kissed by the
people.[7]

Blaise Pascal was there. He probably went to communion after
the community. Mingling with the crowd he kissed the holy
relic with tears in his eyes and joined in the singing of the antiphon.
He was filled with a deep, sober, overwhelming joy. His own

[7] *G.E.*, VI, pp. 96–8.

niece and goddaughter cured by Our Lord's Crown of Thorns!
Thus, right in the middle of the polemics of the *Provincial Letters*,
God himself had approved of him: "Just as God has made no
family happier than ours," he wrote in his notes, "so there is no
family who is more grateful."

With the permission of Mère Agnès, Jacqueline felt that she
must break her resolution to write no more verse. She wrote a
long poem in twenty-five stanzas in the Cornelian style which
she habitually adopted. As we read it, we are sometimes reminded
of the remarks of her brother on "poetic style": they were not
indulgent. But amid some ridiculous lines about "lost sense of
smell" and "gangrene", we find here and there some noble
touches. The lines, for example, which celebrate the "fire" of the
Memorial:

> *Jésus, de ton Autel, jette les yeux sur moi;*
> *Fais-en sortir ce feu qui change tout en soi . . .*

> Jesus, look down on me from thine Altar;
> Make the fire pour out which changes everything into itself.

What are we to think today of the miracle? Catholics have no
grounds for doubting its authenticity. Pope Benedict XIII quotes
it in his *Works* as an example of the continuity of supernatural
interventions in the life of the Church. The ecclesiastical authorities ratified it and committed themselves as far as they do in such
circumstances. In one of the chapters of his *Port-Royal*, Sainte-
Beuve is unable to hide the disgust that he feels at this recrudes-
cence of superstition.[8] According to him, a coalition of fanatics
and rogues tried to make out that a tiny abscess on the eye, which
had been burst by too hasty a movement of Soeur Flavie's, constituted a timely miracle in favour of the Pascal clan. And he
quotes Guy Patin.[9] But he is forced to admit that, at first sight,
"the miracle appears to have all the elements which make it
authentic from an historical point of view".[10] No matter! He
gives history a little twist, exaggerates the unimportance of the
medical consultants, does not mention the necessity of an operation,
the little girl's headaches, the suppuration, and the findings of the

---

[8] *Port-Royal*, VI, pp. 46 *et seq*.   [9] Documents in G.E., VI, pp. 74-5.
[10] *Op. cit.*, p. 49.

doctors. He appears to be ignorant of the fact that Port-Royal was not expecting a miracle, that they were greatly astonished by it, and that the process of verification lasted six months. Pascal's enemies were not fools. They would not have allowed themselves to be taken in by this nasty story of a pimple on the eye which Sainte-Beuve was pleased to invent. Finally, Pascal himself, who was decidedly sceptical about the medical profession, had to take a second look.

The truth is that Sainte-Beuve shows his hand when he quotes Montesquieu. The miracle did not take place because miracles never happen. He treats the miracle of the Holy Thorn as Renan treats the miracles of Jesus and Zola those of Lourdes. Like them he is ready to wipe out the testimony of history in the name of the most short-sighted philosophy that exists.

If the miracle scandalized Sainte-Beuve, Pascal accepted it with the restrained joy of true mystics. He at once had a better understanding of the Gospel miracles and those with which the life of the Church is interwoven. His adherence to Catholicism in those matters which make it unusual becomes, if possible, even stronger. For the experience of miracles, like that of mystical phenomena, divides Catholicism from the religious philosophy introduced by the Protestant Reformation. Catholicism believes in the possibility of miracles today, in the link which connects the miracles that do not cease to adorn the lives of saints to those of the Gospels. There is no break in continuity between the interventions of God in the past and those of our own time. In the same way there was for Pascal a close connection between the miracle of the Holy Thorn and the mystical night of his own conversion. He, too, had felt the touch of the same sovereign hand. The two cures confirmed one another; they illuminated and confirmed those of the Gospels. For this reason Pascal went on meditating on miracles. He set himself to understand the rules in order to avoid both the scepticism of Montaigne and the illuminism distrusted by the Church which drove the degenerate offspring of Port-Royal to the cemetery of Saint-Médard.

Another interior miracle occurred which caused less stir than the healing of Marguerite Périer, but which touched Pascal as deeply because he was its direct agent. The sister of his great friend the Duc de Roannez was converted. Her brother, the Duke, had already been drawn in by Pascal and was in the process of becoming a sort of lay saint. On 4th August 1656, during mass in the chapel of Port-Royal in Paris, Charlotte de Roannez "was so profoundly touched by grace that she burst into tears". She told her brother that she intended to become a nun at Port-Royal. Realizing that there would be opposition from the family and in order to give his sister time to think things over, he took her with him on a journey to Poitou. It was there, from August 1656 to February 1657, that Pascal wrote to brother and sister a series of letters of which unfortunately only fragments have survived. All personal details have disappeared.

The letters to the Duke and to Charlotte de Roannez might be described as the obverse and heart of the *Provincial Letters*. They record the reflections that Pascal could make to himself and suggest to his friends at the most heated moments of the controversy. They throw light on his prayer and his inner monologue.

The first two, written in September 1656, show Pascal returning to his most recent past, to the time of his conversion. He, too, is still a neophyte, full of the consolation of the rescued person who cries his joy aloud. He is still shaken by the effect of the miracle, but he recalls the suffering of being torn from the world. "It is quite certain that we cannot detach ourselves without being hurt."[11] He extols death as a deliverance, but he is already happily aware of the peace of Jesus Christ. Beneath their apparent dryness, the first letters are permeated by deep feeling.

The letters which follow deal with the uneasiness that might be aroused by the threat of fresh condemnations and persecutions of Port-Royal. Pascal reaffirms in them the principles of the spiritual life which he had put into the mouth of Christ in *The Mystery of Jesus:* "I try, as far as I can, not to upset myself over anything and to accept everything that happens as being for the best. . . . I have learnt that everything that happens has something good in it since it reveals the Will of God. I praise him with all my heart for the perfect continuation of his grace because I can see that it

[11] *G.E.,* V, p. 409.

has not diminished in any way. . . ."[12] That does not prevent him in the least from foreseeing the difficulties that the defenders of Grace will have to overcome. He stiffens at the thought. He counts himself among the soldiers of God. Without his noticing it, his October letter reeks of the pride of the elect.

The next letter, written probably at the end of the same month, is an admirable commentary on the miracle of the Holy Thorn. Pascal returns for the benefit of his two friends to his deepest thoughts on the darkness of the hidden God: God "usually hides himself and only reveals himself on rare occasions. . . . This strange secrecy into which God has withdrawn, which is impenetrable to the eyes of men, is a great encouragement to us to cultivate solitude."[13]

We can see that at this time he was already meditating a great deal on the Bible because he at once applies his theory of the "divine secrecy" to the Scriptures. "There are two perfect meanings", he writes, "the literal and the mystical."[14] All things are mysterious; all are "veils which hide God".[15] Pascal sees very clearly that the religious life is a perpetual progress, a series of discoveries, an effort towards the purification of the inner eye. The controversy in which he had become involved in the *Provincial Letters* therefore appears as a battle against priests who connive at the deliberate blindness of hardened sinners. At the price of a continual ascesis we must learn to look on God.

Then the mood changes. The *Provincial Letters* become more and more violent. In a letter to Pascal, the Duke and his sister must have confided in him their fear of a possible rebellion of the friends of Port-Royal against Rome, or a schism. They wanted to remain good Catholics. Pascal approves promptly and wholeheartedly: "From the bottom of my heart I applaud the zeal that I detect in your letter for union with the Pope. The body is no more alive without the head than the head without the body. Whoever separates himself from one or the other no longer belongs to the body or to Jesus Christ."[16]

Serious words that Pascal will repeat several times; every word deserves to be weighed on account of the repercussions they will

[12] *G.E.*, VI, pp. 83-4.   [13] *Ibid.*, p. 88.   [14] *Ibid.*, p. 89.
[15] *Ibid.*, p. 90.   [16] *Ibid.*, p. 216.

provoke later on. He adds this which reinforces his statement: "I do not know whether there are people inside the Church who are more attached to the unity of the body than those whom you call our friends. We know that all the virtues, martyrdom, austerity, and good works are useless outside the Church and out of communion with the head of the Church who is the Pope. I will never leave his communion, at least I pray to God to give me the grace not to do so; otherwise I should be lost for ever."[17]

Nevertheless, the day will come when this fine Catholic mind, this attachment to the papacy, will be subjected to the harshest test imaginable.

Another letter, written slightly later, develops the Jansenist theory of the two forms of delectation, but in a form that makes it acceptable. Pascal shows that Christians find joy "mingled with the sorrow of having given themselves up to other pleasures".[18] As soon as he celebrates this joy which he knows from personal experience he becomes lyrical: "Do not let us succumb to sadness, and do not let us believe that piety consists of nothing but bitterness without consolation. True piety, which only becomes perfect in heaven, brings such rewards that it fills its beginnings, its growth and its completion. It is such a blinding light that it bathes everything that belongs to it, and if there is a touch of sadness in it, particularly at the start, it comes from ourselves and not from virtue. . . ."[19]

Pascal tries to console the girl who is a prey to anxiety and scruples. He invites her, as in his first letters, to live in the present. He confides his own difficulties to her. He admits that he himself is anxious by nature, but "I pray to God when I feel that I am becoming involved in this sort of anticipation, to confine me within my own limits; I collect myself inwardly. . . ."[20]

All in all, these few fragments of letters remain rather impersonal. They are pious writings of the kind common at the time; they recall similar letters written by Pascal to his sisters, particularly the one he wrote at the time of his father's death. His advice is prompted by good sense and a profound knowledge of the

[17] G.E., VI, p. 217.   [18] Ibid., p. 221.   [19] Ibid., p. 222.
[20] Ibid,, p. 299.

problems of conversion; it contained a great deal of humanity and was without anything of the savage spirit that he displayed in his public *Letters* to the Jesuits in which the tone grew more and more heated and which gave vent to one of the most terrible outbursts of the irascible Auvergnat.

CHAPTER V

The Anti-Political Man

THE close of the *Provincial Letters* is an increasingly virulent denunciation of the policy of the Jesuits. Pascal appears to discover their policy in the actual process of writing. There is only a very indirect reference to it at the beginning. Then the allusions become more precise because the *Letters* do not follow a plan drawn up in advance; they develop and become sharper according to the tone of the Jesuits' replies. They grow more serious. At the beginning of the Tenth Letter Pascal writes, "This is not yet the policy of the Society, but it is one of its main principles."[1] He is speaking of the way in which they smooth over the unpleasantnesses of confession. In the Thirteenth Letter the attack becomes more pressing on the question of homicide. Pascal, attacking the distinction between theoretical and practical opinions, concludes: "It is always useful to discover little by little the principles underlying this mysterious policy."

The distinction between speculative and practical opinions started Pascal on the path leading to the discovery of what he regarded as the Machiavellianism of the Jesuits. They have "turned divine laws inside out without the slightest reservation". But they must have shown greater prudence in the treatment of the laws in which the State has an interest. Their system of destroying laws has two distinct stages: they are undermined in theory and then abolished in practice. And this dark design is placed at the service of a single ambition: to rule the world by corrupting Christianity, that is to say, by the reconciliation of religion and human passions. They seek the triumph of a Christianity which comes to terms with duelling, theft, violence and all the vices

[1] G.E., V, p. 249.

to which the Renaissance princes lent their éclat. The Jesuits place "a dagger in the hand of all Christians". And Pascal finishes his letter by accusing them of duplicity and hypocrisy.

Is there not something iniquitous about Pascal's onslaught? In the course of time many readers of the *Provincial Letters* have come to that conclusion and have protested vigorously. "The *Provincial Letters*", said Voltaire, "rest on false foundations."[2] "Pascal is nothing but a slanderer of genius who has left us an immortal lie", said Chateaubriand.[3] Joseph de Maistre was even more violent. He claimed that if what he called Pascal's "lyings" had been written against the Capuchins they would have been forgotten. He failed to see why they could not have been written against them: the Capuchins wielded no political power.[4] In any case, the fact that it was written against the Jesuits has not saved the work of Antoine Arnauld from oblivion. Père de Ravignan has not diminished the force of the blow that Pascal dealt the Jesuits: "Pascal, your genius has committed a great crime: the crime of establishing a link, which is probably indestructible, between the lie and the language of the common people. You have compiled a dictionary of slander; it is still accepted as authoritative."[5] And it is true that the abominable caricatures of Eugène Sue, which would have horrified Pascal, have as their background the shadow cast by the *Provincial Letters*. A few years ago F. Strowski, one of the best Pascalians, while defending Pascal's good faith, subscribed to Voltaire's opinion: "The basic thesis of the *Provincial Letters* is false", he said.[6]

All these writers are more or less right. Pascal allowed himself to be carried away. In his error he was in all good faith the victim of the Jesuits themselves, some of whom like Escobar ended by propagating extravagant theories. The defenders of the Jesuits displayed incredible clumsiness. It was they who put Pascal on the track of the supposed conspiracy by defending willy-nilly

[2] *Le Siècle de Louis XIV*, Ch. XXXVII.
[3] *Études historiques; Analyse raisonnée de l'Histoire de France*, Oeuvres (ed. of 1861), vol. XII, p. 134.
[4] *Soirées de Saint-Pétersbourg* (2e entretien, 1822), p. 131.
[5] Quoted by the Abbé Maynard, *Pascal, sa vie et son caractère* (Paris, 1850), I, p. 472.
[6] *Pascal et son temps*, III, p. 123.

untenable theses. It was idiotic, if you like, but the idea of a conspiracy was a mere figment of Pascal's imagination.

And yet Pascal was only partially wrong. For the policy existed, or more precisely, there were often in Christendom well-intentioned people who did not hesitate to use political means to gain ends which were excellent in themselves and to procure the triumph of good. These people included a number of the most important Jesuits. Pascal, who went astray in Letter XIII, was right in Letter XV. For the word "policy" (see page 140) could be interpreted in two senses. It could be understood as meaning a conspiracy against Christian morality and when applied in this sense to the Jesuits it was false, as Pascal admitted at the beginning. But in the second sense the word meant the solidarity of a very powerful social body, a party entrusted with the defence of truths of a mystical order which did not hesitate to use political means in order to ensure the triumph of its spiritual ends.

An esprit de corps which drove them to treat truth as small beer—such was the essential characteristic of their policy. Take the case of Père Bauny. Pascal attributed a scandalous proposition to him. The Jesuits replied either by justifying the proposition or by claiming that the priest had never defended it:

> When you have said that the axiom is *detestable*, you have at the same time denied that it was by Père Bauny who was therefore innocent; and when you admit that it was by him, you argue at the same time that it is sound and so he is still innocent. With the result that, as the innocence of the Father is the only thing which is common to both your replies, it is plain that it is the only thing you are looking for and that your only concern is to defend your Father by saying of one and the same axiom that it is in your books and that it is not in them; that it is right and wrong; *not according to truth which never changes, but according to your own interests which are changing all the time*. What could I say on that score: for you can see perfectly well that it is convincing.[7]

Thus in so far as the Jesuits formed a party they put into practice the rule of politicians in all ages: defend the party member at all costs and attack its enemies by letting fly with all you've got.

[7] *G.E.*, VI, p. 201 (*italics mine*).

There is no need to be afraid of slander: "It is knowingly and with deliberate intent", Pascal said to them, "that you impute to your enemies crimes of which you know they are innocent".[8] His "you know" would be worth analysing. The sad thing is that in fact the members of a party no longer know. Their greatest misfortune is that they slander in good faith.

To the examples he gives, Pascal adds this:

What can you be thinking about, Reverend Fathers, to testify publicly that you only measure men's faith and virtue by their attitude towards your Society? How is it that you have no fear of being taken yourselves and on your own admission for impostors and slanderers? What, Reverend Fathers, the same man, without undergoing any change in himself, will be *pious or impious; without fault or excommunicate; a worthy pastor of the Church or fit for the stake, in short Catholic or heretic*, according to whether he respects or attacks your Society? In your language, to attack the Society is equivalent to being a heretic! That's an amusing little heresy, isn't it, Reverend Fathers? And so when we see that in your writings so many Catholics are branded as heretics, it only means that *you believe that they have attacked you*. It is a good thing, Reverend Fathers, to be unable to understand such a language. . . .[9]

If we are to grasp the full seriousness of these accusations of heresy, we must not forget that we are dealing with the seventeenth century. Catholicism is the State religion; heresy is a political crime. The easiest way of breaking a man is to cast suspicions on his orthodoxy. To accuse someone of heresy in 1657 was equivalent to a charge of impiety in the Athens of the fifth century; of counter-revolution in 1793, or of "collaboration" in the France of 1946. What Pascal is denouncing is the manoeuvring of those who are engaged in propaganda, who insult and slander their opponent in order to dishonour him before bringing him down. Party manoeuvring of this kind has always existed; it depends on a "line" and measures the orthodoxy that the party propagates by the degree of submission shown towards it.

Having committed one blunder after another, the opponents of Pascal and Port-Royal did something really odious. Already in

8 *G.E.*, VI, p. 188.   9 *Ibid.*, p. 197.

a tract published in 1651, Père Brisacier claimed that Saint-Cyran had imposed on the nuns at Port-Royal secret rules which compelled them to take a vow not to disclose them even on their death and was in fact the founder of an occult society.[10] Père Meynier accused the nuns of not believing in the Eucharist: "We have grounds for doubting their faith in the Eucharist as well as the faith in this same Sacrament of the man who thinks that he is serving God in the House of the Nuns."[11] In the face of this slander Pascal was unable to contain himself any longer. He gave his opponents the greatest lesson that a decent man can inflict: he defended with masterly eloquence the cause of innocent women against those who had attempted to tarnish their reputation:

> There is a piece of imposture worthy of you. There is a crime which God alone is capable of punishing. . . . You fill me with pity, Reverend Fathers. . . .[12] For whom do you think you will convince on the strength of your word alone and without a shadow of proof, and with all the imaginable contradictions, that Bishops and Priests who have spent their lives preaching the grace of Jesus Christ, the purity of the Gospel and the obligations of baptism, have renounced their own baptism, the Gospel and Jesus Christ? . . . Who will believe it, Reverend Fathers? Do you believe it yourselves, miserable wretches that you are? . . . Prove it, Reverend Fathers. . . .[13] You must speak up, Reverend Fathers . . . or put up with the indignity of being treated as liars who are unworthy of ever being believed.[14] Cruel and cowardly persecutors, must we admit that even the most remote cloisters offer no protection against your slanders? . . . The authors of a defamatory work, who cannot prove what they have alleged, were condemned by Pope Adrian *to be whipped*, Reverend Fathers, *flagellentur*. . . .[15]

Hard hitting, but a splendid lesson for all those who go in for writing! It is to the eternal honour of French Catholicism that it inspired this pen, provoked such an outburst by an ardent and

[10] In *Le Jansénisme confondu*, "Slander replied to slander", wrote the Abbé Maynard (*op. cit.*, I, p. 500). . . . "It is difficult to understand why Père Brisacier resorted to such shabby methods."
[11] B. Meynier, *Port-Royal et Genève d'intelligence contre le Très Saint-Sacrement de l'autel* . . . (Poitiers, 1656). Cf. G.E., VI, p. 235.
[12] Sixteenth *Provincial Letter*, G.E., VI, pp. 258 and 274.
[13] *Ibid.*, p. 284.   [14] *Ibid.*, p. 285.   [15] *Ibid.*, pp. 286–8.

loyal spirit, aroused this protestation which is valid not merely in the case of a few obscure Jesuits whose names have been saved from oblivion by Pascal's fame alone, but against the injustice of all slanderers at all times and of all the different obediences. And God knows that the Jesuits in their turn have been victims of the sorry procedure which consists of bias, faking, falsifying and shameless lying.

Thus to borrow the language of Péguy, which is still the most suitable for expressing the essence of the great battle, Pascal denounced "mystics" who were in the process of degenerating into "politicians", forming a party and using the weapons of the parties. "I will talk to you about it one day perhaps, Reverend Fathers," said Pascal, "and people will be surprised to see how far you have fallen away from the original spirit of your organization."[16] In the same way, two hundred and fifty years later at the time of the Dreyfus Case, Péguy will denounce in equally violent terms the lay casuistry and the avatars of the republican mystique.

Pascal went to the heart of the problem, but he was in difficulties with his explanations. Could he accuse the Jesuits of doing everything in their power to become the King's confessors, of being the propagators of a smart, spineless, diluted religion, which was the religion of the Court? He could not denounce Mazarin and Louis XIV. He could embark on this path only with prudence. But he put in his notes what he was unable to publish:

> I do not know whether they could do better with individuals who did not wish to rule by the sword. . . .
> Constitutions.—Poverty, ambition. Mainly princes, great noblemen who can help or hinder.—Useless rejects. Good complexion. Wealth, nobility, etc. . . .
> Give his capital to the Society for the glory of God. Union of feelings. *Decl.* submit to the Society and in this way preserve uniformity. . . .
> A universal and immortal body.—Affection for the community great and without scruple, dangerous.[17]

This time Pascal opens the case for the prosecution. Certain

[16] Thirteenth Letter, *G.E.*, VI, p. 41.
[17] *Pensées*, Brunschvicg 956. Sounder text in Lafuma 779. They are notes on the *Historica Jesuitica* of Rodolphe Hospinianus, Tiguri (Zurich), 1619.

Jesuits of his day had not organized a conspiracy, but wanted the power to do so and had it. It was the revival of an ancient drama of which Huxley became the historian in *Grey Eminence*. Looked at from this point of view, the *Provincial Letters*, which are the breviary of the anti-political man, take their place beside *Notre jeunesse*.[18] They bear witness to the unending struggle, at the very heart of Christendom, between the spirit of St Francis of Assisi and that of Machiavelli.

Alas! The Jesuits ended by triumphing over Port-Royal through Port-Royal itself. In its turn Jansenism became embittered, turned into a religious party, a political party—they were one and the same thing in the seventeenth century. And the *Provincial Letters*, paradoxical though it may appear, drove it in that direction. They were written against one party and became the weapon of a different one. Soon, men will be judged at Port-Royal only according to the degree of their Jansenist orthodoxy. The hour of intrigues, conspiracies and secret manoeuvres necessarily follows. As he tells the story of the two Capuchins who visited the monastery, Racine makes the same accusation against Port-Royal that Pascal made against the Jesuits. People were treated there as a party always treats people: first of all they are interrogated in order to find out whether they are "the friends of truth", meaning the official truth of the party. The other truth—truth pure and simple—becomes less and less important. Differences of opinion are concealed; people correct, twist and mutilate texts. They indulge in casuistry. They scarcely hesitate at defamation. Port-Royal withers and dies, not by the Pope's hand or by the hand of Louis XIV. Sainte-Beuve felt it and expressed it admirably on the last page of his *Port-Royal*.

But though he was defeated at Port-Royal itself and by its direct descendants, this does not alter the fact that Pascal was right in delivering a violent attack on the party spirit. Above all he was right in the Sixteenth, Seventeenth and Eighteenth Letters where he speaks to the Society of Jesus as a whole, and more directly still to Père Annat, one of the most powerful men in France. So much so that the *Provincial Letters* end in a duel between the representative of freedom and the representative of power.

[18] Charles Péguy.

CHAPTER VI

The Duel with the King's Confessor

IN Père Annat Pascal found an opponent who was almost of the same calibre as himself, not perhaps intellectually, but by reason of the post he held. Through concentrating on a single man his violence appeared to increase. Escobar lived in Madrid; it was a very long way away. Pères Meynier, Brisacier or Le Moyne were men of straw, whereas this time the duel was a real one.

Père Annat loftily undertook the defence of the Jesuits, but disdaining to reply to Pascal's challenges he confined himself to accusing him of heresy without knowing him and brought the controversy back to the theological aspect of Jansenism.

Pascal replied to the charge of heresy:

> I ask what proof you have. When did anyone see me at Charenton? [That is to say, at the Protestant church.] When have I missed mass or failed in the Christian's duties to his parish? When have I made any move to join the heretics or schismatics? What Council have I contradicted? What rule of the Pope's have I violated? It is up to you to reply, Father, or . . . you understand what I mean.[1]

Père Annat's argument could be reduced to a syllogism: "Port-Royal is heretical: but the author of the *Provincial Letters* belongs to Port-Royal: therefore the author of the *Provincial Letters* is a heretic."

Pascal begins by attacking the minor premiss and replies that he does not belong to Port-Royal. It is a surprising statement. We are conscious of a mental reservation.[2] Because for us today

[1] Seventeenth Letter, *G.E.*, VI, p. 342.
[2] See the comment, whose tone is unpardonable, of C. Gaillardin quoted by E. Jovy, *Études pascaliennes*, III, pp. 118–19.

Pascal does belong to Port-Royal. But according to contemporary opinion things were different. To belong to Port-Royal meant to be a member of the community of nuns or the group of the Solitaries. Now if Jacqueline belonged to Port-Royal, Blaise did not. He had gone there in order to make a retreat, as the Duc de Saint-Simon used to go to a Trappist monastery. There is the evidence of Arnauld's letters: at Port-Royal itself Pascal was regarded as an outside sympathizer, a visitor, a friend—a rather more intimate friend than other people—but one who had never sold his goods in order to take up residence at the Granges and who remained free to leave whenever he chose. He took advantage of his freedom and had ample reason to protest against Père Annat's gratuitous allegation.

He knew very well how to make the best use of the testimony of a free man, the freest man who existed, "single-handed against thirty thousand", unknown and without any credentials except his eloquence and his loyalty. What pride in his declaration of independence in the face of the whole world! It begins with a profession of the Catholic faith: "I have no attachment to anything on earth except to the Catholic, Apostolic and Roman Church in which I desire to live and die, in communion with the Pope, its sovereign Head; outside of which I am convinced there is no salvation."[3]

This profession of faith, made without any ambiguity, with the most obvious sincerity and repeated by Pascal at the same time, as we have already seen, in a letter to the Duc and Charlotte de Roannez, placed him in a position to assert his complete independence:

I am not afraid of you either for myself or anybody else because I am not attached to any community nor to any individual whoever it may be. Whatever your credentials, they are useless so far as I am concerned. I hope for nothing from the world; I am afraid of nothing in it; I want nothing from it; by the grace of God I do not need the goods or authority of anyone. Therefore, Father, you have no hold over me. You cannot get at me from whatever angle you try. You can get at Port-Royal, but not at me. People have certainly been dislodged from the Sorbonne, but that does not dislodge me from

[3] Seventeenth Letter, *G.E.*, VI, p. 343.

5. JEAN DUVERGIER DE HAURANNE, Abbé de Saint-Cyran.
Portrait by Philippe de Champaigne.

7. MÈRE ANGÉLIQUE ARNAULD.
Portrait by Philippe de Champaigne.

(*Above, left*) 6. The Abbey of Port-Royal des Champs. Engraving from a drawing by Marguerite de Hortemels. (*Below*) 8. MÈRE AGNÈS ARNAULD AND SISTER CATHERINE DE SAINTE SUZANNE. Painting by Philippe de Champaigne (father of Sister Catherine).

Mre Antoine Arnauld
Docteur de Sorbonne

9. ANTOINE ARNAULD.
Engraving after a portrait by Philippe de Champaigne.

my home. You can take violent action against Priests and Doctors, but not against me as I do not possess these qualifications. And it may well be that you have never been involved with anyone who was so far out of your reach and so fitted to fight against your errors because *I am free*, without commitment, without attachment, without connections, without relations, without business, with quite a good knowledge of your axioms and firmly resolved to pursue them as far as I believe that God has called me to do, without any human considerations being able to halt or slow down my pursuit. . . . In short, I declare clearly and loudly that no one is answerable for my Letters but myself; and that I am answerable for nothing except my Letters.[4]

It is the tone of Socrates's *Apology* and not even Bossuet has surpassed the perfection of the style or its eloquent simplicity.

After proclaiming his own freedom, Pascal proceeded to attack the major premiss of Père Annat's syllogism: Is Port-Royal heretical? He takes up again the problem of the five propositions and states afresh with the greatest possible clarity the position adopted by those known as Jansenists. Nicole had prepared the draft Pascal used in order to demonstrate the method to be followed in distinguishing between those things which were the objects of science and faith respectively. Pascal's plea is solid and well documented because Nicole and Arnauld had a thorough knowledge of the question. It is a model of the way in which this kind of argument should be conducted. In the Eighteenth Letter Pascal distinguishes the order of truths which are not dependent on faith. Whether the earth revolves or not, whether Origen was or was not a heretic, are questions of fact which are not tied to supernatural Revelation and on which the Church only has to take disciplinary action without her infallibility being in any way affected.

Pascal had a very good understanding of the essentials of Revelation. The errors of fact committed by the Church which her enemies were to babble about in the eighteenth century— errors which can be as numerous as you like—only prove that she is human. Pascal knew perfectly well that he did not detract in any way from her strength, that he was fortifying the Church by emphasizing them. His faith had no need to come to terms with deliberate blindness. And to transform these remarks into objections against Catholicism would be to admit that Pascal's Jesuit opponents were right.

During the long interval between the last two Letters, it was learnt that Rome had once again pronounced. A bull of Alexander VII's, dated 16th October 1656 but presented to the King by the Nuncio on 10th March 1657, condemned the five propositions not this time in themselves but in the sense given to them by Jansen. "We declare and define", wrote the Pope, "that these five propositions were taken from the book of the said Cornelius Jansen, Bishop of Ypres, entitled *Augustinus*, and that they have been condemned in the sense in which the Author explained them . . ."[5] This was a stroke at the roots of Arnauld's doctrine. It would have been possible to appeal against the Pope's judgment, but the whole of the Church accepted it. The Assembly of Clergy in France not only subscribed to the bull, but called in the State to support it in the action it took.

Why did not the theologians of Port-Royal abandon Jansen purely and simply, since they maintained that in their opinion the author's real meaning scarcely differed from the teaching of the Thomists which was not condemned? Had not Jansen himself solemnly submitted his work to the judgment of the Holy See, retracting in advance anything that might be condemned? Pascal preferred to claim that by "sense of Jansen" the Pope meant a Calvinist sense and that in consequence the condemnation did not in practice affect the theology of Jansen or Arnauld. He was making use of a distinction which was as fine as those of the casuists. According to impartial witnesses like Bossuet there was room, between the meaning of Calvin on the one hand and on the other that of the Thomists and Augustinians, for a meaning which was Jansen's and which the Pope and the Church in France meant to condemn.

People were very conscious at the time of the weakness of Pascal's defence. Nicole reports a dialogue, which may have been fictitious but is decidedly plausible, that at the time of publication of the last of the *Provincial Letters* he exchanged with a man of the world who was indifferent to the subtleties of theology:

[5] *G.E.*, VI, p. 61.

Tell me, I beg you [it is Nicole who is speaking] whether, if I stop at this point, there is anything clearer or more elegant or truer than what [Montalte] says about efficacious grace, which bends and turns the will as it pleases without depriving the will of its power of consent?[6]

Allow me to tell you [he replied] that it is the very passage which did not strike me as convincing or as worthy of Montalte. I know that such things are the impertinent remarks of the Thomists and I know, since Montalte himself says so, that it is also Jansen's view. But I cannot stand seeing Montalte imitate them. He ought to have left these puerile arguments to the Scholastics; they are as far removed from the character of his own mind as they are from truth. And if you want me to tell you simply what I think, it is that he has in fact convinced me that he is a Thomist, but he has convinced me at the same time that he is not incapable of occupying himself with petty matters.[6]

The sophisticated public which had been encouraged by Pascal to regard the arguments of the doctors of theology as frivolous were disconcerted to find Montalte himself wearing the doctor's hat.

After defending Jansen, Pascal did not feel that it was incumbent on him as a layman to go any further. He affected, as he had done at the beginning of his campaign, a slightly insolent attitude of indifference over the substance of the controversy which he treated as a question of minor importance.

Your quarrel is beginning to be a matter of indifference so far as I am concerned. When I thought you were arguing about the truth or falsity of the Propositions I listened carefully to what you had to say, for that was a question of faith; but when I realized that you were simply arguing whether or not they were to be found *word for word* in Jansen, since it was no longer a matter that affected religion, I lost interest too.[7] . . . Your quarrel means nothing to me as it means nothing to the Church. . . .[8] It may be that the doctors of Port-Royal are too favourable in their interpretation of Jansen;

[6] *Les Provinciales* . . . *avec les notes de Guillaume Wendrock* (Amsterdam, 1767), vol. IV, pp. 448–9.
[7] Seventeenth Letter, *G.E.*, VI, p. 352.   [8] *Ibid.*, p. 354.

but it may be that your interpretation is not favourable enough. I do not propose to go into that.[9]

At the end of the last of the *Letters*, he treats the controversy as being much ado about nothing, *"pro nihilo*, Father, as St Bernard says".[10] It was a return to the *leitmotiv* of the first *Letters*. The Sorbonne and the Jesuits had got together in order to produce a mouse. But Pascal will soon take a very different view. He will realize what is illogical and untenable in the position of the logicians of Port-Royal.[11] He will live through the most agonizing drama of his spiritual and religious life. His attachment to the Church, which he had proclaimed so proudly, will be at stake.

A draft of the beginning of a Nineteenth Letter to Père Annat has been found among his papers. Pascal admits in it that he had been vanquished by the Jesuit in the ecclesiastical field. "Come and look at what you have done", he seems to be saying, as he describes the plight of Port-Royal. The Letter was never finished. The vast press campaign begun on 23rd January 1656 came to an end on the 24th March 1657. But Pascal was simply changing his weapons. He considered that public opinion was sufficiently aroused and informed. The next step was to go on to direct action, to turn against the Jesuits their own methods of warfare and to replace verbal by ecclesiastical condemnation. It was a fight to the death.

What survives today of the *Provincial Letters*? According to Alain, "they are no longer read, but people certainly read the *Pensées*. I am not thinking here of teachers and students who are obliged to read them, but of the ordinary Reader. . . ."[12] It would be interesting to discover whether the *Provincial Letters* are much less read than Homer, Ronsard or Montesquieu. It is perfectly true that they have dated, that they seem to deal with controversies which are well and truly dead. The general public no longer understands them and the Jesuits have lost the political power which once made Pascal's caricatures entertaining. The *Provincial*

[9] *G.E.*, VI, p. 373.   [10] Letter XVIII, *G.E.*, VII, p. 55.
[11] See Sainte-Beuve's pages at the end of Chapter VIII of Book III on Pascal, *Port-Royal*, vol. III, pp. 185–90.
[12] *Propos sur le christianisme* (Paris, 1928), No. XLV, p. 149.

Letters derive their life from the fame and the indirect illumination of the *Pensées*. But they enable us to judge what the *Pensées* would have been like if Pascal had lived to finish them. More than anything, they provide us with an indispensable knowledge of the character and genius of Pascal. It is through its failure to read them that the general public has formed the impression of a sad and romantic Pascal when in fact he was gay, witty, biting, mocking and took a lively pleasure in reading Scarron, and was imbued with such impeccable taste that he seems to anticipate the best aspect of the eighteenth century.

Sainte-Beuve wondered whether the *Provincial Letters* were the equal of Demosthenes' *Philippics*. He decided that they were, but thought that the Greek orator was more human.[13] The Abbé Maynard went to a good deal of trouble to prove that the letters were inferior to the *Dialogues* of Plato.[14] But Bossuet was such an admirer of their elegance that he did not agree with him.[15] Nor did Mme de Sévigné who found them delightful. Molière drew on them and so did Boileau. Racine learnt style from them and so, in our own time, did Mauriac in his journalism.

We must repeat that, as has been said a hundred times before, the *Provincial Letters* are the letters patent of nobility of classic French in all its forms. The language is extraordinary and enchanting. Pascal the mathematician has suddenly arrived at the moment when his genius blossoms and becomes fused in his irrepressible and unpredictable maturity. He wrote in the worst possible conditions, a hurried work which was put together as he went along. But like Newman the heat of controversy excited him and made his conversational gifts sparkle like a firework display.

He possesses already [observed Mgr Calvet] the incisive phrasing of Voltaire, his detachment, his shafts like the sting of a wasp, and his acute sense of the comic . . . . Voltaire's method in his anonymous pamphlets is precisely the same and he, too, congratulates himself on "letting fly at evil-smelling beasts without exposing himself". That is the difference between them; it lies in the "evil-smelling beasts". There is a touch of vinegar in Voltaire; there is none in

[13] *Port-Royal*, vol. IV, p. 26.   [14] Abbé Maynard, *op. cit.*, vol. I, p. 374.
[15] "Bring back the elegance of the *Provincial Letters*", he wrote in 1698 in his *Réponse à quatre lettres de l'archevêque de Cambrai*.

Pascal. It is for this reason that his pamphlets against the Jesuits, prompted by passion and anger pushed to the point of mockery and invective and even to insult, always preserve the dignity of pleas written in a noble cause by a man who stakes his very soul on what he writes.[16]

The reply to the *Provincial Letters* did not come for ten years. The Jesuits had raged and fulminated, but simply made people laugh at them. The shot was fired from Port-Royal. It came from the "little Racine", as Monsieur Lemaistre called him. He alone dipped his pen into the same ink as Pascal in order to attack Port-Royal in the way in which Pascal had attacked the Jesuits and set to work, in the pithy words of his son, "to wallop the Gentlemen in the bloodiest and most ferocious manner". In a reply to Nicole, Racine was conducting the defence of poets, but what venom:

If you did not approve of them it was not a reason to start insulting them. You could have used gentler terms than words like *public poisoners*, and *people who are horrible in the sight of Christians*. Do you expect people to take your word for it? No, Sir, no: people are not accustomed to believe you as lightly as that. Twenty years ago you were saying every day that the five propositions were not in Jansen, but people still don't believe you.

But we know the austerity of your morality. We do not find it strange that you damn poets: you damn a lot of other people besides. What is surprising is to discover that you want to prevent men from honouring them. Come, Sir, be satisfied by awarding them places in the next world: don't try to decide on their rewards in this one. You left it a long time ago: let it judge the things that belong to it. Pity it, if you wish, for spending its time on trivialities and for having a good opinion of those who fabricate them; but don't envy them the petty honours that you yourselves have renounced.

In another place: "Not everybody can write against the Jesuits, but there are other paths that lead to glory."[17]

Racine criticizes Port-Royal on the same grounds as those on which Pascal criticized the Jesuits: for turning into a party.

[16] J. Calvet, *La Littérature religieuse de François de Sales à Fénelon* (Paris, 1938), pp. 209–10.
[17] *Lettre à l'auteur des Hérésies imaginaires et des deux Visionnaires*, Racine, *Oeuvres complètes* (Bibliothèque de la Pléiade), vol. II, pp. 19–20.

Although a woman may be leading an irregular life or a man may have plunged into a life of debauchery, if they call themselves your friends you must always hope for their salvation: if they were not your friends, however virtuous they were, you would always fear the judgment of God for them. Knowledge was treated as if it were a virtue; it was not enough in order to be learned, to have studied all one's life and to have read all the writers; you had to have read Jansen and not to have found the Propositions in him. . . . When we look at what you have been doing for the last ten years—your Disquisitions, your Dissertations, your Reflections, your Considerations, your Observations—we find nothing except that the Propositions are not in Jansen. Come, Gentlemen, leave it at that. Don't go on saying it. Let me be frank. We on our side are more disposed to believe the Pope and the French clergy than you.

And at the end of the second letter, Racine gives them a piece of advice: "Take my word for it, go back to the Jesuits. They are your natural enemies."[18]

Every shot went home. Pascal had acquired this most unexpected disciple. What is more, Racine's *Letters* reveal the scale of Pascal's victory. They are only comic because, in the eyes of the public, Port-Royal was literally the victor, just as the *Provincial Letters* had owed their success to the power of the Jesuits. But unlike the *Provincial Letters*, the *Lettres à l'auteur des Hérésies imaginaires* ("Letters to the author of the Imaginary Heresies") were odious for several reasons. It is true that everything about Nicole was bound to irritate Racine. But in spite of the favour it enjoyed with the public, Port-Royal was persecuted whereas Père Annat had never been. Moreover, Racine should never have forgotten that when he was an orphan he had been the favourite pupil of Monsieur Lemaistre, that his aunt was a nun at Port-Royal. But if he had continued his battle with Nicole in this tone, he would undoubtedly have made up for and matched the *Provincial Letters* in the sphere of the comic and of good sense. It was necessary to recall the cruel dialogue between Pascal and Racine, the two wittiest and most sensitive men of the seventeenth century.

[18] Racine, *op. cit.*, pp. 23–31.

CHAPTER VII

After the "Provincial Letters"

ALTHOUGH the *Provincial Letters* had ended, the battle was far from being over. On the contrary, a sequence of serious events made it fiercer than ever.

As we have already seen, the event which had the most far-reaching consequences was the fresh condemnation of Jansen by Pope Alexander VII. Although dated 16th October 1656, the bull did not reach France until March of the following year. The Assembly of Clergy proposed a formula of submission to the bull which ecclesiastics and religious should be required to sign. The supporters of Port-Royal did not intend to submit to the decree from Rome. They attempted to negotiate, but without success. The interpretation given by Pascal to the papal decisions was condemned. There was only one way of preventing Port-Royal from being regarded as heretical and treated accordingly: it was to appeal to members of Parliament not to accept the bull and in that manner prevent signature of the formulary being required under pain of sanctions. With this end in view, Pascal collaborated with Antoine Lemaistre in drawing up the *Letter from an Advocate in Parliament to one of his Friends relating to the Inquisition which is being established in France on the Occasion of the new Bull of Pope Alexander VII.*[1]

The *Letter* is a work of pure propaganda which sets out the arguments that were likely to move members of Parliament. The author claims that if Parliament "receives" the bull, it will provide the Pope with the means of taking political action in fields where Parliaments have always shown themselves jealous of their independence. He wants to frighten the lawyers by showing that

---

[1] G.E., VII, pp. 198–218.

acceptance of the bull will result in their children being deprived of their ecclesiastical benefices. This attempt to create panic among the middle classes by an appeal to their interests is decidedly unedifying.

So far as the substance is concerned, it is a Gallican plea. The bull is an infringement of the freedom of the Church of France. It is an attempt to implant the dogma of papal infallibility. At the end of the *Letter* the author attacks the papal condemnation itself and repeats the objections which had been made a hundred times before by Arnauld and taken up again in the last *Provincial Letters:* the five propositions are not in Jansen.

Pascal must have provided the arguments without himself writing the *Letter*. The style is unworthy of him: loose, slipshod, wordy, without any of the vigour of the *Provincial Letters*. Not only, as Louis Lafuma observes, did Dom Clémencet omit it from the list of Pascal's works, but he definitely attributed it to Lemaistre: an attribution which is suggested by the title itself.[2]

The *Letter* was condemned by an order of the King as containing "several propositions contrary to the honour and reverence which are due to our Holy Father the Pope and the Holy Apostolic See, scandalous and tending to sedition, injurious to the government and to the administration of the State. . . ."[3] It failed to prevent the registration of the bull by Parliament, but was effective in tempering the measures taken against the Jansenists.

The *Provincial Letters* were condemned in their turn. They had been burnt by the public executioner on 9th February at Aix in the Place des Prêcheurs by virtue of a parliamentary decree.[4] As the authorities had been unable to obtain a copy of the *Letters*, the public executioner had had to make do with an almanac.[5] On 6th September Rome put the *Provincial Letters* on the Index.[6] But it is a fact that at this time to put a book on the Index did not have the same effect as today. Thousands of Catholics continued to procure, read and have the *Provincial Letters* printed without the slightest twinge of conscience. Pascal himself does not appear to have been unduly affected by a decision which in his eyes was a

[2] Lafuma, II, p. 186: *Vie inédite de Pascal par Dom Clémencet* in E. Jovy, *Études pascaliennes*, VI, p. 33.

[3] G.E., VII, p. 220.

[4] *Ibid.*, p. 377.

[5] *Mémoires d'Hermant*, III, p. 292.

[6] G.E., VII, pp. 231-2.

form of police action by the Holy See. It would be an anachronism to infer from his attitude that in 1657 he was involved in a rebellion against the Pope.

A few months later he was to reopen the controversy over the *Provincial Letters*, but this time on the more propitious terrain of casuistry and moral theology. Towards the middle of December 1657, Père Pirot, a Jesuit, published anonymously and against the advice of many of his colleagues a book entitled *Apologie pour les casuistes contre les calomnies des Jansénistes* ("Defence of the Casuists against the Slanders of the Jansenists"). In the form of question and answer, the Jesuit sets out to reply to Pascal and to do so by dealing in detail with each of the decisions of the casuists attacked in the "Little Letters". He might have written a fine, serious, humane defence which would have cleared the ground, but which would have defended the casuists' aspirations towards a humane moral system. If not this, he could have emphasized the good intentions of his colleagues and their personal integrity. Instead of doing either he set out not merely to justify everything, but to attack Pascal. He claimed that Port-Royal had the intention "like Luther and Calvin in earlier times to get rid of the celibacy of the clergy".[7] He accused Antoine Arnauld of being "marvellously skilful in the art of collecting alms". He went on to accuse Pascal of attacking the Blessed Virgin: "The historians tell us that God has often avenged the dishonour done to his Mother by extraordinary punishments. The *Letters* give us grounds for fearing similar ones. . . . Paris already has major diseases which may only be the prelude to things more dangerous. . . ." The insinuations of the Jesuit became even more scabrous: "I should like to believe, Gentlemen, that you are chaste," he said, addressing himself to Port-Royal, "but the severity you affect is not a reliable proof of it. . . ." He claims equally that Pascal, the secretary of Port-Royal as he calls him, had got himself "debagged" by harlots. "He has given the reader grounds for supposing that he was not quite so chaste as Joseph. . . ."

[7] The extracts from the *Apologie des casuistes* which follow are taken from the catalogue drawn up by Nicole in Mlle de Joncoux's edition of the *Provincial Letters* (Amsterdam, 1768), IV, pp. 233-40.

But there is no end to the list of the good father's compliments. They reflect the tone of the controversies of the age, throwing into relief and enabling us to appreciate the taste and nobility of Pascal. The stupid remarks about Port-Royal seemed a proof of the truth of Pascal's complaint that the casuists defended slander. The *Apologie des casuistes* caused a scandal.

Pascal had learnt from experience. Instead of replying, he set out to get his new opponent condemned. The procedure was simplicity itself. Port-Royal shrewdly sought the assistance of the secular clergy. The parish priests of Paris decided to refer the *Apologie* to the ecclesiastical judges and to Parliament. They invited Pascal to defend their case in a tract called *Factum pour les curés de Paris*.

In a few pages the factum gives a résumé of the entire controversy over the *Provincial Letters*, brilliant pages which are the equal of the boldest and most mordant in the "Little Letters". They open with a roll of drums: "Our cause is the cause of Christian morality. Our opponents are the Casuists who corrupt it. Our interest is the interest of the consciences in our charge."[8]

We can see that the tone is clear and energetic. The picturesque details which enliven the *Provincial Letters* are suppressed. Like a great classic orator, Pascal goes straight to the essentials.

He shows that if men have always been sinners, up to that time sin had always been recognized for what it was. He accuses the casuists of corrupting the rules of morality and of substituting reason for the Gospel: "It is by this horrible reversal that we have seen those who style themselves Doctors and Theologians replace true morality, which should only have for principle the divine authority and charity as its aim, by a morality which is purely human and which has no other principle but reason. . . ."[9]

He sets out the most reprehensible of their axioms in a single page. In the same way he summarizes the methods used by the casuists to bolster up their views, enumerates the previous condemnations pronounced against them, and with great skill brings together the different points in an attack on Père Pirot.

The battle had evidently blazed up again more violently than before. The preachers in the Paris parishes denounced the casuists. The Jesuits defended themselves and published a *Refutation*.

[8] *G.E.*, VII, p. 278.   [9] *Ibid.*, p. 280.

The very next day Pascal suggested that eight priests, as delegates of their colleagues, should put their signatures to a *Second Statement* which he had written in great haste in a single day. He was angry and anger is an inspiration. In its vehemence his second statement is the finest he produced. He repeats in identical terms the political criticisms of the Jesuits made in the Fifteenth of the *Provincial Letters* on the grounds that they treat the secular clergy differently according to whether they wish to conciliate them or think that they are being attacked by them. "In the *Apologie* they hate us as though we were *ravening wolves;* here they love us as *People of piety and virtue.*"[10]

Pascal's attack is ferocious and without the slightest restraint. It can be judged by this philippic:

[The Casuists] will have placed poison and daggers in the hands of the furious and the vindictive by declaring in these terms: *That private individuals have the same right as Sovereigns to decide by the sole light of reason when it is forbidden or permitted to kill their neighbour,* and we dare not submit to the Ecclesiastical Judges these murderous axioms and make representations to them by means of a Factum about the monstrous effects of this bloodthirsty doctrine.

They will have given everyone without distinction the right of life and death which up to the present has been the sole prerogative of the sovereign, and we shall not dare to tell our people that it is a monstrous, a diabolical falsehood to say that it is permissible for them to take the law into their own hands. . . .

They will have put up for sale all the offices in the Church and thrown open the entrance of the House of God to every form of simony through their distinction between *price* and *motive;* and we shall not dare to proclaim that it is impossible without being guilty of crime to enter the ministry of the Church except by the one and only door, which is Jesus Christ. . . .

They will have permitted judges to keep the bribes they have taken for perpetrating an injustice; women to rob their husbands; servants to rob their masters; mothers to desire the deaths of daughters for whom they cannot find husbands. . . .

In short, they will have encouraged Christians to do all those things that Jews, Pagans, Mohammedans and barbarians hold in execration, and will have plunged the Church into the deepest dark-

10 *G.E.*, VII, p. 310.

ness ever to emerge from the Abyss; and we shall not dare to allow the faintest gleam of the light of the Gospel to penetrate the darkness without the Society rising up as one man and declaring that people who speak this way against their moral code are no better than rebels and heretics.[11]

After a passionate defence of ideological warfare when it is necessary, Pascal turns on the Society once again:

> We see the largest and most powerful organization in the Church, an organization which is the keeper of the conscience of nearly all the greatest in the land, conspiring to propagate the most appalling slogans under which the Church has ever laboured. In spite of all the charitable warnings which have been given both in public and in private, we find them obstinately approving vengeance, avarice, sensuality, pride, a false conception of honour and all the passions of fallen human nature, the profanation of the sacraments, the corruption of all the offices of the Church and a contempt for the Fathers who are replaced by the blindest and most ignorant of writers; and though we see that the Church is on the point of being submerged beneath this sea of corruption, for fear of disturbing the peace we dare not cry out to those who are leading it: *save us for we perish.*[12]

The campaign against the casuists was felt throughout France. The *Écrits des curés de Paris* ["Statements by the Parish Priests of Paris"] drawn up by Arnauld and Nicole followed one after another. The parish priests of Rouen, Nevers, Amiens, Évreux and Lisieux asked their bishops to condemn Père Pirot's book and the propositions of the casuists.

The Protestants of course were delighted. Did not this torrent of pamphlets prove the moral corruption of the Catholic Church, the Great Whore of Babylon, "the Scarlet Woman"? Pascal wanted to reply to the attack by Calvinist ministers. This time the controversialist of the *Provincial Letters* was one with the man who wished to convert Protestants and unbelievers. With this aim in view he wrote the *Cinquième écrit des curés.* His argument was a simple one: Calvinists and Jesuits were both wrong. The Church condemned the excesses of the casuists which could not claim

[11] G.E., VII, pp. 314–16.   [12] *Ibid.*, p. 323.

the support of any conciliar definition or any papal decision. The protestations of the clergy showed that by attributing to the Church the moral code of the casuists, Protestants and Jesuits were making a mistake. Pascal, however, drew a distinction of capital importance between the two categories of opponent. He makes the priests say:

> We do not wish those whom he has entrusted to our care to be so carried away by anger at the excesses of the Jesuits that they forget that the Jesuits are their brothers, that they are part of the unity of the Church, members of our body, and that we therefore have an interest in keeping them, whereas the heretics are members who have been cut away and form a body which is an enemy of our own. This puts an infinite distance between them and us; because the schism is a great evil, is not only the greatest of evils, but it is impossible according to all the Fathers of the Church to find any good where there is schism.[13]

At the same time Pascal prepared a draft of an episcopal summons against the *Apologie des casuistes*. He, too, was the author of the *Sixième écrit des curés de Paris*, written on 24th July 1658.

The Jesuits, anticipating a condemnation, disowned Père Pirot. In this they were sincere. Many of them had criticized and disowned the *Apologie des casuistes* as soon as it appeared; but instead of condemning it openly, they announced that the Society refused to be drawn into the dispute. Pascal was indignant over what he regarded as a subterfuge. "Come, Reverend Fathers, the whole of the Church is in a ferment over the present controversy. The Gospel is on one side, the *Apologie des casuistes* on the other. Prelates, Pastors, Doctors and the people make common cause on one side; and the Jesuits, when pressed to choose, announce that they do not intend to *become involved in the war*. What a criminal form of neutrality!"[14]

The controversy was brought to an end by Rome itself. On 21st August, on the instructions of Pope Alexander VII, the Inquisition put the *Apologie des casuistes* on the Index with an express prohibition against printing and circulating it.[15] Much

---

13 *G.E.*, VII, pp. 368–9.   14 *Ibid.*, p. 47.
15 Text in *G.E.*, IX, p. 343.

more than that, twenty years later, in 1679, Pope Innocent X condemned the suspect propositions of the casuists.

It has been said that Pascal was finally vanquished in the Church, that today probabilism is still triumphant in the books used by confessors. It is quite true that the tendency of some theologians to treat moral matters juridically has not disappeared, nor have they lost their taste for solving the most imaginary and the most extraordinary cases of conscience. To be sure, the Church encourages a kind of casuistry which is likely to develop the powers of judgment of confessors: she warns them against undue severity which would only be a form of Pharisaism. Her sexual morality is none the less of exceptional severity in the eyes of Protestants or lay people who boast of being on the side of the *Provincial Letters*. Pascal was therefore partly in the right and partly in the wrong. His readers must not forget that the greatness of the Christian soul is not to be found in books dealing with mental and moral disease. The way of sanctity is not to be learnt from legal treatises or the illustrations in anatomical works. The *Provincial Letters* and Pascal's *factums* still possess the extreme usefulness of reminding us of the gravity of these questions and inviting us to deal with them with tact and prudence. It is thanks perhaps to Montalte and Bossuet, who have done no more than lend their voices to so many mystics and saints, that the Church in France today as in the seventeenth century preserves its seriousness, its touch of severity, its slightly austere atmosphere, its taste for frankness which make it attractive and which Renan himself had observed in the course of his clerical education.

CHAPTER VIII

Writings on Grace
and Treatises on the Roulette

P ASCAL had no illusions. Prelates, men of the world, a large
number of serious Christians and even atheists had followed
his efforts with sympathy and had approved of the *Provincial
Letters*. They were far from being as definite when it came to the
theology of Jansen. They found it repellent; it seemed to them to
be odious and frightening. They approved of Rome for condemning it.

Pascal made up his mind to clarify the question, to show the
public at large what he called "the truths of grace" in such a way
as to overcome its repugnance. He also had to explain his position
to correspondents who raised the objection of the decisions of the
Council of Trent. For this reason there is a collection of treatises by
him on grace which were copied out by his friends, but not published during his lifetime.

An educated person of today who is capable, for example, of
reading and understanding a book on the circulation of money
would find these treatises more or less unreadable. Should we forget
that the spiritual problem of the very meaning of Christianity was
involved in his commentaries on St Paul and St Augustine, that
it was a question of the greatest mystery that can test the human
intelligence, the mystery of man's relations with God? The
sixteenth-century Reformation had no other cause. Now, Pascal
sensed in Cartesianism the emergence of a philosophy whose
aim was to suppress the action of God in human life, to invite
man to work out his salvation alone. He saw in it the resurrection
of the work of the Pelagians. On the other hand, he believed that

in the Augustinianism of Jansen he had found a rampart against the rising tide of atheism. In his eyes, God not only remained the master but grace, which was a form of divine action, exerted such immense power that it acted almost alone and drew man along in its wake.

Without mentioning Descartes, in his treatises Pascal compares the solutions produced by Protestants, by the Jesuits who were followers of Molina, and by St Augustine. According to him, for the Protestants man does not participate at all in grace. It is from outside and without their participation that God rewards the righteous through the merits of Jesus Christ. On the other hand, the Molinist teaching makes the divine action depend on the determination of the human will. Between these two errors, St Augustine asserts that before original sin man was free in the Molinist sense. Now that man is fallen God saves whom he pleases. As long as he gives man efficacious grace, which is victorious over the will, man is capable of doing good, but as soon as God withdraws grace man is inevitably dragged down to evil by a victorious sensuality.

As for the analysis of the free action, Pascal did not spend much time on it. He did not believe in what he called the "liberal will" in fallen man.[1] The will inevitably follows what attracts it most powerfully: concupiscence or grace.

Thus fallen man is even more of a slave than the slaves in chains of Michelangelo. For their souls could remain free. What is more, Pascal is not afraid of using the word slavery when applied to the state in which grace places man. We are the instruments of the all-powerful will of God. The damned, to be sure, have willed their damnation, but God has willed that they willed it, or rather has not willed to draw them to him with his irresistible chains. He has abandoned, deserted, forgotten them.

That is the purest Jansenism. Pascal claims of course that he is basing it on a strict analysis of the human act and the traditional proofs which have the authority of St Augustine. He tries to correct its disastrous effects. He recalls that "those who are saved

---

[1] There is a play on words in the French. The French for free will is *libre arbitre* from the Latin *liberum arbitrium*. Pascal coined the phrase *libéral arbitre*. —*Trans.*

wanted to be saved . . . those who are damned wanted to commit the sins which deserved damnation."[2] But we know that in the competition between the two wills, human and divine, the divine will is victorious. Pascal asserts no less energetically that the judgment by which God abandons the damned is *just* though mysterious; in short, that "all the men in the world are forced to believe, but with a belief mixed with fear which is not accompanied by certainty, that they belong to the small number of the Elect whom Jesus Christ wishes to save".[3]

Pascal thought that he was giving an accurate summary of Catholic doctrine. He regarded himself as a strict disciple of St Augustine. On both these points he was mistaken. If he had published his *Écrits sur la grâce* during his lifetime, he would have had difficulty in convincing unbelievers and he would have at once exposed himself to the same condemnation as Jansen, Arnauld and later Quesnel.

If Pascal and his friends were so mistaken about the meaning of St Augustine's work, it is not fair to hold it against him. He was not a professional theologian or a scholar. He wrote hurriedly at the dictation of his masters. He had no time to work out his own theory of grace.

Moreover, his life like that of his masters often acted as a corrective to the extravagances of theory and system. At Port-Royal prayer and the reception of the sacraments were scarcely different from what they were at Saint-Sulpice or the Oratory. The lofty conception of the action of God on the soul through grace lost its rigidity in prayer.[4] There remained only a profound sense of religion which permeates his *Écrits sur la grâce* and gives life to their finest pages. We feel the presence of a sort of inner fire. It is through this inner experience of prayer and union with God that the *Écrits sur la grâce* still live and serve as a preface to the *Pensées*.

---

[2] *Premier écrit*, G.E., XI, p. 128.   [3] *Ibid.*, p. 137.
[4] The somewhat tendentious arguments of Henri Bremond in his volume on "L'École de Port-Royal" in his *Histoire littéraire* . . . are corrected by two fine essays: "En Prière avec Pascal" and "Pascal et les mystiques" in *Autour de l'humanisme* (Paris, 1937).

Eloquence, controversy, theology, the study of St Augustine and prayer were not sufficient to satisfy Pascal's devouring thirst for action. When he was most fully occupied with his theological work he suddenly returned to pure mathematics and brought off the most brilliant discovery of his life as a scientist. In fact, he had never really given up science. While he was writing the *Provincial Letters*, we find him carrying on a long correspondence with Sluse, Canon of Liége and a good mathematician.[5] He suggests some problems which will lead him to those of the centres of gravity of volumes engendered by curvilinear curves. Sluse was also a Hebrew scholar. Pascal asked him questions about the Hebrew text of Isaias, the choice which should be made in the Massorah between the *ketiv* or text, and the *qere* or marginal corrections, as well as certain confusions on the part of scribes between the negative and the positive pronoun in the third person. Sluse replied admitting that he found it difficult.[6]

Now, one night, possibly in May 1658, Pascal was unable to sleep owing to a violent toothache. In order to take his mind off the pain, he began to think about Sluse's solution of the problem of surfaces and the centre of gravity of certain curves. He applied them to a curve that Mersenne had mentioned to him which was known as the *roulette* or cycloid. It was none other "than the passage through the air of the hub of a wheel when it turns in the ordinary way" and describes the form of the arch of a bridge.[7] It was the half of the ellipse traced by the planets revolving round the sun. Pascal had a sudden perception of the path to follow in order to discover the centre of gravity. It was not fortuitous, but the result of an earlier piece of research which he had to abandon in favour of more urgent demands made on him.

Shortly afterwards he discussed his discovery with Roannez. The Duke advised him to put his calculations into writing and first and foremost to establish a date in accordance with the usual practice of the scholars of the age—that is to say, to send a circular letter to other geometers containing a statement of the problems

[5] Sluse's first letter is dated 6th April 1658, but it is a reply. Pascal's correspondence with Sluse must therefore have lasted for some time.
[6] Letter from Sluse to Pascal, *G.E.*, VII, pp. 331–6.
[7] *Histoire de la roulette*, *G.E.*, VIII, p. 195.

to be resolved, fixing a time limit for the receipt of solutions by the judges and offering a nominal prize of forty *pistoles* to the first person who produced a set of correct solutions. Carcavi was chosen to judge the competition. Six questions were set in Latin and circulated.

Now, Pascal did not find out until it was too late that his intimate friend Roberval, who was always very secretive about problems he had solved, had already solved the first four on the list. Sluse wrote to say that he had long ago solved the first problem.[8] At this juncture a Jesuit from Toulouse, Père Lalouère, set to work with a few hints from Fermat. He had soon solved the first three problems and claimed to have solved the others by applying the same principles and to have discovered in addition the quadrature of the circle.[9] Pascal altered the rules of the competition, suppressing the four problems already solved by Roberval and only retaining the last two.

At the beginning of October Pascal sent out a third circular confirming the time allowed for the competition and naming Paris as the place to which the entries were to be sent:

I realise that this gives an advantage to the French, particularly those living in Paris, but by favouring some I have done no injustice to the others. I leave to all comers the honour of their discoveries. I do not confer the honour: it is the result of merit; I have nothing to do with it. I control nothing but the award of the prizes and since they are due to my own liberality, I was free to decide on the conditions: I have done so in this way; no one has any grounds for complaint; I owed nothing to Germans or Muscovites; I might have offered them to the French alone; I can offer others to the Flemings alone or to whomever I choose.[10]

He replied to the criticisms of the Englishman, Wallis, who found the time allowed too short. Then Pascal attacked Lalouère for the miscalculations he had admitted. "There are only two ways of showing that you have solved the problems: to give the solution with paralogism or the calculation without mistakes."[11]

[8] *G.E.*, VIII, pp. 4–11.
[9] Introduction to the letter from Lalouère to Fermat, *G.E.*, VIII, pp. 24–5.
[10] *Ibid.*, pp. 161–2.   [11] *Ibid.*, p. 168.

On 10th October, with the assistance of Roberval, Pascal published his *Histoire de la roulette*. In it he was unjust to Torricelli by accusing him of plagiarizing Roberval and he overlooked the works of Galileo. He gave first place to the discoveries of his friend, examined the solutions put forward, added some other problems and indicated which were his own discoveries.

The judges met on 24th November. Père Lalouère saw that he was disqualified as he had admitted errors in his own calculations. The solution of the Englishman, Wallis, was not considered rigorous enough. The prize was therefore awarded to Pascal himself, who until then had preserved his anonymity, since no one else had submitted a satisfactory solution. In December there appeared the *Suite à l'histoire de la roulette* which was directed against Lalouère who persisted in maintaining that he had found the solution, but refused to reveal his method or his calculations. Then under the pseudonym of Amos Dettonville, which was an anagram of Louis de Montalte, Pascal published his own results in the form of a *Letter to M. de Carcavy, followed by a Treatise on Geometry*.

Throughout the entire affair of the competition Pascal's attitude seems to have been decidedly rigid: very certain that he was right and indulging in biting comments at the expense of those who made mistakes. He was ill-informed about the abilities of some of the foreign scholars, but very ready to pay tribute to those who really were his peers. One could only wish that he had been able to demonstrate his superiority in a way that was less wounding to other people.

It was by the method of the infinitely small that he was able to resolve the problems relating to the cycloid. In this way he reached the threshold of integral calculus and obtained his results by purely geometrical means.

His work in pure mathematics won the admiration of contemporary scholars and the admiration is still felt by present-day specialists. The results show that at the very moment he was translating Isaias, composing the *Pensées*, writing the last of his *factums* for the parish priests of Paris and practising his religion with ardour, Pascal had preserved intact his marvellous intellectual powers and his extraordinary capacity of carrying on simultaneously tasks which were so different from one another as to appear irreconcilable. In a sick body his mind maintained the perfect equilibrium necessary for the exhausting researches which demanded the sustained attention of the subtlest and most flexible of pure reasons.

Part III

GETHSEMANE
(1658–1662)

Jesus will be in agony until the end of the world. We must not sleep during that time.

Pascal

CHAPTER I

The Composition of the "Pensées"

THE year 1658 was a time of feverish activity for Pascal. He not only prosecuted unflinchingly his war against the casuists by inspiring or writing the *factums* of the parish priests of Paris, but he also found time to write a considerable number of notes on pure mathematics. He carried on an assiduous correspondence with Sluse, Carcavi and Huyghens. This year also saw the composition of the essential parts of the *Pensées*. In fact, it was mainly in 1658 that Pascal covered with his spidery handwriting the five hundred large pages, half of which were intended to serve as the plan for the Apology for the Christian religion that he dreamed of writing.[1] It was the book that he wished to be more eloquent, more vibrant and more passionate than the *Provincial Letters*. He would address himself to Méré, Miton, Bourdelot and Le Pailleur. It seems that there were many atheists in Paris. Père Mersenne had put their number at 20,000. Later on Saint-Simon actually discovered a few in Louis XIV's immediate entourage. They even included cardinals like Retz. The sermons of the preachers, the allusions of Bossuet, the success of Montaigne's *Essays*, La Bruyère's chapter on the *esprits forts*, prove that, in the second half of the seventeenth century, the eighteenth was already present in embryo. Pascal knew perfectly well that he was not tilting against windmills.

For the purpose of his book he had at his elbow his Bible and Montaigne—that atheist's bible. But first and foremost he thought. And since he no longer trusted his prodigious memory, he took

[1] L. Lafuma has proved that the essentials of the *Pensées* were written in 1658. Cf. *Recherches pascaliennes*, pp. 70, 99; *Controverses pascaliennes*, pp. 14–15, 46ff., 83; and Lafuma I, p. 13. Finally, and most important, *Histoire des Pensées de Pascal* (Paris, 1954), pp. 11–28.

notes on everything: textual references, new translations of the prophets, plans. He was drafting a great work, wrote out some pages of it and later, on days of extreme fatigue, he dictated ideas that came into his head to his sister.[2]

When the Gentlemen of Port-Royal learnt that he was working on an apology for Christianity, they burned with envy to be the first to read it. Blessed curiosity that forced Pascal to complete some pages of his book.

It was probably about October-November and at Port-Royal des Champs that in the presence of Arnauld, Nicole and the Duc de Roannez the most brilliant of lecturers spoke "for at least two hours" with extraordinary success.[3] "Although those present were the sort of people who were not much given to admiration . . . they still admit that they were carried away by it . . ."[4] Pascal was in particularly good form and the warmth of his eloquence aroused the enthusiasm of his audience: "Whether something of the union of head and heart, which warms and brings new power, was added to what was effective on both sides, or whether it was simply one of those lucky moments when the most gifted of people surpass themselves and when impressions become so vivid and profound, everything that M. Pascal said has remained in their minds until the present day."

Thus spoke Filleau de la Chaise.[5] Unfortunately, this member of Pascal's audience did not possess the talent and the accuracy of the worthy Fontaine. More than eight years after the event he wrote down a summary of the lecture without having any notes at hand, replacing them by a copy of the manuscript of the *Pensées* which obviously influenced him considerably.[6] This is apparent from what he wrote. When he stopped using the written text, he was very far from the engaging eloquence, the pathos and the directness which give such life to the *Entretien avec M. de Sacy sur Epictète et Montaigne* ["Discussion with M. de Sacy on Epictetus and Montaigne"].

[2] According to Marguerite Périer, Lafuma, III, p. 63.
[3] *Discours sur les Pensées de M. Pascal*, Lafuma, III, p. 91. On the *Discours sur la condition de l'homme* reconstructed by P. L. Couchoud, see Lafuma, *Controverses . . .* pp. 76-9, 87.
[4] Lafuma, III, p. 91.   [5] Lafuma, III, pp. 91-2.
[6] Lafuma, *Controverses pascaliennes*, p. 18; *Recherches*, p. 83.

But if Pascal's observations appear swamped in a wordy, nerveless discourse compared to the original in his own notes marked "A.P.R." (At Port-Royal), we nevertheless find in the *Discours* a few echoes of the impact that Pascal's ideas made on the audience. The listeners had a vivid impression of discovering an absolutely new world, reminding them of the surprise and delight that they had experienced the day they read the first of the *Provincial Letters*. Pascal produced a complete upheaval inside apologetics. A revolution as important as that of Descartes, but in the reverse sense which consisted in detaching the proofs of Christianity from their traditional metaphysical foundations and replacing philosophy by psychology and history. Such was the *instauratio magna* of Pascal.

He wanted an apologetic which would pursue the atheist into his lair, into the place where the roots of his affections and his feelings reached, into the unconscious depths of his heart. Méré boasted that he was the arbiter of the human heart and knew its secrets. It is in fact in this mysterious crypt that according to Pascal the drama of salvation is played out. The rest—proofs, refutations, metaphysical discourses—were without any power to convince. Before Freud, in a very different way and by a much broader method, Pascal sets out to discover in the depths of man the key to the religious problem. He uses the dark lantern of the seekers of subterranean things. He is determined to track down the unbeliever.

The fact is [he said to his friends] that it is less important to prove the existence of God than to make people feel his presence, which is the most useful and, taken all round, the easiest job. And in order to feel him, we must seek him in those feelings which still remain in us and which are a legacy of the greatness of our first nature. For if God has left signs of himself in all his works, as we cannot doubt, we shall find them rather in ourselves than in external things which do not speak to us and of which we see only the merest surface because we are prevented for ever from knowing their depths and nature. And if it is inconceivable that he has not imprinted in his creatures what they owe him for the being he has bestowed on them, it will be rather in his own heart that man will find the important lesson than in inanimate objects which accomplish the will of God without

knowing him and for which being does not differ from nothing-
ness.[7]

Pascal therefore invented what was known fifty years ago as
"the method of immanence", and discovered in man what is
necessary to enable him to rekindle in his heart the fear of what he
is and the longing for what he could be with God.

It is in the Bible that we must seek the divine reply to this
tragic appeal of a humanity whose incurable anguish if God does
not exist was seen by Pascal alone in the seventeenth century.
Here, again, Pascal made a vivid impression on the minds of his
audience by the novelty and by what one might almost call the
brutality of his highly original views. He makes a clean sweep of
everything except men's dream of finding an all-powerful God who
will love and heal them. When faced with a man reduced to
"despair", Pascal opens his Bible. Now what he begins by
emphasizing is the harmony between the Bible and the human
heart. The fundamental contradictions of man are well described.
He sees "the portrait of his heart in an infinite number of places".[8]
He also sees a magnificent image of God. He finds the answer to
the central problem of his life: What is man? What must he do?
Above all he discovers a strange invitation to love God, father
and saviour, healer and doctor of man.

In the course of his examination of the Bible, Pascal makes some
observations on the infinite as part of his approach to the
mysterious element in religion. The dimensions of the world
permit us a glimpse of the divine transcendence.

Pascal then comes to the argument from the internal coherence
of the Bible, that is to say, the way in which its miracles fit in
with the harmonious development of its laws and dogma. He
brings out the admirable way in which the Old and New Testaments complete one another. The aim of the prophecies is to
serve as a prelude to the foundation of the kingdom of charity.
Their progressive character is well noted.

When he comes to the Gospels Pascal once again surprises his
audience. The words that Filleau de la Chaise attributes to him
are a clear indication of his method:

[7] Lafuma, III, pp. 90–1.   [8] *Ibid.*, p. 97.

Even if there had been no prophecies foretelling Jesus Christ and he had performed no miracles, there is something so divine in his life and teaching that we could not help being charmed by them; and as there is no true virtue and no uprightness of the heart without the love of Jesus Christ, so there is no high degree of intelligence or true delicacy of feeling without the admiration of Jesus Christ. . . . Let Socrates and Epictetus appear and at the same time that everyone in the world yields to them in moral questions, they themselves recognize that all their justice and all their virtue vanishes like a shadow and disappears before that of Jesus Christ. . . .[9]

According to Filleau de la Chaise, Pascal finished his lecture with some general observations on the fundamentals of the religious problem and the proofs of religion which look back to what he said at the beginning. Not only do the proofs of Christianity in their own order depend on the heart, but the same is true of their efficacy. "Not only the things that must be felt depend on the heart, but also those belonging to the mind when the heart may have some part in them."[10] For Pascal there was nothing very extraordinary about it. Since God is personal, the relations between hate, indifference or love towards him place all the proofs in a different light. A stripping of the self is necessary as a prelude to any examination of Christianity. Filleau de la Chaise was therefore under no illusion about the effectiveness of the *Pensées*, and Pascal himself may have intended to suggest in advance that his efforts were doomed to failure with the great majority of his readers. He divined, he pointed the way to the eighteenth century with its feverish desire for amusement, its follies, its materialism, its care-free attitude, its emptiness. It might seem as though he had Voltaire's *Remarques* on the *Pensées* in front of him: "How sad and cruel these truths, which are such a consolation to many, will seem to them. . . . They will appear at most like those empty phantoms that we brush away when we pass our hands over our eyes. . . ."[11]

And Pascal attacks the humanism which without knowing it was still permeated by Christianity, but a Christianity without dogmas, without the infinite God, the faint perfume clinging to an empty bottle; he attacks, too, the morality without religion

[9] Lafuma, III, p. 107.   [10] *Ibid.*, p. 108.   [11] *Ibid.*, p. 114.

which was to triumph in the eighteenth century and whose total collapse we are witnessing today.

The two treatises *Sur les preuves des livres de Moïse* ["On the Proofs of the Books of Moses"] and *Où l'on fait voir qu'il y a des démonstrations d'une autre espèce et aussi certaines que celles de la géométrie* ["Where it is shown that there are proofs of another kind which are as certain as those of geometry"] are not connected with any particular lecture given by Pascal. But the Gentlemen of Port-Royal had a reason for including them later in their edition of the *Pensées*. There are echoes in them of the conversation and personal views of Pascal.

The *Discours sur les preuves des livres de Moïse* evidently belongs to a period in which people had scarcely even begun to realize the difficulties raised by the authenticity of the Pentateuch when understood in the strict sense. We know today that Genesis and Deuteronomy did not come to us from Moses in the same simple and direct manner that the *Pensées* came from Pascal. What does it matter? Pascal may well have shared the point of view of his age on primitive history, but he continually rises above it, and though the form in which he stated them needs amending, his arguments in favour of the internal coherence of the Bible and its value as evidence have lost none of their value.

It should be observed that Pascal's interpreter joins issue with the theory that reason has been corrupted to such an extent that it abdicates completely in face of faith. "God", he says, "has not endowed man with reason and intelligence with the idea of making such a great gift useless and even harmful by only offering as objects of faith things against which the proper means of knowledge are in a state of continual rebellion."[12] He shows that in his opinion the Christian mysteries are linked to other demonstrable truths, that they are even linked to all fundamental truths which are the common legacy of the human race.

According to the same interpreter, Pascal turned next to history. For him no amount of theory is worth a fact and religion is based on facts. He undertakes to establish the firmness of "the fact of Moses" with the assistance of very acute historical, moral,

[12] *Discours sur les preuves des livres de Moïse*, ed. V. Giraud, p. 103.

psychological and social proofs. What would he not have achieved if he had been armed with all the discoveries of criticism and archaeology at our disposal today? He has, at any rate, shown the order to which historical proofs belong and which gradually gathers in the supporting evidence until certainty emerges. But why do some people resist "the Christian fact"? Their will and heart refuse to submit to it. Indifference and disaffection precede doubt. For there is a certain "uprightness of the heart" which is necessary if we are to cultivate within ourselves a "taste for truth".

The richest and most suggestive part of the *Discours sur les preuves des livres de Moïse* is incorporated in some of the pages on "proofs of another kind which are as certain as those of geometry". Golden pages which anticipate the whole of Newman's *Grammar of Assent*. Pascal distinguishes two kinds of certainties: those that are the result of geometrical demonstrations and those that are the result of testimony. "The fact, for example, that the city of London was burnt down a few years ago[13] is no truer in itself than the proposition that the angles of every triangle are equal to two right angles; but it is, so to speak, truer so far as men in general are concerned."[14] It is the difference between abstract and concrete. Our lives do not depend on the former, but on the certainties which come from the testimony of other men. In order to criticize their testimony we unconsciously apply the laws of probability. When they are convergent they finish by creating certainty. Pascal explains how the addition of testimonies which are in conformity with one another never produce anything but a greater and greater degree of probability. In order to go beyond probability and take a leap into the realm of certainty, there must be an element of trust in human nature, a sense of the veracity of the witnesses, the value of the control they exercise over one another. Nobody who has not seen the city of Rouen doubts its existence because to do so would mean accusing all men of duplicity or madness. Truths of this nature are innumer-

[13] The Fire of London took place on 2nd September 1666. Pascal could not therefore have been speaking of it. See G. Chinard, *En lisant Pascal* (Paris, 1948), pp. 18–34.
[14] *Traité où l'on fait voir* . . . , p. 147.

able and we constantly appeal to them; to reject them would be tantamount to refusing to go on living.

According to Pascal, the proofs of religion belong to this order of certainty. The witness of history, that of the great saints and mystics, the coherence and supreme value of the great Christian dogmas, the excellence of Christian morality, the permanence and duration of the Church, are proofs which, when considered in isolation, may not perhaps create more than a probability of truth; when considered collectively they form such a phalanx, "such a great accumulation of proofs of our religion, that there is no more convincing demonstration and it would be as difficult to doubt it as a proposition of geometry even if we had nothing but the help of reason."[15]

Pascal's conversation with his friends on the nature of proof in matters of religion is of capital importance for an understanding of the Pensées. If Pascal moves away from metaphysics, it is the result of deliberate choice. He wanted to deal with man as he is. That is the secret of his power of persuasion which his work has preserved intact.

He did not stop there. One day he had the opportunity of giving three little lectures or talks. It was a question of the education of an aristocrat, probably the young Duc de Chevreuse. The subject was a fashionable one. With the advent of the royal absolutism everyone was wondering what form the education should take of a future monarch, reigning without any sort of control over a kingdom as large as France. After Pascal's death, Nicole published a Traité de l'éducation d'un prince "Treatise on the Education of a Prince".[16] Duguet did the same thing. We know Fénelon's dreams. A hundred years later Jean-Jacques Rousseau, taking up the threads of Montaigne and Rabelais in his turn, looked to the pedagogues for the resurrection of the golden age.

Some of the fragments of the Pensées are linked to these three talks of Pascal's. For everything served him as a pretext for

---

[15] Discours sur les Pensées, ed. Giraud, p. 156.
[16] Essais de morale, vol. II, pp. 251ff., of the edition of Desprez and Desessartz of 1714. It was in the volume at the end of the treatise on Grandeur that the Discours de feu M. Pascal sur la condition des Grands were first published.

returning to the great truths that he was meditating. Man was a fallen prince. A young aristocrat was therefore a perfect image of man. To discuss his education was a heaven-sent opportunity for developing a number of very daring political ideas.

In the first discourse Pascal demolishes the very idea of aristocracy and natural right. It was nothing but the fruit of chance encounters, marriages and the fantastic operation of human laws. By what right do hereditary fortunes exist? "It is a matter of indifference to your soul and your body in themselves," he says to the young prince, "whether their status is that of a boatman or a duke." You possessed nothing which set you above other people. The sole truth is "perfect equality between all men".[17]

But Pascal was not so naïve as to imagine that men are really equal even outside the artificial distinctions established between them by society. In the second discourse he returns to the distinction drawn in his *Letter to Christina of Sweden* between greatness of establishment and natural greatness. The first is factitious; the second is founded on genuine superiority: knowledge, intelligence, virtue, strength. The first is honoured by external ceremony: "You have to speak to kings on your knees."[18] As for respect, it is confined to natural superiority. "If you were a duke without being a man of parts . . . when I paid you the respect that the human order has established as being due to your birth, I should not fail to have for you the inner contempt dictated by the baseness of your mind."[19]

Finally, in the third discourse Pascal draws a distinction between the order of charity and the material order. You are monarch of the possessions which engender and satisfy cupidity, he says to his youthful listener. Do not rule by means of force, but by political skill placed at the service of an equitable distribution of your possessions. If you stop at that, you will be damned, but damned as a man of parts. It is better than being damned as a rogue. It is for someone other than myself to lead you along the paths of charity. If you follow them, my advice, which is purely human, will at least have saved you from an inelegant stupidity and brutality.

Pascal's three talks express towards earthly greatness the faint contempt of the superior man who knows how to put things in

[17] *G.E.*, IX, p. 367.   [18] *Ibid.*, p. 369.   [19] *Ibid.*, p. 370.

their proper place. We feel the breath of the Socratic mind of which there are so many traces in the *Pensées*.

During the years of gestation of the *Pensées* Pascal, who was constantly preoccupied with his educational interests, wrote a few pages of a treatise on logic which was intended for the instruction of the older pupils of Port-Royal. They have been preserved under the title of *De l'Esprit géométrique* and *De l'Art de persuader* ["The Mathematical Mind" and "The Art of Persuasion"]. It is a part of Pascal's *Discours de la méthode*.

In his eyes the ideal order is the mathematical order. Not every thing is defined in it because there are some ideas which are so clear that all definition of them is useless and impossible. But we define everything that is not self-evident. Pascal subscribes to the Cartesian theory of evidence. In his view space, time, movement, equality, the majority, the whole and reduction are indefinable concepts. It is pointless to cast doubt upon them like the sceptics. Nature gives us a clear intuition of their reality.

Pascal insists firmly on the infinite divisibility of geometric space. He refutes Méré who laughed at the idea of the infinitely small and treats his difficulties as "absurd" and "fatuous".[20] He even seems to grudge the time spent on proving it. "It is tiresome to be held up by these details; but there are times for playing the fool."[21] And he develops at great length an argument based on the idea of number.

In *The Art of Persuasion* he shows that there exists a whole order of truths which depend less on demonstration than on an effort of the will. Everything that risks causing us displeasure demands, in order to be believed, the consent of our hearts. The truths which are at once evident and agreeable easily carry conviction. Conversely, "that which bears no relation to our beliefs or our pleasures is importunate, false and completely alien to us".[22] There is "a dubious balance between truth and pleasure."[23]

It appears from this that whatever the subject we wish to discuss

[20] *G.E.*, IX, p. 260.   [21] *Ibid.*, p. 262.
[22] *Ibid.*, p. 275.   [23] *Ibid.*, *loc. cit.*

with someone, we must pay regard to the person whom we are to convince, whose mind and heart must be known to us, what principles he accepts and what things he likes; then, in the matter that concerns us, point out its relation to accepted principles or to the pleasant objects through the charms it brings to it. So that the art of persuasion consists as much in that of making agreeable as in that of convincing, so much more are men governed by whim than by reason.[24]

Where do we find the rules for pleasing? Pascal considers that it is impossible to know them absolutely. Man is too changeable. "No man is more different from another than he is from himself at different times."[25] "Everyone has his fads . . . and it is a peculiarity which strikes the wrong note."[26]

Pascal therefore confines himself once again to drawing up the rules for mathematical demonstration. He takes advantage of it to move away from both Descartes and the Scholastics. He pays tribute to Descartes. In a reference to the *Cogito* he remarks on the admirable consequences that the philosopher deduces from it. He alone, however, has shown himself capable of "perceiving in this word an admirable succession of consequences which prove the distinction between spiritual and material natures and of establishing a firm principle supported by a complete system of physics as Descartes *claimed* to have done. For, without considering whether he has been completely successful in his claim . . ."[27] We observe the reservation. At the close of this short work he attacks the Scholastics and the abuse in philosophy of a barbarous vocabulary. These incomparable paragraphs summarize Pascal's entire intellectual programme and formulate the code that he describes as *honnêteté*:

> Excellence of whatever kind is not to be found in things that are extraordinary or peculiar. We raise ourselves to reach them and move away from them: more often we have to stoop down. The best books are those whose readers feel that they could have written them themselves. Nature, which alone is good, is completely familiar and commonplace. I am therefore in no doubt that these rules, being the true ones, should be simple, unsophisticated, natural, as they are.

[24] *G.E.*, XI, p. 277.   [25] Laf. 962: Br. 106.   [26] *G.E.*, IX, pp. 285–6.
[27] *Ibid.*, pp. 285–6.

It is not *barbara* and *baralipton* which form our reasoning processes. We must not allow our minds to be awkward: tense, clumsy manners fill it with a sort of foolish presumption by an elevation which is foreign to it and by a vain and ridiculous inflation instead of a solid and vigorous nourishment. And one of the main reasons that drive those who embark on this kind of knowledge from the true path they ought to follow is the idea we have that good things are out of reach by calling them great, lofty, elevated, sublime. That ruins everything. I should like to call them low, familiar, common; these names are more fitting; I hate those inflated words. . . .[28]

The text ends with a row of dots.

Now, in the first discourse included in *La Logique ou l'art de penser* ["Logic or the Art of Thought"] Nicole delivers a vigorous attack on Pascal. "There is sometimes a tendency", he said, "to overdo the charge of pedantry and we may fall into it ourselves by attributing it to other people."[29]

It was evidently a subject on which Pascal and Port-Royal did not see eye-to-eye. It seems that he was laughing at Arnauld for writing his *Logique*.[30] He and his friends differed no less on literary questions.

In the *Pensées* Pascal expressed his intense dislike of the pompous style and of pedantry. He attacks false eloquence, antitheses produced "by forcing the meaning of words".[31] He criticizes the "false beauties" of Cicero.[32] He goes for the lack of taste in the poetry of his time. He compares pompous sonnets to peasants tricked out with sham jewelry.[33] In the baroque jargon he sees the effect of lack of taste. He gives precise examples of the style that he considers bad, but he maintains that in art "there is no general rule".[34]

It is known today that most of these observations were aimed at his friends at Port-Royal. We learn from an anonymous manuscript that Pascal laughed at the fact that Antoine Lemaistre had "written well for the dullards at the law courts who did not

---

[28] *G.E.*, IX, p. 289.
[29] *La Logique ou l'art de penser*, 9th ed. Amsterdam, 1718, pp. 14–15.
[30] See *G.E.*, IX, p. 237 note 1.   [31] Laf. 971: Br. 27.
[32] Laf. 966: Br. 31.   [33] Laf. 933: Br. 33.   [34] Laf. 988: Br. 38.

understand a word".[35] And d'Andilly produced grandiloquent sonnets.

He argued about it with Nicole who had been associated with the composition of the *Provincial Letters* and had written a dissertation, *De vera pulchritudine et adumbrata*, together with a collection of epigrams which had been published by Savreux in August 1659. The author conceded much to the aesthetics of Pascal, to his taste for a simple, natural style, but he remained resolutely Cartesian and for him it was reason itself which "will enable us to discover true beauty in the works of the Spirit".[36] The dissertation was preceded by a preface in which Pascal's influence is referred to in the clearest terms, the author admitting that he had "discovered these rules of taste not in his own mind or simply in the works of the Ancients but, what is far preferable, in the talk of men who were remarkable for their general culture and whose wide experience had taught them true politeness."[37]

But in spite of Pascal's influence on Nicole and possibly on Arnauld, the miracle of the *Provincial Letters* was not repeated. The genius of controversy was lacking in the author of the *Imaginary Heresies*. He became bogged down in his straggling sentences, piling up the dimmest of jokes. Once the brilliant parenthesis of the "Little Letters" was closed controversy began again in the theological style, which says everything. The shaft of flame which for a moment had lighted up the whole sky of Port-Royal was extinguished for ever.

[35] Z. Tourneur, *Beauté poétique*, p.128.   [36] *Ibid.*, p. 134.
[37] *Ibid.*, p. 34.

CHAPTER II

Martyrdom

Pascal's health had always been precarious, but from 1659 onwards his illness grew steadily worse. He was thirty-six. He left youth behind him in order to learn how to die.

Some people only achieve their particular form of perfection through excessive suffering. Appalling physical and moral ordeals which plunge the second-rate into a state of terror and rebellion open up new horizons for them. They are revealed to themselves and other people. Pascal was one of those people who become greater through suffering. As he was subjected to his terrible martyrdom, we see him growing still more perceptive, breaking his own pride, becoming more pitiful. He never complained. He only spoke of the pain in passing and to assert that to him it seemed a rich, fine and just thing. Above his work he set his very being which without a murmur climbed the steps of sanctity.

And yet what torture it was!

In August 1660 he was at Bienassis, a small château not far from Clermont, which belonged to the Périers. It was a delightful place standing in the middle of vine-covered slopes. The ancient house had some charming arches dating from the middle ages. Pascal was able to rest. He received a letter from Fermat while he was there inviting him to a meeting and suggesting a place roughly half-way between Clermont and Toulouse, for Fermat, too, was ill.[1]

Pascal's reply is a masterpiece of courtesy. He professes the greatest admiration for Fermat: "Monsieur, you are the most gallant man in the world and I am certainly among those who are best able to recognize your qualities and admire them

[1] *G.E.*, X, p. 3.

infinitely. . . ."[2] Pascal suddenly displays a complete indifference towards geometry. But he was well versed in the graces; his apparent contempt for science can be explained on the grounds that he was completely absorbed by his psychological and religious researches.

I must also tell you that though I regard you as the greatest Mathematician in Europe, that is not the quality which would have attracted me; but I found so much wit and such uprightness in your conversation that it was for this reason that I sought you out. For to speak frankly, I consider Geometry the highest form of intellectual exercise, but at the same time I know that it is so useless that I draw little distinction between a man who is merely a Geometer and a skilled workman. Thus I call it the finest profession in the world, but in the last resort it is no more than a profession, and I have often said that it is excellent for testing one's faculties, but not for the application of one's full strength, so that I would not go a yard for Geometry, and I am sure that you are of the same opinion as myself.[3]

We should be clear about the meaning of these sentences which must have made Fermat shake his head. Pascal is less contemptuous about geometry than he appears, but he has done with training his mind, and if time is granted to him he will be something very different from a scientist: his ambition is to become a connoisseur of the human soul and a saint. Does he sense that even in terms of the fame he despises the *Pensées* will carry more weight in the eyes of posterity than the *Letters from Amos Dettonville to Carcavi*? Surely not, but he has a presentiment that he has other discoveries to make in a realm which is not that of mathematics to which he hastens to bid farewell. It has taken up too much of his time.

The rest of the letter to Fermat contains some moving information about the state of his health: "I am so weak that I cannot walk without a stick or sit on horseback." He has returned to the time when he needed crutches. He adds: "I can only do three or four miles at most even in a carriage, that is why it took me twenty-two days to travel here from Paris."[4] What a long agony. Almost a month to reach Clermont. Sleeping at inns, being worn

---

[2] *G.E.*, X, p. 4.   [3] *Ibid.*, pp. 4–5.   [4] *Ibid.*, p. 5.

out by fatigue and exhausted by the jolts of the carriage. But he hopes to recover. In September he has to go to the waters of Bourbon for a cure, then push on to Saumur, and he has it in mind to stay with the Duc de Roannez until Christmas.

What was the illness which forced him to admit that he had never passed a day without pain and which has made him so weak again by 1660 that he can scarcely walk? The doctors of today diagnose intestinal tuberculosis complicated by chronic and serious rheumatism. Some speak of cerebral cancer which caused spells of paralysis. In this case cancer might have been preceded by another neoplasm in the intestine.

In the nineteenth century Lélut and others spoke of acute neurasthenia. That was the time when all mystics were regarded as neurasthenics and madmen. An absurd hypothesis in the present instance and refuted by all the evidence, particularly by the autograph manuscript of the *Pensées* which proves without possibility of error Blaise Pascal's perfect mental equilibrium at the worst periods of his illness.

Pascal not only overcame his illness heroically, he celebrated it in his writings. For him it was the power which raises up the Christian, detaches him from the world and enables him to penetrate the inner realm of love. He often said to his sister, Gilberte, "that illness is the natural condition of the Christian". People have sometimes protested when reading this sentence that it is Jansenism, forgetting that Péguy, the least Jansenist of men, agreed with Pascal. Replying to Laudet who made out that Joan of Arc was a sick woman, he wrote: "Illness is such an integral part of the mechanism of sanctity that we do not know whether the saints who were ill were not the greatest among the saints. . . . You simply pull Christianity to pieces if you take away from it wretchedness, poverty and sickness. . . ."[5] But we must be clear about what we are saying. "It is not at La Salpêtrière that we should look for saints." In bodies which were often shattered, the great mystics had souls of iron. There was nothing of the neurotic about them. A clear mind, more than the usual ration of good sense, all the characteristics of the most robust mental health.

"Illness is the natural condition of the Christian." When Van

[5] *Un Nouveau théologien: M. Laudet* (Paris, 1936), pp. 71-2.

der Mersch had to describe illness—the same illness as Pascal's—
torturing another great mystic, St Thérèse of the Child Jesus, who
also saw in her appalling sufferings not the natural condition of
the Christian, but the special vocation of certain souls for martyrdom, he several times called his heroine "a little Pascal".

Pascal celebrated his suffering in an extraordinary canticle. The
"canticle to the sun" of suffering is called *Prayer to God for the
Good Use of Sickness*. Five stanzas in prose, but a prose vibrating
with music. Addressing himself to Jesus, to the Lord "whose
spirit is so good and gentle in all things", he praises him in soaring
litanies for destroying the world in his eyes and permitting him to
anticipate the Last Judgment:

O God to whom I must render an exact account of my life, at the
end of my life, and at the end of the world.
O God, who only allows the world to go on and all the things in
the world in order to exercise your elect and punish sinners.
O God, who leaves hardened sinners in the delicious and criminal
use of the world, and the pleasures of the world.
O God, who causes our bodies to die and who at the hour of
death detaches our soul from all that it loved in the world.
O God, who tears me, at this last moment of my life, away from
all the things to which I have become attached and in which I have
placed my heart. . . .
I shall bless you all the days of my life because it has pleased you
to anticipate in my favour that terrible day by destroying for me all
things in the state of weakness to which you have reduced me. . . .[6]

Then comes the canticle exalting the victory of grace in the
same terms in which St Paul celebrated charity:

. . . Illness no more than health,
neither discourses nor books,
neither your Sacred Scriptures, nor your Gospel,
neither your holiest mysteries,
neither alms nor fasts,
neither mortifications nor miracles,
neither the use of the Sacraments nor the sacrifice of your Body,

[6] *G.E.*, IX, pp. 324–5.

can do anything at all to bring about my conversion,
unless you accompany all those things
with the wholly extraordinary help of your grace.[7]

In order to receive grace, the poor invalid cries his distress
aloud to his Saviour, and is suddenly delighted by a vision of the
face of divine love:

O my God, how happy is the heart which can love so delightful
an object that does not dishonour it . . .[8]

His voice trembles with joy. He is on the threshold of a solid
and lasting happiness, but his sins prevent him from entering.
Stanzas VII, VIII and IX are cries of repentance, a long confession.
Pascal, to be sure, admits that his life has been "free from great
crimes", but he knows very well that it is due simply to favourable circumstances. He blames himself bitterly for his carelessness,
his coldness, his false judgments: "I have said: Happy are those
who enjoy a measure of wealth, a great reputation and robust
health."[9] But illness has driven him back into himself. "For,
Lord, your Kingdom is among your faithful, and I shall find it
within myself if I find there your Spirit and your sentiments."[10]
Then like a new Job he seeks to move God to pity:

Consider therefore, O Lord, the ills that I suffer and those which
threaten me.
Look with an eye of mercy upon wounds that your hand has
inflicted on me.
O my Saviour, who have loved your sufferings in death:
O God, who only became man in order to suffer . . .[11]

And the litany starts again. Gasping with pain, Pascal offers
God his bleeding, mutilated body. He begs for a little consolation
to mitigate the atrociousness of his agony. He does not ask for
death or glory, but only for the strength to bear his martyrdom
and never to lose hope. He discovers the means: it is the memory
of the Agony in Gethsemane, and in terms which are identical
with those of the *Mystery of Jesus*, the faithful Christian unites

[7] *G.E.*, IX, p. 327.   [8] *Ibid.*, p. 328.   [9] *Ibid.*, p. 332.
[10] *Ibid.*, p. 333.   [11] *Ibid.*, *loc. cit.*

himself with the blood and sweat of his master: "What is more shameful and at the same time more ordinary in Christians and in myself than that, while you are sweating blood for the expiation of our sins, we live a life of pleasure. . . ."[12] And the end of the prayer is completely in keeping with the Gospel:

> I do not ask for health or sickness or life or death: I ask that you dispose of my health and sickness, my life and death, for your glory, for my salvation, and for the use of the Church and your Saints of which I am a part. You alone know what is expedient for me: you are the sovereign Master: do what you wish. Give to me, take away from me; but make my will conform to yours: that in a humble and perfect state of submission and in holy trust, I may prepare myself to receive the commands of your eternal Providence; and that I adore equally all that comes to me from you.[13]

This is the corrective to his axiom on sickness. In the eyes of the Christian, sickness is not better than health if God wills health for him. He does not ask for sickness; there is no sign of dolorism; he joyfully accepts the ineluctable, seeing in the circumstances the action of a divine and fatherly hand, a true idea of prayer, which some unbelievers imagine on the strength of caricatures to be a perpetual begging for earthly goods, which leads them to write an apology for the serene wisdom of Spinoza as though the joyful acceptance of a Pascal were not at least as pious, as wise and the generator of more light and peace.

Pascal is not alone. He suffers with Jesus Christ, with the saints, with the humblest of Christians. We may think that he was wrong to believe, that is to say, to be Pascal, for his faith was a part of him. He lived it. He may have been guilty of errors of detail in his theology of grace: he was a fallible human being. There was no error in his prayer. It is an insult to him and an admission that his worst enemies were right to cast him from the Body of Christians; it is to forget that, with all his strength, he did not wish to be anything but the suffering and pitiful brother, not of the philosophers and the scholars, at whom he laughed, but of those among the members of Jesus Christ whose sufferings were greatest.

[12] G.E., IX, p. 336.   [13] Ibid., pp. 337–8.

CHAPTER III

The Drama of the Signature

THE years 1659 and 1660 passed with Blaise Pascal doing hardly anything except suffer. The controversy over the *Provincial Letters* was at an end. The persecution of Port-Royal had died down. Two years earlier, under the pseudonym of Wendrock, Nicole had published his Latin translation of the *Provincial Letters* to which he had added notes. Referred by the Council of State to the ecclesiastical authorities, the translation was condemned by an edict of 23rd September 1660. On the strength of a report by the Bishops of Rennes, Rodez, Amiens and Soissons, the book was declared to be heretical.

It is so obvious that if anyone denies it, it can only be because he has not read it or has not understood it; or, what is worse, because he does not believe that something is heretical which has been condemned by the Sovereign Pontiff, by the French Church and by the sacred Faculty of Paris. In addition, we declare that these three Authors [Jansen, Pascal and Nicole] are so insolent and so bold in evil-speaking, that if we except the Jansenists, they spare no one, not even the Sovereign Pontiff, nor the Bishops, not the King nor the principal Ministers of the Kingdom, nor the sacred Faculty of Paris, nor the Religious Orders, and for this reason the said book deserves the penalty ordained by the law against defamatory and heretical Books.[1]

As a result of the decree, the *Provincial Letters* were torn up and burnt by the public executioner in the Carrefour de la Croix-du-Tiroir at noon on 14th October 1660.

On his return to Paris Pascal, who was still living just outside and close to the Porte Saint-Michel, Rue des Francs-Bourgeois-

[1] *G.E.*, X, p. 18.

Saint-Michel, in the parish of Saint-Cosme, took to live with him the eldest of his nephews, Étienne Périer, who was reading philosophy at the Collège d'Harcourt. He was surrounded by a collection of children: his other nephew, Louis Périer, aged nine, whom Gilberte had entrusted to him when he was seven and whom he alone had managed to educate; the little Rs . . . whom he took in, which gave Jacqueline the opportunity of congratulating him on 16th November 1660 on becoming "father of a family in one of the ways in which God is our father".[2]

In agreement with Jacqueline, Pascal had already been encouraging the signs of a religious vocation in his nieces. He opposed plans for the marriage of one of them and continued his correspondence—the correspondence of an unofficial spiritual director —with his eldest sister Gilberte.

He also continued to see old friends. Roannez was still the most intimate of them. He paid numerous visits to the Marquise de Sablé who was very fond of him, admired him and trusted him completely. He thanked her by letter for providing him with an opportunity of making the acquaintance of Dr Manjot, a Calvinist.[3]

But Pascal was soon immersed again in theological controversy. For the past three years the heretical nature of Jansen's teaching had been a dead letter. Alexander VII's bull had been accepted by the Church in France, but the acceptance had remained theoretical. Some coercive measures, to be sure, had been taken against the Jansenists, but the handling of the matter had been distinctly dilatory. Now, at the beginning of the year 1660, the battle flared up again. In September the Assembly of Clergy, under pressure from Mazarin, decided to embark on an energetic policy and wipe out Jansenism.

At that time the theologians of Port-Royal were very divided on the tactical methods they ought to adopt in order to defend what they regarded as Augustinian orthodoxy. Some of them, like Guillebert, parish priest of Rouville, M. de Sacy and M. du Mont, the group which was headed by Barcos, the nephew of the Abbé de Saint-Cyran, considered that Jansen was an *historian* of theology. He had no system of his own. There could be no

[2] *G.E.*, X, p. 18.   [3] *Ibid.*, p. 38.

question of defending the man himself. Discussion should be confined to St Augustine. People should submit to the papal condemnation of Jansen. The problem of the meaning of St Augustine's writings remained intact. It was a remarkably judicious solution.

The first group was opposed by another group led by Arnauld and more still by Nicole who both favoured a fanatical defence of Jansen. They had decided to prove that the teaching of the Bishop of Ypres was substantially the same as that of the great Scholastics, in particular of St Thomas Aquinas. Singlin was divided between the two attitudes with a preference for the first. Pascal, on the other hand, was completely on the side of Arnauld for whom he had acted as advocate in the "Little Letters". He described the paper in which Barcos attempted to defend his position as "ridiculous". "M. Pascal", wrote Racine, "was respected because he spoke out strongly, and M. Singlin gave in as soon as anyone spoke to him with strong conviction."[4]

When the bishops, one after another, insisted in their dioceses on signature of the formula of submission to Alexander VII's bull, the friends of Port-Royal decided to take the initiative and in the absence of Cardinal de Retz to suggest to the vicars-general of the Diocese of Paris a formula which would aim at satisfying everybody and which the Jansenists could sign without raising any objection. The first formula, dated 8th June 1661, was ingenious; if Pascal did not actually draft it, it seems that he approved it. "We order and enjoin [wrote the vicars-general], that with regard to the facts decided by the said Constitutions [the Pope's] and contained in the said Formulary, everyone maintains the sincere and complete respect due to the said Constitutions . . . and that the signature of the said Formulary by everybody will be a testimony . . . that they undertake to accept it as a pronouncement of Faith. . . ."[5]

It amounted to an official sanction of Arnauld's distinction between "law" and "fact".

The authorities proceeded forthwith to obtain the signature of the two convents of Port-Royal. On the advice of Arnauld the

[4] Racine, *Oeuvres*, ed. R. Picard (Bibliothèque de la Pléiade), II, p. 153.
[5] *G.E.*, X, p. 85.

nuns at the Paris house signed. Those at Port-Royal des Champs hesitated. The resistance was led by Jacqueline Pascal. It seemed to her that to sign amounted to a mental reservation, that it smacked of equivocation and was lacking in frankness. In a letter to Mère Angélique de Saint-Jean, she maintained that by signing one condemned Jansen, "a holy bishop", and "that his condemnation definitely involved the condemnation of the grace of Jesus Christ."[6] "What difference do you see", she asked, "between these subterfuges and incensing an idol on the pretext that one has a cross up one's sleeve?"[7] She commented sharply on the bishops: "I know perfectly well that, whatever may be said, it is not for girls to defend the truth by an unhappy wrangle, that since the bishops have the courage of girls, the girls ought to have the courage of bishops; but if it is not our job to defend the truth, it is our job to die for the truth and to suffer everything rather than abandon it."[8] After being advised by Arnauld to submit, the nuns finished by signing.

On 6th August Mère Angélique Arnauld died, to use ecclesiastical language, "in the odour of sanctity" in Paris. At this stage the diocesan authorities appointed a new superior of Port-Royal who embarked on a canonical visitation and an interrogation of the nuns. Soeur Sainte-Euphémie's interrogation took place on 22nd August. M. Le Bail asked her:

"Were you taught as a child that Jesus Christ died for all men?"

"I do not remember this being in my catechism."

"Since you have been here have you not been taught about it?"

"No."

"What is your opinion?"

"I am not in the habit of going into these matters which do not affect the practice of religion. Nevertheless, it seems to me that we must believe that Our Lord died for everybody. For I remember two lines of verse which are in the Book of Hours that I had when I was in the world and have kept all the time I have been here, where it is said in speaking of Our Lord: 'You did not disdain, in order to save the world, To enter into the humble womb of a pregnant Virgin.'"

[6] *G.E.*, X, p. 106.   [7] *Ibid.*, p. 107.   [8] *Ibid.*, p. 108.

"That's right. But how comes it then that there are so many who are eternally lost?"

"I must confess, Monsieur," replied Jacqueline, "that it often causes me pain and that when I am praying in the ordinary way, particularly when I am in front of a Crucifix, it comes into my mind and I say to Our Lord in my heart: 'O God, how can it be after you have done so much for us that so many should perish wretchedly?' But when these thoughts come to me, I put them out of my mind because I do not think that I ought to probe the secrets of God. That is why I confine myself to praying for sinners."

"That is very well said, my daughter."[9]

A few weeks later the state of Jacqueline Pascal, who had probably suffered for a long time from tuberculosis, was desperate. She died suddenly at Port-Royal des Champs on 4th October 1661.

Gilberte Périer had come to Paris. It seems that Blaise was prevented from going to the Abbey of Port-Royal des Champs to see his younger sister: "When he heard the news of her death, he said nothing except: May God grant us the grace to die as Christian a death as hers! And later on, he only spoke to us of the graces God had bestowed on my sister during her life and of the circumstances and time of her death; then, raising his heart to heaven, where he believed her to be among the blessed, he said to us with a touch of ecstasy: Blessed are they who die like that in the Lord."[10]

In fact, Pascal was deeply affected by his sister's death. He knew how profoundly upset she had been by putting her signature to the formula and decided to defend passionately what he believed to be the truth.

Even before the death of Soeur Sainte-Euphémie matters had become complicated. On 1st August a brief from Rome had condemned the conciliatory formula of the vicars-general of Paris. In October they prepared a second formula ordering the condemnation of the five propositions "as heretical in the sense in which they were understood by Jansen".[11] This removed anything

[9] G.E., X, pp. 129–30.   [10] Lafuma, pp. 57–8, Eng. tr., p. 61.
[11] G.E., X, p. 163.

which could be interpreted equivocally. The new formula was published on 20th November and all ecclesiastics were required to sign it within a fortnight.

A week later the nuns put their signatures to it preceded by a statement to the effect that "in our ignorance of everything that is outside our vocation and our sex, all that we can do is to bear witness to the purity of our faith".[12] It was a very guarded way of preserving the distinction between "law" and "fact".

It was at this point that Pascal intervened. Three parties had been formed at Port-Royal at the time of the publication of the second formula. Du Barcos continued to favour a simple signature. Arnauld and Nicole accepted the signature accompanied by the reservation: "I only subscribe to these constitutions in so far as they relate to faith." Pascal maintained very energetically that law and fact were linked in the minds of the Pope and the bishops. What the bishops wanted to reach by the condemnation, he said, was not the Calvinist interpretation of the propositions, but the actual meaning given to them by Jansen. To submit in so far as it affected faith was therefore to accept the condemnation of "efficacious grace, St Augustine and St Paul".[13] Pascal denied that there was any validity in Arnauld's arguments which he himself had recently adopted in the *Provincial Letters*.

A sharp and bitter controversy followed. With the support of Domat, Pascal composed his very brief *Écrit sur la signature* which has been preserved. Nicole and Arnauld replied. They treated the arguments of Pascal and Domat as "sophistries". Pascal retorted very harshly with a *Grand écrit sur la signature*. He accused the logicians of Port-Royal of changing their views for political reasons, of concealing the truth from themselves by hair-splitting, and of using abominable forms of "equivocation". It was a new *Provincial Letter*, written this time against Arnauld and Nicole.

There was a meeting at Pascal's house. Arnauld, Nicole, the Duc de Roannez, Domat, Mme Périer, Étienne Périer her son, and other theologians debated the problem. Pascal defended his view in violent terms. He was clear about Rome's intentions. In his opinion it was indeed Jansen who was condemned. No

[12] G.E., X, p. 165.   [13] *Écrit sur la signature*, G.E., X, p. 171.

further subterfuges were possible. Nicole and Arnauld retorted
that to follow Pascal was tantamount to accusing the Pope and
the bishops of condemning efficacious grace and of creating a
schism. Pascal agreed. The Pope, the bishops, everybody who had
signed—Carmelites, Dominicans, Oratorians, the secular clergy—
had condemned grace and sunk into semi-Pelagianism. The whole
of the Church had fallen into error. Pascal hesitated no longer
over the prospect of open rebellion against Rome.

Naturally, the majority of those present went over to Arnauld's
side and strongly condemned Pascal. He was "so deeply pained
that he was taken ill, was unable to speak and fainted".

The theologians left and members of his family gave Pascal
first aid. When he regained consciousness, "Mme Périer asked
him what had caused the incident. He answered: 'When I saw
all those people, whom I regarded as those to whom God had
made known the truth and who should have defended it, crack
and give in, I confess that I felt a pain which was past bearing and
to which I succumbed'."[14]

Later Port-Royal went to great trouble to remove all evidence
of the quarrel in which Pascal had exposed the fundamental
ambiguity of Arnauld's theology. By putting pressure on Domat,
they obtained an undertaking that he would burn the *Grand
écrit sur la signature* and ensure that every trace of it disappeared.[15]

It so happens that there are two pieces of evidence of Pascal's
anger. In the first place, extracts from a letter written to an
unknown correspondent in which he said:

> What! Behave as though their mission were to ensure the triumph
> of truth whereas our mission is only to fight for it. The desire to
> conquer is so natural that, when it is hidden under the desire to
> secure the triumph of truth, we sometimes mistake one for the other
> and imagine that we are working for the glory of God when we
> are really working for our own. . . . I am furious with those who are
> determined that people shall believe the truth when they demonstrate
> it, a thing that Jesus Christ did not do in his created humanity
> . . . .[16]

[14] Lafuma, III, p. 65.   [15] *G.E.*, X, pp. 193–4.   [16] *Ibid.*, pp. 156–7.

And a sentence from the draft of the nineteenth *Provincial Letter* dryly sums up the position of Arnauld and his friends: "They are witnesses to the unpleasantness of finding themselves between God and pope."[17]

It is a fact that Pascal alone had grasped the implications of the decisions taken by Rome. He refused any sort of equivocation or compromise. He maintained that if Jansen were right, the Pope and the whole of the Church were wrong. He alone perceived that logically the position of Arnauld would drive the partisans of Père Quesnel, fifty years later, to appeal to the council against the decision of Rome and would lead finally to the schism of the Jansenists in Holland. We must not minimize the extent of his aberration. He found wide open in front of him the way of all heretics. In his rage he contemplated breaking with the Church.[18] Arnauld told him so. Since the bishops agreed with the Pope, he explained to Pascal that nothing less than the infallibility of the Church in matters of faith was at stake: an infallibility which up to that point no one at Port-Royal had for a moment dreamed of doubting.

Such was the drama of conscience with which Pascal grappled from the end of the year 1661 to the beginning of 1662. It was true spiritual anguish. Pascal found himself torn until death between his attachment to the Church and what he regarded as divine truth. At one moment he believed himself to be the solitary witness of God against the Pope, the bishops and the King; against all other Christians and even his dearest friends. The apparently technical nature of the argument should not be allowed to hide its tragic grandeur. Pascal would never have

[17] Lafuma, I, p. 543; *G.E.*, VII, p. 174, give as the presumed date April–May 1657. But Lafuma, II, p. 202, observed that the third sentence is similar to the *Écrit des curés de Paris* of 1st April 1658. It seems that the final sentence is aimed at Arnauld and Nicole.

[18] Sainte-Beuve was perfectly clear on the point: "Arnauld", he wrote, "pleaded the orthodoxy of the Pope which Pascal *denied*. That is what all the Jansenist explanations have sought to obscure. . . . This obstinate determination to know better than the popes what the popes thought and defined is the favourite theme of the Jansenists from Arnauld onwards . . . " (*Port-Royal*, III, ch. XIII, pp. 185–7). On the view of Du Barcos, see Besoigne, *Histoire de l'abbaye de Port-Royal*, IV, pp. 238ff., and the *Correspondance* quoted above. And on Pascal's opposition, Racine's notes, *Oeuvres*, Pléiade, II, p. 153.

imagined that such suffering could be in store for him: to find himself caught like the young Antigone and Joan of Arc between his humble submission to the laws of the terrestrial City of God and his highest duty. But in the end his humility carried the day.

In fact, after the meeting with his friends, Pascal retreated into silence. He had only a few more months to live. It was then that he decided to give up theological controversy and put his trust in the Church. A *volte-face*? Not at all: a confession of ignorance and weariness. He may have come to the conclusion that he was mistaken in attaching so much importance to the disputes. If, as Arnauld and Nicole claimed, neither the Pope, the bishops nor any of the signatories of the formula intended to condemn St Paul, St Augustine and efficacious grace (a dogma that the Catholic Church still teaches today), it might have been that Jansen himself was in error when he contended that his work was an accurate résumé of St Augustine's teaching. Pascal no longer felt that he had the strength or the time to undertake the necessary research. He wanted to prepare himself to die in peace.

CHAPTER IV

A Saint Like Another

As he waited for death, Pascal lived his last months like a saint: not as a canonized or, indeed, a canonizable saint, but an anonymous one lost in the crowds which swarm into the churches on feast days. A saint like millions of other saints.

Compelled by his illness to seek distraction, to go for walks, he used a cruel method of bringing himself continually back to meditation: a spiked belt worn next to his naked flesh. Sometimes he gave himself a jab with his elbow. He would return home after visiting several churches where he had spent hours on his knees. He ate absentmindedly and without appetite. His ration of vegetables cooked in water was fixed in advance. He would not allow his household to make sauces for him or give him orange juice to which he was very partial. He swallowed the most horrible medicines without betraying any signs of disgust. He recited the breviary and re-read his Bible. In the morning he made his own bed. His room was stripped of everything: no carpets or ornaments and practically no books. He had sold his books. He swept his room, took his plates to the kitchen, lived like a pauper. He provided lodging at his home for a family named Bardout. They had fallen on hard times. He was the godfather of one of the children, the Little Blaise. He fed them and gave them firewood in winter.

He had visitors. There were long conversations about religion. In the main it was the unbelievers who came to see him most frequently. He was very gentle with them, but as soon as he began to speak he was so brilliant that he distrusted himself and set out to punish himself for his own eloquence. He visited the poor and comforted them. One day he saw a pretty girl begging outside

Saint-Sulpice where he had gone for his devotions. He questioned her about her position and sensed the dangers to which she was exposed. He took her round to the seminary, placed her in charge of one of the priests, then sent a woman to look after her. He did not mind whether the priest whom he had seen was an enemy of the theology of Port-Royal. His only concern was charity and poverty.

He still enjoyed a laugh and a joke, but detested bawdiness and had begun to distrust irony. He was very strict in the matter of behaviour and was offended at hearing people talk about pretty women, good cooking, wealth and money. His sister noticed in him a rather over-sensitive modesty, and an extreme delicacy. He had an acute sense of truth, of the true value of life, of the distinction of manners in the Christian so that when he was on his knees in church wearing shabby clothes he still preserved the grand manner of an aristocrat of the spirit who would take umbrage at the mere suggestion of a mean action or coarse language.

The source of his sanctity lay in a merciless knowledge of himself and other people. By nature he liked luxury, beautiful things, wealth, intellectual success, faultless language. He was affectionate and exceptionally sensitive. He knew that he was terribly proud and impatient; he spoke in a harsh tone; irony came too easily to him and was cruel. He was liable to fall into sudden violent rages, but he made up his mind to control himself.

He did not share the naïve errors about mankind which were to fill the *sottisier* of the following centuries. He knew—it has recently been discovered afresh—that man is naturally a beast of prey, that if he follows his instincts he can easily degenerate into a cruel and lubricious animal. Pascal put his ferocity down to original sin. He knew that the most brilliant civilization was simply the art of concealing, in an agreeable way beneath delicate and deceitful appearances, man's basic animality. But he was determined to root out his own pride, his love of money, his hardness, his sensuality. He was very conscious of his genius: he knew what immense successes this genius had achieved. He could excel at anything, but he wanted to master himself. It was a hard thing. He had to battle with himself and give up illusions.

Anyone who harboured illusions was playing at being an angel: a thing that Pascal detested. The spiritual battle left him with a little of his own blood on his hands. Voltaire and Sainte-Beuve speak with disgust of the Pascal who swept his own room, did the washing up, cared for a child suffering from smallpox and wore a spiked belt, but it is they who were the hypocrites, who pretended to forget the beast inside them, who appeared to think that it did not exist and secretly let it have its way. That Pascal was right to use extreme methods in order to master himself was the view proclaimed by all the saints of the Church and all the mystics of all ages and all the different religious observances.

There is no trace of Jansenism in this austere life. The same or even more drastic mortifications give beauty to the lives of the Desert Fathers, the great monks and in our own time of St Thérèse of the Child Jesus, the Curé d'Ars, or Père de Foucauld. Nor did Pascal overdo these harsh practices. His asceticism remained human and balanced. He avoided excesses and remained mentally relaxed. He was well informed about the ways of genuine sanctity and used penance as a means of attaining those two essential virtues: poverty and charity.

In following the path of poverty he imitated St Francis of Assisi. He loved the poor, wished to live with them and "help the poor poorly".[1] It was an admirable axiom which led him straight to the heart of Christianity. Not a noisy, but a hidden charity. For Pascal the poor man was man in the nakedness of his condition, the true man deprived of the amusements which are so effective in hiding the face of suffering and death. By deliberately reducing himself to poverty in the midst of a humanity in love with wealth and comfort, he asserted the truth of the God of Jesus Christ and translated the *Pensées* into practice. The sight of Pascal smiling at a sick child, visiting a garret, repairing the straw mattress himself on which in the evening he stretched out a body broken by suffering, is a living commentary on the pages on the two infinites, on distraction and on the sovereignty of the order of love. His charity revealed itself by preference in dealing with the poor in spirit who are the unbelievers. He spoke to them with gentleness. He did his utmost to help them, to understand

[1] Lafuma, p. 55. Eng. tr., p. 58.

their doubts, to sympathize with their anxieties, to suffer with them. His sister emphasizes his affection, his goodness and gracious-ness, his courtesy, his smile; the repeated victories over himself by a person who was by nature stiff and provocative. His humanity warmed people's hearts. They felt that he was accessible to pity, fragile, easily broken. "He did not see any great difference between affection and charity any more than between charity and friend-ship."[2] Marvellous words which show what a Christian humanism can be when it is founded on an heroic and ascetic battle against oneself.

Like all saints he prayed without ceasing. For that purpose he nourished himself on the Bible to the point of knowing it literally by heart. He continually turned it over in his mind, made an inventory of its treasures. He acquired a sensibility for the Bible, found in the Psalms, in the prophets and above all in the Gospels and St Paul the living source of all Christianity. He said his breviary composed entirely of biblical texts. He never wearied of praising Psalm 118. This long and fastidious eulogy of the law written by a scholarly Jew in an early period is not, to be sure, a masterpiece of literature. But Pascal found in it the whole of his theology of grace. He was carried away by it in the same way as M. Hamon, the doctor of Port-Royal, who was later to write a whole book of effusions about the psalm-poem whose author seeks God and sings of the delightful favours of the Almighty.

With Pascal a love of the Bible was inseparable from Catholic devotion to the offices of the liturgy, relics and the memory of the saints. His sister gives a picturesque example: "His chief amuse-ment, particularly in the last years of his life when he was no longer able to go on working, was to visit churches where relics or other pious objects were displayed, and he had provided him-self for the purpose with a *Spiritual Almanac* from which he found out the places where all these devotions were practised."[3]

Ernest Jovy, the great Pascal scholar, has found the *Spiritual Almanac* which was written by Père Martial du Mans, a penitent religious. It was published every year. Copies for the years 1651, 1652, 1654, 1667 and 1670, etc., are extant. Each day of the year lists the Paris ceremonies: processions, vespers, exhibition of

[2] Lafuma, p. 59. Eng. tr., p. 62.   [3] *Ibid.*, p. 64. Eng. tr., p. 68.

relics, sermons.[4] There was hardly a day without a procession going through Paris. Pascal followed it.

At the end of a few months he must have known all the churches in the capital. He followed the prayers in his missal, gave alms to innumerable beggars, visited the poor at the Hôtel-Dieu, a practice which was highly recommended by the author of the *Spiritual Almanac.*

The anonymous pilgrim of the streets of Paris and old churches, the passer-by who revered the innumerable statues of Our Lady and the saints in the back streets of the great city, reminds us of Péguy saying his rosary in the streets, praying to the saints who have given their names to the boulevards, streets and underground stations. Both of them, Pascal and Péguy, have become inseparable from old Paris. They were both laymen a little off the beaten track of official canonizations, both poor, both affectionate towards their friends, and in possession of a faith which was so total that it resembled the faith of little children: a simple faith which enjoys pilgrimages. It is in this respect that Pascal, who belongs to modern times, is close to the middle ages. He had a feeling for external devotions; he liked the traditional gestures, holy water, burning candles, litanies taken up by the crowd. He wanted to unbend, to humble himself among little people, mix happily with the poor and the lowly. The exceptional man, the prince of intellect, brought off the paradox of submerging himself completely in the crowd of his brothers and sisters in Christ.

At the end of his life the engineer reappeared in Pascal. At the sight of the diligences which linked the different towns with one another, he had the idea of introducing in the interior of Paris carriage-omnibuses which would follow a fixed itinerary at regular intervals. The fare was to be five *sols.*

On 6th November a veritable joint-stock company of shareholders was formed consisting of Pascal, the Duc de Roannez, the Marquis de Crénan, the Marquis de Sources and Arnauld de Pomponne. The shareholders obtained the King's licence on

[4] *Études pascaliennes*, VII, pp. 59-70: "*L'Almanach spirituel* de M. Pascal".

7th February 1662. On 26th February a note, which was probably signed by Pascal, reports the first attempts with horses and a hired carriage. After an initial *succès de ridicule*, Parisians began to take a lively interest in the venture. Everybody began to hope that the carriages would pass through his district. On 18th March the first line of seven carriages was inaugurated under police protection, its itinerary running from the Porte Saint-Antoine to the Luxembourg. The coachmen wore blue cloaks "with the arms of the King and the city embroidered on the stomach". By midday on the first day there were queues at the stopping-places of the carriage-omnibuses. Gilberte wrote: "You see people in the streets waiting to get into a carriage, but when it arrives it is full. It is annoying, but we can take comfort because we know that there will be another in seven or eight minutes. Nevertheless, when the next one arrives it is full, too, and when that happens several times running you have to walk."[5] Poor Gilberte missing the bus like a Parisian in 1900! For she adds: "Don't think that I'm exaggerating. It has happened to me. I was waiting at the Porte de Saint-Merry in the Rue de la Verrerie, very much hoping that I should be able to go home by carriage because it is rather a long way from there to my brother's, but I had the annoying experience of seeing five go by without being able to get a seat because they were all full."

The King took an interest in the venture and encouraged it. "On 11th April a second line was started from the Rue Saint-Antoine to the Rue Saint-Honoré", and a month later a third from the Rue Montmartre to the Luxembourg.[6]

Pascal, who was very much of a realist, regarded his venture as a surer means of making money than the calculating machine, but this time it was less on his own account than to help the poor. He wanted to borrow against future profits in order to assist the poor of Blois and by his will left a part of his rights to the hospitals of Paris and Clermont.

But the authorization had been granted with the proviso that "soldiers, pages, lackeys and other people wearing livery, as well as manual labourers could not use the said carriages". "The exclusion of part of the population gradually made the carriages

[5] *G.E.*, X, p. 277.   [6] *Ibid.*, p. 279.

unpopular and they disappeared about 1679 after an existence of seventeen years."[7]

As evidence of the part played by Pascal in the introduction of public transport in Paris, it was the practice of Paris omnibuses about 1930 to sell books of tickets with a minute portrait of Pascal on the outside.

[7] *Palais de la Découverte, l'oeuvre scientifique de B. Pascal*, Paris, 1950, p. 34.

CHAPTER V

Death

AT THE beginning of July 1662, Pascal suddenly began to suffer from terrible bouts of colic. He had no temperature, but was unable to sleep and lost weight in an alarming fashion. He had to leave his house which stood "just outside the Porte Saint-Michel". Gilberte nursed him and the child of the poverty-stricken family living with him who had smallpox. He had himself taken to a little house belonging to the Périers "on the bank [of the river] between the Portes Saint-Marcel and Saint-Victor, in the parish of Saint-Étienne-du-Mont" on the site of what is now 77, Rue du Cardinal-Lemoine where Gilberte lived.

On 3rd July, Guénaut, the Queen's physician, the man whom Molière was to put into *L'Amour médecin* under the name of Macroton, was called into consultation. He wrote out the following prescription: "*M. Pascal laborat infarctu viscerum ab humore melancolico; qui humor, dum fermentatur, vapores emittit, symptomata producentes varia, prout partes quas attingunt, diversae sunt; ideo fermentatur quia ebulliunt et a calore fit haec ebullitio; ideo mittendus sanguis ex utroque brachio, postea purgandus. . . .*"[1] The language recalls that of Père Noël and the titbits of Bachelierus:

> *Clysterium donare*
> *Postea saignare*
> *Ensuitta purgare.*

Guénaut, indeed, goes on: "*Mittatur sanguis ex pede; deinde purgetur ut supra, ter aut quater. . . .*" The dying Pascal was to be douched, purged and bled until death supervened. If the diagnosis

[1] G.E., X, p. 306.

208

of the doctors of our own time is to be trusted, it made no difference whether Pascal was suffering from intestinal tuberculosis or generalized cancer: the tortures that his doctors inflicted on him did nothing but hasten the final stages of his illness. He might have recalled the words that Jesus spoke to him shortly after his conversion: "The physicians will not cure you." He was to battle for two months, delivered into the hands of the imbeciles of the Medical Faculty.

At the beginning of this bout, his sister tells us, "being a very courageous man, he did not fail to get up every morning and took all the remedies himself as he did not wish anybody to perform the least service for him."[2] The doctors said "that there was not the slightest danger". In spite of this reassuring opinion, Pascal felt that his condition was very grave. On the fourth day of his illness he sent for Père Beurrier, a religious of the Order of St Geneviève and parish priest of Saint-Étienne-du-Mont, Gilberte Périer's parish.

Beurrier has described his talks with Pascal. "After exchanging greetings, he told me that as he had always loved the order God had established in his Church and as I was his pastor, he had asked me to come and see him so that he could put his soul and conscience in my hands. After some further talk about his illness which was a bilious colic . . . he asked me whether he should make a general confession or an ordinary one."[3]

Père Beurrier advised him to make a simple confession. Pascal replied that "two years previously he had made a spiritual retreat", which probably meant the end of 1660. The retreat was followed by the decision to "sell his carriage, his horses, his carpets, his fine furniture, his silver and even his library, with the exception of his Bible, St Augustine and a very few other books. . . ."[4]

The conversation continued. Pascal spoke at length about atheists and the methods of convincing them. He reiterated energetically his condemnation of the moral theology of the casuists. Beurrier did not know that the man in front of him was the author of the *Provincial Letters*, but he agreed with Pascal in condemning the casuists. As for dogma:

[2] Lafuma, p. 66. Eng. tr., p. 70.   [3] Lafuma, III, p. 52.
[4] *Ibid.*, p. 54.

He told me [said Beurrier] that he groaned with anguish at the sight of the divisions between the faithful who, whether they were speaking or writing, grew so heated and decried one another with such vehemence that it was prejudicial to unity and charity . . . adding that people had tried to involve him in these controversies, but that two years ago he had prudently withdrawn from them, considering the great difficulty of the complicated questions of grace and predestination which even St Paul himself admitted when he cried: O *altitudo* . . . .[5]

And when it came to the question of the authority of the Pope, he thought it was important and very difficult to get to know its limits; that not having studied Scholasticism . . . he had come to the conclusion that he ought to withdraw from controversies and disputes which he regarded as prejudicial and dangerous, because he might have erred by saying too much or too little, and so he held to the views of the Church on these great matters and wished to make a complete submission to the Vicar of Jesus Christ who was the Sovereign Pontiff. I replied that he had acted very wisely. . . .

He added that so far as the new relaxed moral code was concerned, it was not in conformity with the Gospel, the canons of the Councils or the views of the Fathers of the Church, and that it should certainly be condemned; that it was very dangerous because it encouraged cowardice, vice, debauchery and the corruption of morals, that it was very prejudicial to the Church and that he had a great horror of it. . . .

Then he asked my advice on several matters which I gave him so that he would be in a state to receive devoutly the sacraments of penance and the Holy Eucharist which he ardently desired, and the talk ended with the request that he made to me to offer him to God and to ask his divine Majesty to give him the grace to live and die a good Christian and in all things to accomplish his divine will, which was the one thing he desired. . . .[6]

Three years after the death of Pascal, the parish priest of Saint-Étienne-du-Mont was summoned by the Archbishop of Paris to give an account of Pascal's opinions at the end of his life. He told the Archbishop that "during an informal talk [he had admitted] that in earlier days he had become involved with the party of the Gentlemen [of Port-Royal], but that two years previously he had

[5] Lafuma, III, pp. 52–3.   [6] *Ibid.*, pp. 53–4.

withdrawn from it because he had observed that they went too far into the question of grace and appeared to be less submissive than they should be to Our Holy Father the Pope".[7]

In spite of a promise not to do so, the Archbishop disclosed this information. It produced a vigorous protest from Pascal's friends who sought evidence to refute it. Nicole, Arnauld, Sainte-Marthe, the Duc de Roannez and Domat declared that, on the contrary, Pascal had only detached himself from Port-Royal because the Gentlemen were too conciliatory. Beurrier himself wrote to Gilberte Périer telling her that he had misunderstood some of the things his penitent had said to him.[8] But twenty years later, in his memoirs, he went much more deeply into the question and gave an account of his talks with the dying Pascal. He maintained that Pascal had withdrawn from the controversies on grace and, *without speaking of a break with Port-Royal*, had declared his complete trust in the Church and his submission to the Pope.

For the past forty years there have been lively discussions about the value of his testimony. The supporters of Beurrier have sometimes accused Port-Royal of duplicity, which is false and unjust. Scholars have replied by trying to prove that Beurrier had completely failed to understand the subject of the quarrels between the theologians of Port-Royal and that his *Memoirs* are riddled with inaccuracies. These inaccuracies in no way invalidate the repeated testimony of an upright and loyal person. Beurrier wrote badly and put his material together without any sort of order. He misunderstood—it was easy enough to do—certain of Pascal's references to differences which were unknown to the general public, and he freely admitted his mistake in a letter to Mme Périer of 12th June 1671. But since he had no feeling against Port-Royal, he certainly did not invent Pascal's statements on the authority of the Pope, on his withdrawal from controversy, which did in fact date from 1660, and on his determination to remain silent in the dispute about grace.

The protests of Arnauld and Nicole are valid in so far as they relate to Pascal's views at the end of 1661. But it is precisely because at the moment Pascal was prepared to go much further

[7] G.E., X, p. 338.
[8] *Lettre du Père Beurrier à Mme Périer*, G.E., X, p. 360.

than Arnauld and Nicole in organizing open opposition to Rome that, realizing the ultimate consequences of the position he had adopted, he had to choose between schism and complete submission to Rome. In his eyes there was no longer room for half-measures. The distinction between "law" and "fact" seemed to him to be valueless. He simply decided to give up trying to solve an insoluble problem.

He had in no sense quarrelled with Port-Royal. He did not cease seeing Arnauld, Nicole and Sainte-Marthe or treating them as friends. But he realized that submission to the Church must be in the sense understood by Beurrier, his confessor, who had signed both the formulas, and for this reason would have appeared to the Pascal of 1661 to be guilty of semi-Pelagianism. They both spoke of grace. Pascal declared his submission to the Pope without any ambiguity or reservation. His loyalty as a dying man prevented him from adopting any subterfuge to receive the last sacraments which would have seemed shocking to him and which is contradicted by every detail of the accounts of his death. At the time of Beurrier's first visit his mind was clear and he was in full possession of his faculties.

A statement by the parish priest of Saint-Étienne, which is not suspect because it comes to us from Gilberte Périer, confirms the impression of authenticity that we get from his final talks with Pascal: "He's like a child; he's as humble and *submissive* as a child."[9]

All through the month of July the sick man continued to grow worse and became steadily weaker. On the morning of 3rd

[9] I have given what I believe to be the only solution that takes into account *all* the evidence about Pascal's attitude which has given rise to so much controversy. Insufficient attention has been paid to the extent to which the evidence of the two chief witnesses, Gilberte Périer and Beurrier, coincides. Everything that Gilberte Périer says about her brother's poverty and his devotions must relate to the last six months of his life. It is she herself who reports Beurrier's statement: "He's as submissive as a child."

There was no retraction by Pascal, but a *withdrawal*. Pascal did not become an exponent of infallibility. There was no question of that and it would never have occurred to Beurrier to ask him to do so. But Pascal confessed of his own free will to a priest who was known to have signed the formula and in whom six months earlier he would have seen as an unfortunate man who had consented to the condemnation of efficacious grace, of St Paul and St Augustine.

Those interested in the reliability of Beurrier's evidence should read E. Jovy, *Pascal inédit*, II, and the same author's *Études pascaliennes*, V, which contains (pp. 1-78) P. J. Monbrun's "La Fin non janséniste de Pascal".

LETTRE
ESCRITE A VN PROVINCIAL
PAR VN DE SES AMIS.
SVR LE SVIET DES DISPVTES
présentes de la Sorbonne.

De Paris ce 23. Ianuier 1656.

MONSIEVR,

Nous eſtions bien abuſez. Ie ne ſuis détrompé que d'hier, juſque-là j'ay penſé que le ſuiet des diſputes de Sorbonne eſtoit bien important, & d'vne extrême conſequence pour la Religion. Tant d'aſſemblées d'vne Compagnie auſſi celebre qu'eſt la Faculté de Paris, & où il s'eſt paſſé tant de choſes ſi extraordinaires, & ſi hors d'exemple, en font conceuoir vne ſi haute idée, qu'on ne peut croire qu'il n'y en ait vn ſuiet bien extraordinaire.

Cependant vous ſerez bien ſurpris quand vous apprendrez par ce recit, à quoy ſe termine vn ſi grand éclat; & c'eſt ce que ie vous diray en peu de mots aprés m'en eſtre parfaitement inſtruit.

On examine deux Queſtions; l'vne de Fait, l'autre de Droit.

Celle de Fait conſiſte à ſçauoir ſi Mr Arnauld eſt temeraire, pour auoir dit dans ſa ſeconde Lettre; *Qu'il a leu exactement le Liure de Ianſenius, & qu'il n'y a point trouué les Propoſitions condamnées par le feu Pape; & neanmoins que côme il côdamne ces Propoſitiôs en quelque lieu qu'elles ſe rencontrent, il les condamne dâs Ianſenius, ſi elles y ſont.*

La queſtion eſt de ſçauoir, s'il a pû ſans temerité témoigner par là qu'il doute que ces Propoſitions ſoient de Ianſenius, apres que Meſſieurs les Eueſques ont declaré qu'elles y ſont.

On propoſe l'affaire en Sorbonne. Soixante & onze Docteurs entreprennent ſa defenſe, & ſoûtiennent qu'il n'a pû reſpondre autre choſe à ceux qui par tant d'écrits luy demandoiét s'il tenoit que ces Propoſitions fuſſent dans ce liure, ſinon qu'il ne les y a pas veuës, & que neantmoins il les y condamne ſi elles y ſont.

Quelques-vns meſme paſſant plus auant, ont declaré que quel-que recherche qu'ils en ayent faite, ils ne les y ont iamais trou-

11. ANTOINE LEMAÎTRE.
Portrait by Philippe de Champaigne.

12. ISAAC-LOUIS LEMAÎTRE DE SACY.
School of Philippe de Champaigne, wrongly supposed
to be a portrait of Pascal.

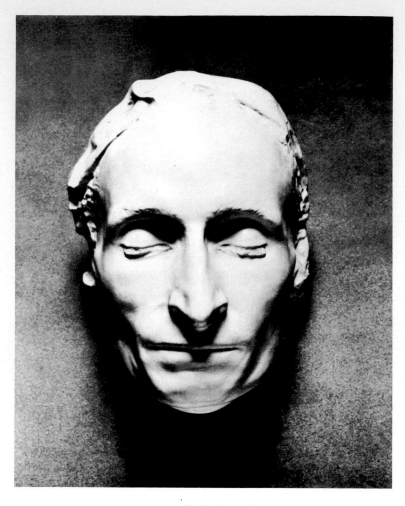

13. Pascal's death mask.

August he took advantage of a short respite to send for the lawyers
Guéneau and Quarré, so that he could dictate his will to them.
He began with a profession of faith: The testator, "as a good
Catholic, Apostolic and Roman Christian in the first place has
recommended and recommends his soul to God, begging that by
the merits of the precious blood of our Saviour and Redeemer
Jesus Christ, it will please him to forgive him his faults and
receive his soul when it departs this world, imploring to this end
the intercession of the glorious Virgin Mary and of all the
Saints in Paradise. . . ."[10] He desires that his body shall be buried
at Saint-Étienne-du-Mont and entrusts himself to his brother-in-
law, Florin Périer, for the funeral ceremonies.

He leaves twelve hundred *livres* to Françoise Delfault, sister of
his father's housekeeper who had brought him up; one thousand
livres to Anne Polycarpe, the servant "of the said lady"; an income
of one hundred *livres* to his cook Esdune. He gives legacies to his
nephew Étienne Périer and to his nephew's nurse, to the hospitals
of Paris and Clermont, to his friend Domat, and appoints Florin
Périer, his brother-in-law, to be his executor.

He felt that death was imminent and desired ardently to receive
Holy Communion. About 8th August an important medical
consultation brought the big guns of the day to his bedside:
Brayer, Renodot, Valot and Homes. The first three were Mazarin's
physicians. The consultation took place at Pascal's bedside in the
farcical style which Molière borrowed from them word for
word:

M. Homes strongly advised M. Pascal to take ten to twelve
grains with half-an-ounce of diaphrenic . . .
M. Pascal was bled five times in the arms for his colic . . .
M. Brayer suggested that he should have a purgative . . .
M. Renodot was of the opinion that he should be purged with two
or three drams of senna in a decoction of tamarind and chicory . . .
. M. Homes, to purge him with an infusion of two drams of senna
dissolved in six drams of catholicon. . . .[11]

Valot and Renodot prescribed emetic wine in a douche.

[10] *G.E.*, X, pp. 295–6.   [11] *Ibid.*, p. 307.

Homes was against it. They all agreed that his condition was not serious. The sick man, on the contrary, was very conscious that his strength was ebbing and his life slipping away. He protested in vain against the doctors' diagnosis. He wanted the Last Sacraments but his family, putting their trust in the doctors, considered that it was inopportune to disturb the parish priest of Saint-Étienne so that he would have to bring the Blessed Sacrament with the solemn ceremonial which was customary under the Ancien Régime.

He felt an ardent desire to receive Communion, but the doctors were against it because they did not consider that he was sufficiently ill to receive the viaticum, and they did not think that it was fitting that it should be brought to him at night, when he had to be fasting, unless his condition took a turn for the worse. Since the colic persisted, however, they prescribed waters which brought him a few days' relief, but on the sixth day of the waters he suffered from severe giddiness accompanied by a violent headache. Although the doctors were in no way surprised by the incident and said that it was only the vapour from the waters, he lost no time in making his confession and demanded, with the greatest urgency, that he should be given Communion and that in the name of God they should find some way of removing all the obstacles that they had put in the way of it; he was so pressing that someone who was there said it was not a good thing and that he should abide by the views of his friends, that he had scarcely any temperature, and that he should judge for himself whether it was right to have the Blessed Sacrament brought to the house because he was better, and whether it was not more suitable to wait and receive Communion in church where he would soon be well enough to go. He replied: "They do not feel my illness; they are mistaken; there is something extraordinary about my headache." Nevertheless, seeing that his wish was meeting with such opposition, he dared not say any more about it. But he said to me: "As this grace has been refused me, I should like to make up for it by some good action, and since I cannot have Communion in the Head I should like to do so in the members, and for that I thought that I might have here some poor sick person to whom the same services can be rendered as to me. For I am distressed and confused at finding myself with such assistance while a vast number of poor people, who are sicker than I, are deprived of the barest necessities. Let a nurse be engaged for the purpose and let there be no difference between him and me. It will lessen the pain which I feel at finding that I lack nothing, and which I can no longer bear without the consolation of knowing that there is a poor man here who is being as well cared for as I. . . ."[12]

Gilberte sent to ask Beurrier whether he knew an indigent person who was in a fit state to be moved to the house. There was no one, but he promised that as soon as Pascal was well he would send him an old man of whom he could take care for the rest of his life. Pascal then asked to be moved to the Hospital for Incurables. He had decided to die among the poor and displayed his customary tenacity in order to attain his ends. His family brought up the medical objections. On 13th August the pain became worse and Pascal suggested another consultation. "The doctors ordered him to drink a little milk and kept on asssuring him that there was no danger, that it was only the effect of his migraine and the vapours from the waters. Nevertheless, no matter what they said, he did not believe a word."[13]

His condition grew worse. On the evening of 17th August Pascal felt so desperately ill that he again begged the family to send for a priest to spend the night with him. Since they could not get Beurrier, who was at Nanterre, they sent in great haste for Claude de Sainte-Marthe, one of the priests from Port-Royal, who heard his confession. Gilberte, who was alarmed and realized that it was the beginning of the death agony, secretly prepared the candles, altar linen and holy water so that her brother could be given Communion the following morning.

Suddenly, during the night, Pascal went into convulsions and a coma caused by cerebral haemorrhage. The family sent urgently for the parish priest of Saint-Étienne who had returned to Paris in the course of the evening. When he arrived and "as though by a miracle" the convulsions died down and Pascal regained consciousness.

When M. le Curé came into his room with Our Lord, saying: "Look, I am bringing you Him whom you have so greatly desired",

[12] Lafuma, pp. 68–9. Eng. tr., pp. 71–2.
[13] Ibid., p. 69. Eng. tr., p. 73.

his words woke him. M. le Curé went towards him to give him Communion; he made an effort and half raised himself on his own in order to receive it with greater respect; and when M. le Curé interrogated him, in accordance with his usual practice on the principal mysteries of the faith, he replied devoutly: "Yes, Monsieur, I believe them with my whole heart." And afterwards he received the Holy Viaticum and Extreme Unction with such devotion that tears came into his eyes. He replied to everything and, at the end, thanked M. le Curé, and when he blessed him with the Blessed Sacrament he said: "May God never abandon me!" which were, so to speak, his last words. For the moment that he had made his thanksgiving, the convulsions returned and did not leave him a moment's respite; they continued until his death which took place twenty-four hours later: that is to say, on the nineteenth of August 1662 at one o'clock in the morning, at the age of thirty-nine years and two months.[14]

When Pascal was dead his sister closed his eyes. Two women, Françoise Delfault and Esdune the cook, washed his skeletal body and fastened the jaws together with a chinstrap. An appalling scene that people always try to hide. The disciple must have attained a perfect resemblance to his Lord after the torture!

But the final act was still to be played, a miracle to be performed and an act of sacrilege committed.

The family decided to have a death mask made.[15] In the course of the centuries to so many of the written Pensées was to be added like a living illustration the very image of the thinking organ, the reflection of God on the face of the most movingly religious man left to us by the France of the Ancien Régime. Pascal's mask reminds us of Napoleon's with something less feminine, less dreamy and more regally intelligent about it. Peace suffuses the features of the dead man who is still young; the face is half-paralysed by hemi-

[14] Lafuma, p. 70. Eng. tr., pp. 73–4.
[15] U. Moussali, Le Vrai visage de Blaise Pascal, Paris, n.d. Ch. III, p. 10, states that the mask was found at the home of Duvivier, the maker of the mould, at the end of the eighteenth century. He observes that the weight of the plaster had slightly crushed the nose and that the chinstrap had caused a clenching of the jaws. Medical analyses have been made of the mask: Dr. Gilles de la Tournette, Nouvelle iconographie de la Salpêtrière, mentioned by Z. Tourneur, Une Vie avec Pascal, p. 28; Dr Just Navarre, op. cit., remarks: "The face is clearly asymmetric, but only to the same extent as all expressive human faces." (Plate II.)

plegia; as different as it could well be from those last drawings of the aged Voltaire with his grimacing face, surmounted by the pleated bonnet, of an old termagant sucking in the sneering lips.

The act of sacrilege was to hand over the mortal remains of a saint for a post-mortem. In a closed room in front of doctors as inquisitive as a bunch of necrophiles, Valland-Macroton cut open the belly of the corpse, pulled out the intestines, prodded them, sawed through the skull, performed his bloody butcher's task. What need had we to know that the dead man had a "withered stomach and liver and gangrened intestines"?[16] We might have guessed it. The frontal joint and the other crack-brained notions were Broca's contribution. The path was open to those whom Suarez dubbed "those scientific hounds" who try to explain the *Pensées* by means of phrenology.

The Pascal family must have been deficient in a sense of awe to allow Diafoirus to mess about with one of the most marvellous of human brains to the accompaniment of farcical comment.[17]

The funeral took place at Saint-Étienne-du-Mont on Monday, 21st August, at ten o'clock in the morning. Pascal's friends were invited to attend in these terms:

> You are invited to attend the Funeral procession, Service and Burial of Blaise Pascal, Esquire, deceased, son of the late Messire Étienne Pascal, Counsellor of State and Judge of the Cours des Aydes of Clermont-Ferrand; died at the house of M. Périer, his brother-in-law, King's Counsellor at the same Cours des Aydes, at the boundary of the Porte Saint-Marcel, close to the Fathers of Christian Doctrine; which will take place on Monday, 21st August, 1662, at ten o'clock in the morning at the Church of Saint-Étienne-du-Mont, his Parish and place of burial, which the Ladies may attend if they wish.[18]

Fifty friends were present at the ceremony which was very solemn. He was buried in the church itself "behind the High

[16] Lafuma, III, p. 66.
[17] Diafoirus was one of the doctors in Molière's *Malade imaginaire* and was used as a symbol of medical incompetence.—Trans.
[18] Lafuma, III, p. 75.

Altar near the Lady Chapel, on the right hand side".[19] Later, a Latin inscription was placed on the grave on the instructions of Florin and Gilberte Périer. It still exists, but has been moved from its original place.

According to a piece of tittle-tattle of Mme de Genlis, which Michelet carried into his *Histoire de la Révolution Française*, Pascal's body is supposed to have been secretly exhumed in 1789 and burnt at the Palais-Royal to assist the Duc d'Orléans in his ventures into alchemy.[20] The truth is less macabre and more prosaic. Behind the choir of the church were two marble plaques with two short inscriptions on the pillars standing on either side of the Lady Chapel. The left-hand one states that Jean Racine is buried there. The right-hand one says that Pascal's grave is there. It is possible that Pascal's leaden coffin is still intact because the graves in the church of Saint-Étienne-du-Mont were not desecrated at the time of the Revolution. Pascal wished to be buried in the communal paupers' grave. He is not buried in the golden casket of the saints or in the freezing, laicized vaults of the Panthéon. His remains are mixed with those of millions of Christians which lie beneath the turf of the hill of Sainte-Geneviève in the very heart of Paris.

[19] *Nécrologie de l'abbaye Notre-Dame de Port-Royal des Champs* (Amsterdam, 1723), p. 342.
[20] Ed. de la Pléiade, I, p. 126 note 3.

Part IV

THE *PENSÉES*

"Outside the domain of thought, you sometimes find a dog and sometimes a tiger, or a hen if you like; always a beast. All men eat, sleep and fornicate, to be sure; but do not eat the same things or dream of the same things. All they have in common is sleep when their sleep is dreamless, and death. "Whether there is a permanency of nothing matters little if it is precisely the thing which constitutes man's nobility that is condemned. If the passion of the best of them merely attains what is most perishable . . ."

"This passion, at any rate, is durable, my dear Möllberg," said Comte Rabaud. "Something eternal remains in man— in the man who thinks. . . . Something I will call the divine spark; it is his ability to call the world in question."

André Malraux, *Les Noyers de l'Altenburg*

CHAPTER I

Pascal's Drafts

MANUSCRIPT No. 9,202 in the main collection of French manuscripts at the Bibliothèque Nationale is a fat volume of 500 large pages measuring 23 by 35 centimetres and bound in green morocco. It has the appearance of a ledger from a provincial lawyer's office. When we open it, we sometimes find stuck on to sheets of thick vellum large pages covered with regular handwriting often riddled with crossings out or sentences which have been obliterated, and sometimes odd scraps and strips of paper covered with an illegible scrawl. Almost everywhere we find the imperial, unforgettable handwriting of "an angry cat"; subtle, spidery, compressed, nervous, with flourishes that recall those of Napoleon or Beethoven. In other places, there are fragments which look as though they had been written by the wise pen of the mother of a family, a few lines written in a childish hand and others which might have been written by a peasant or an almost illiterate housewife. Such is Pascal's spiritual testament: the manuscript of the *Pensées*.

There is a little of everything in this ledger: fragments of the drafts of the *Provincial Letters* and the *Treatise on the Vacuum*, the texts of religious meditations, notes on Pascal's reading of the Bible, Montaigne, Charron, Grotius, the *Pugio Fidei*, St Augustine, translations of passages from the Prophets, a draft of the lecture given at Port-Royal on the future *Apology for the Christian Religion*, some pages corrected and rewritten for the definitive version of the *Apology*. The whole does not add up to a book or, at any rate, not according to the rules of literary composition as they were formulated in the seventeenth century.

All writers have somewhere in their library, or buried in the corner of a desk, one of those little cemeteries for papers. They bury in them ancient plans for books which remain unwritten, lecture notes or notes that they gave up the idea of publishing. After their death they are tied into a dusty, yellow bundle which is burnt by one of the heirs or is discovered by the rag-and-bone man in the dustbin and tossed into an old sack with a pointed stick. The *Pensées* are nothing but Pascal's "lumber room". Sainte-Beuve described the manuscript as "immortal drafts". A beautiful untruth! They are mortal drafts of which a third has perished.

After Pascal's death several bundles of papers were found among his belongings. Some of them had been classified by him, numbered and fixed together on threads. Others were loose. They were the manuscripts of his scientific writings, drafts of public lectures, letters he had received and copies of those he had written, possibly a draft of the *Provincial Letters*.The papers which dealt mainly with religion, we are told by Étienne Périer, were copied in the state in which they were found. This was the way in which manuscript 9,202 (and its duplicate 12,449), known today as the *Copy of the Pensées*, came into being. The manuscript provides us first with papers divided logically into twenty-seven chapters, and then with thirty-three or thirty-four collections of writings which are unclassified.[1]

Long extracts from the *Pensées* were published in 1670. In 1711 Louis Périer, Pascal's nephew and adopted child, considered publishing a more complete edition. He had begun work with a Benedictine, Dom Touttée, but had to abandon his plan and deposited three collections of manuscripts in the library of the Abbey of Saint-Germain-des-Prés. At this time the bundle containing the *Pensées* was in the form of a bound ledger because Louis Périer had had all the papers of differing sizes stuck on to large white sheets to prevent them from being lost. Twenty years later the collection was bound. The other two bundles disappeared, but it is not known when this happened.

When the Revolution broke out the manuscript narrowly

[1] See specially Z. Tourneur in the preface to his edition of the *Pensées* published by the Éditions de Cluny, Lafuma's preface to his great edition of the *Pensées*, Lafuma, I, pp. 5–17, and more recently his *Histoire des Pensées de Pascal*, Paris, 1954.

escaped destruction in the fire at the abbey on 19th August 1794. It was saved by Dom Poirier and deposited at the Bibliothèque Nationale. In 1842 Victor Cousin drew attention to its existence with considerable fanfare. From 1844 onwards people set to work to produce a correct edition. Several followed one another until in 1905 Léon Brunschvicg published an enormous folio volume containing a photographic copy of each page of the autograph manuscript.

The preservation of the manuscript collection is almost miraculous. Naturally enough no original manuscripts have come down to us from antiquity or the middle ages: nothing of Shakespeare's or Rabelais's; a few corrections in Montaigne's handwriting in the margins of one of the editions of the *Essays;* a few of Racine's notes, but nothing of Molière's or La Bruyère's, and very little of La Fontaine's. The seventeenth century only admired finished works. It had no use for drafts, plans, corrections, or an author's crossings out. Manuscripts were burnt. If Gilberte Périer had not regarded the papers left by her brother as relics and if Louis Périer had not taken it into his head to deposit them at the Abbey of Saint-Germain-des-Prés, the *Pensées* would have followed the drafts of the *Provincial Letters*, the manuscripts of Plato, St Paul, Virgil, Racine and Molière into the fire or would have been eaten by the rats. In the case of Racine and Molière or the *Provincial Letters*, it would not have mattered because the essentials have been preserved; but if the *Pensées* had been destroyed without a copy being made, the posthumous Pascal whom we love would have vanished.

The edition of 1670, known as the Port-Royal Edition, was produced in poor conditions. The public were in a cautious mood. It was the time of the Peace of the Church. The Jansenist controversies had died down for the moment. The Jesuits and Port-Royal had signed a truce. It was therefore necessary at all costs to ensure that Pascal's writings, whose publication was eagerly awaited by his enemies, did not cause an uproar. The editors of the Port-Royal Edition had to present a neutralized, attenuated Pascal: a Pascal without the prickles.

It was also necessary to give shape to the shapeless fragments. The classics regarded unfinished work with horror and contempt.

Pascal's executors thought that they would do serious damage to the reputation of the author of the *Provincial Letters* if they gave to the public work which they regarded as imperfect, ill-proportioned and written in a style that was sometimes harsh and grating. What would become of his reputation as a skilful organizer, the creator of a subtle and balanced prose style? Readers of the *Pensées* would simply find themselves in a writer's workshop and Romanticism had not yet discovered the nostalgic poetry of ruins.

A committee set to work. It consisted of the Duc de Roannez, Filleau de la Chaise and Goibaud du Bois. At the end of 1667 it was joined by Brienne who acted as liaison officer with the Périer family. Nicole and Arnauld, the official theologians of Port-Royal, were responsible for approving the work of the Duc de Roannez who personally examined all the manuscripts.[2] Their work ended with the production of the Port-Royal Edition which appeared in 1669–70.

The classic Pascal of this edition was the only one known to Bossuet, Fénelon, Dugnet, Voltaire, Rousseau and Chateaubriand. We have to wait for Prosper Faugère's edition in 1844 to see the resurrection of the authentic Blaise Pascal. The Port-Royal Edition marked the beginning of "the Pascal problem". For since that time the autograph manuscripts have never ceased to exercise the sagacity of the critics. There is no end to the discovery of the erroneous readings, the blunders and misprints of the editors of what is the most exacting of French texts because of its traps and the difficulty of deciphering it. Zacharie Tourneur complained that the great Brunschvicg edition contained "more than 300 misreadings". "Strowski", he said, "corrected about 90, but was guilty of about 470 new ones."[3] Most of them are only of minor importance. There are, however, a number of serious and celebrated blunders. *Les trognes armées* is probably a misreading of *troupes armées* and an unfortunate one.[4] The people prefer the hunt, not "to poetry", but to "the kill".[5] An editor had put

---

[2] On the work of the committee, see the study by C. H. Boudhors in *Écrits sur Pascal* (Paris, 1959), and Lafuma, *Histoire des Pensées de Pascal*.

[3] Z. Tourneur, *Pensées*, I, p. L. The author returns to the charge in *Une Vie avec Blaise Pascal*, p. 18.

[4] *Trognes* means "bloated faces".—*Trans.*   [5] Laf. 269: Br. 139.

"pronouncements which bear fruit" whereas Pascal had written "seeds"; "no one calls himself a Cartesian" when Pascal had written "courtier".

But these misreadings, which have sometimes caused a good deal of fuss about nothing, are less serious than the contradictory interpretations of some of the most famous sentences in the *Pensées*. The "dialogue" or "dramatic" form which the finished *Apology* would have had has become more and more evident. Commentators have realized that we need to be highly circumspect and not in too much of a hurry to attribute to Pascal himself some remark taken from Montaigne, some fragment or sentence of the manuscript in which Pascal is reporting a saying not of his own, but of one of the participants in his imaginary conversations or one of his characters. Victor Cousin invited misinterpretation on a large scale when he began to speak of Pascal's scepticism and faith, "a bitter fruit which grew in the desolate region of doubt under the arid breath of despair".[6] This was the starting-point of the whole of Maurice Barrès's exegesis. Bremond and Valéry were guilty of the same mistake in believing that they detected a personal admission in the famous sentence: "The eternal silence of these infinite spaces terrifies me", which was a reflection that Pascal put into the mouth of his atheist.[7] And G. Duhamel goes equally astray when he speaks of Pascal's groans of anguish and of "the battle between intelligence and faith in his soul".[8]

A correct interpretation of the *Pensées* needs more prudence and less "literature".

Pascal is not a living author merely because of the irritating problems raised by his manuscripts, but also because of the touching and seemingly disorderly nature of his work. He crosses out, scratches out and restores. His sentences, warm with the breath of life, preserve something of the nervous haste of the hand that writes while engaged in the battle against death. We can

[6] *Blaise Pascal*, p. 217. Commenting on "the eternal silence", he observes: "Is not this sinister line standing by itself like a mournful cry which suddenly bursts from the depths of the soul?" (p. 226).

[7] See Valéry, "Variation sur une Pensée", *Variété* (Paris, 1924), pp. 137–53.

[8] G. Duhamel, *Les Confessions sans pénitence* (Paris, 1941), p. 181.

choose between several versions or "states" of the text.[9] The incomplete state of the *Pensées*, their dramatic abbreviations, are admirably suited to the very nature of their message. The work appears stripped of everything that is not essential. If it were a philosophical treatise or a work based on logical deductions, its fragmentary condition would damage its coherence irretrievably, whereas in fact the *Pensées* celebrate the union between genius and human wretchedness. Form and content harmonize and by a sort of miracle the style itself retains a living contact with sickness. Suffering forced Pascal to go further than Montaigne who wishing to draw a portrait of himself in his diversity, did so by sketches and fragments, but did it light-heartedly. He loiters along the path, he stops where he pleases, and the path leads nowhere. Pascal carries out a rescue operation. In the heart of a storm he creates words for us which are carried aloft and ripped apart by the gusts of his own sufferings. All that reaches us from the navigator of the infinite are words which are sometimes as disconnected as the S O S of a shipwrecked man. Gide claimed that he only liked "books whose authors had almost come to grief". Pascal was broken by the superhuman efforts of a martyr.

Yet even when his sufferings were greatest, his handwriting never betrayed the slightest sign of mental disorder or suggested that his intellectual faculties were in any way impaired. The eighteenth-century philosophers, who used the words "idiot" or "demented" when speaking of Pascal, have received a crushing reply from the graphologists and specialists in mental pathology. Pain may have racked his body, tortured his mind and paralysed his limbs, but it never affected in the slightest degree the lucidity and mastery of his miraculous intelligence, or caused the hand which was so firm and sure of itself to falter. His handwriting has aroused the admiration of the specialists for its balance, its simplicity and its aesthetic sense.[10] It gives us an incomparable insight into the state of Pascal's soul when he wrote and when he prayed. By means of manuscript 9,202 in the Bibliothèque

[9] See Chap. IX below.
[10] We owe the best study of Pascal's handwriting to M. de Rougemont quoted by F. Strowski, *Les Pensées de Pascal, étude et analyse*, pp. 59–61.

Nationale and the photographs of it, we come into the closest contact with the most personal genius of the golden period of literature and of the mystical and religious life in France as well as the one who is nearest to us.

It would be a vain undertaking to try after so many others to reclassify all the *Pensées*. It is impossible to discover the order in which they were written for the very good reason that not all his notes were intended for the *Apology* and that the plan of the work had not reached finality at the time of his death. It is true that he threaded together twenty-seven bundles, but he had stopped doing it and would probably have refused to go on to a methodical classification of *all* his drafts with the idea of publishing them. We do not know the precise date at which Pascal began the classification of his notes. Nevertheless, if we wish to discover the chronological order of each of the fragments contained in each of the bundles, we have to read all of them, beginning at the end.[11]

Editors of the *Pensées* who try to reconstruct the *Apology* in accordance with their own ideas perform a service for Pascal's readers. The very diversity of their classifications confirms the incomplete nature of the book and the freedom left to everybody to read Pascal in his own way. They highlight this or that fragment which in the case of another writer might remain obscure. Pascal appears in a changing light, varying his discourse according to the position assigned to this or that saying or its "follow up". The fifteen or twenty separate books which could be produced by varying the order of the *Pensées* are like the same number of avenues of approach which enable us to illuminate the central mystery of Pascal's thought in the way that varying lighting effects are concentrated in the attempt to light up the silent, enigmatic face of genius.

But if it is impossible to restore the thread of the *Apology*, it must be recognized that links exist between the fragments of the *Pensées*. Without in any way prejudging the order which Pascal

[11] This was understood by Z. Tourneur before he died. In his edition A. Anzieu says that he does not understand why Tourneur reversed the order of the fragments in the first bundle and reproduced the traditional order of the others.

would finally have chosen, we are entitled to draw up an inventory of these nubs: the role of the atheist, the idea of the infinite, human contradictions, the meaning of the Bible, the nature of the Church—such are the axes of Pascal's thought.

When we meditate on the *Pensées*, we see that beneath the apparent disorder of the draft, which corresponds involuntarily though perhaps providentially to Pascal's refusal to commit himself to a systematic presentation, we catch a glimpse of a higher order. Not the false symmetry, the mathematical order of a Descartes or a Spinoza. Human reason is not the measure of the world: Pascal seeks a true order which is not only resigned to mystery, but loves it. He prefers the halting exploration in the dark to the confident stride of the man in love with himself who goes round in circles like a caged animal.

CHAPTER II

The Atheist

PASCAL's works were always written with a particular group of readers in mind; they are all works of circumstance. The *Pensées* continue in writing the long conversations between Pascal and the atheists of his time who were among his friends.

The place occupied by the atheist in Pascal's mind is of such importance that it might almost be said that the *Pensées* were written for him alone. They present an argument *ad hominem*. In the *Pensées* the atheist speaks; he interrogates the Christian and answers him. At least a score of the fragments are in dialogue form. In this respect the book recalls the *Provincial Letters* and the work of Plato.

Pascal's atheist is not the ordinary kind. He is no monster of debauchery like des Barreaux who was for years the lover of Marion Delorme, ate meat on Good Friday and composed obscene songs one of which ended like this: "*Et par ma raison je butte A devenir bête brute.*"[1] [And by my reason I strive To become a brute beast.]

Pascal's atheist is not the old goat who cures himself of metaphysical anguish by tipping up girls: the old goat of whom Aldous Huxley paints a revolting picture in *After Many a Summer dies the Swan* and who resembles the sort of person that Anatole France would have become at the age of 200. This atheist is the *honnête homme*: he belongs to those whom Pascal describes as "very shrewd". For there are the simpletons, the semi-shrewd and the very shrewd. The simpletons have never interrogated themselves about anything. They take the world as they find it without having the brains to question it. The semi-shrewd have learnt their way round. They are out-and-out sceptics, the slaves of fashion. They

[1] See E. Chamaillard, *Pascal mondain et amoureux*, p. 330.

have just enough wit to contradict the opinions of the simpletons, but not enough to break with snobbery. Their efforts seem to have exhausted them, made them rigid and incapable of overcoming doubt or seeing things from above and from a distance. Pascal never stops taunting them: "They pretend to be knowing, upset people and misjudge everything."[2]

Simpletons and the semi-shrewd make up the bulk of the human race. The very shrewd are only a small *élite*, a grain of sand lost on the banks of a humanity which is scarcely distinguishable from animals. The *Pensées* were written for 10,000 in each generation out of 2,000,000,000. It is in this that the book differs from the Gospels or La Fontaine. It will never be a book for the mass audience.

Thus Pascal conceived the character of the atheist as a perfect man of the world, who enjoys a laugh, conversation, jokes and frequenting the salons where he knows how to make the most of his brilliant, scintillating mind. He is affable, has a knowledge of mathematics without knowing too much about it, or at any rate knowing how to forget it; possibly a writer but one who never talks about his own work. He is also an artist who is adept at hiding his anguish behind a veil of humour, a gambler but not a fanatical one. In love he is detached, is modest and human, avoids anything which appears foolish or exaggerated. Above all else, he is intelligent and takes pleasure in the subtleties and beauty of a style which is permeated by poetry. He is sensitive, open to conviction, and ready to follow anyone who is skilful in "the art of persuasion". He is broad-minded enough to kneel and dip his fingers in holy water if he finds in these gestures, which appear absurd, a means of reaching truth. All in all, a fine fellow; upright, strong in his clarity of mind, courageous, a doubter when doubt seems called for, believing if he must, never taken in, least of all by himself, never a slavish follower of public opinion, rather independent in his views, but with an independence which is capable of surrender when brought face to face with the majesty of God, if God is presented in the manner that he should be: a manner worthy of God's glory or of himself.

This kind of man is a thinker. His one really human function,

2 Laf. 173: Br. 327.

his only form of nobility, is the ability to think. Pascal makes him look upon man as a "thinking reed". A lapidary definition which in its condensation gains in penetration and depth what it loses in variety and breadth.[3] For man is also a loving reed, a reed which acts, a suffering reed. But when it comes to reflecting on the essential nature of man, Pascal strips his atheist of everything: philosophy, poetry, painting, science, sport, conversation, politics, love—all yields in his eyes and in those of his interlocutor to his function as a thinker. No one has provided such a simple and at the same time such a lofty definition of the nature of man.

Pascal was completely ignorant of the biological origins of man and his probable evolution. What difference would it have made to him? If he had known about them he would have rejected the blandishments of the *élan vital*. In this sense he was a Cartesian and a mechanist. He regarded the human body as a machine that was more complicated than the calculating machine, but a machine all the same. He would not have been among those who are continually dazzled by the findings of biology and botany. What would have interested him, if he had been able to look for a moment through the eye-pieces of our microscopes, would have been not the tricks of the mysteries of life, but the mystery of the man who invented the microscope, the tragedy of the scientist who seeks and questions. He was fascinated less by the results of geometry than by the existence of the geometer: that ultimate example of human greatness. Man is a thinking machine. You boast in vain of the pleasure of entertainment: Pascal laughs at the importance people attach to such moments which for him do not rank among those given up to the exercise of man's powers of reflection.

Pascal's atheist admires and enjoys Montaigne more than Descartes. Montaigne is his chosen master. Pascal approves of his choice. He accepts the wager and gives the enemy a good showing. He uses the *Essays*, that breviary of religious indifference, as his starting-point for guiding his atheist to faith. Not by the tricks of an apologist who is too clever by half; he has a horror of cheating. If he takes Montaigne as his starting-point it is because

[3] Laf. 391: Br. 347.

he is fond of him. He loves the succulent prose of this amiable companion who is never boring, who is a connoisseur of tall stories and of the Tartarin who laughs at himself. What variety and finesse, what a sense of humour! What irony and judgment! There is nothing about Montaigne of the velvety Machiavelli, the anti-Christian in sheep's clothing invented by Sainte-Beuve.[4] Pascal has an immense relish for his Gascon verve and the suggestion of leg-pulling. He at any rate is certain not to bore his reader.

Moreover, he accepts the rules of the game, restricts the horizon, puts on the spectacles of the old radical-socialist, preserves the tone of the *Essays*, which is that of a frank conversation but never about unpleasant subjects. Neither Lucretius nor Dante nor Hamlet! He chooses from the material of the human comedy only those details likely to amuse someone who enjoys a cosy life and who, in a château surrounded by vineyards, enjoys the spectacle of the immortal folly of mankind. For Montaigne, man is a learned ape whose tricks deserve to be appreciated. Judges, priests, kings, doctors and regents must lay aside their frills and furbelows, their robes and collars, and the ribbons which hold their decorations. Let them undress and Montaigne will plant the human animal stark naked, white and ridiculous, in front of us. He also wants moral nakedness, wants to catalogue the fantasies of self-esteem, imagination, all the foolish, ridiculous or indecent customs, all the grotesque teaching, the baroque superstitions, and when he sees the thousand clownish tricks he does not bellow with laughter like Rabelais, but very gently and slyly he smiles.

Once he has opened the *Essays* with his atheist, Pascal follows with his finger the inventory of the mountebank's tricks. The pair of them go round the circus, that is to say, they betake themselves to the Jeu de Paume, the Courts of Justice, the barracks, the Court, the ball, the hunt, the baccarat tables. They stop at the cobbler's shop to admire a well-turned heel. They hear one of the regulars shout out in the tavern: "What a lot that fellow drinks! What a thimbleful this one drinks!"[5] One entertaining detail—they are

---

[4] This view of Montaigne is criticized by M. Raymond, *Génies de France*, Neuchâtel, 1942, pp. 50–67.
[5] Laf. 72: Br. 117.

astonished to learn that the Turkish Grand Seigneur works. They move backwards in time and are amused to see Alexander drunk and chaste, Pyrrhus indefatigable, Caesar in the process of conquering the world and forgetting himself in the arms of Cleopatra, Herod more cruel to his sons than his pigs, Cromwell killed by a stone in his bladder.

In short, under the guidance of Montaigne, Pascal, in the company of his atheist, discovers a thousand ways in which man plays the clown in order to achieve happiness, eggs his dogs on after a hare, is bowled over by a woman's nose, applies his mind to dancing in step, becomes a judge, a king or a conqueror and not possessing a sufficiency of these absurd benefits, proceeds to create for himself an infinity of imaginary ones, pursues them with passion, and after a life of agitation drops down dead with a stone in the ureter or an abscess under the armpit.

Not only does Pascal simply summarize Montaigne with broad strokes, but out of all the wealth of observation in the *Essais* he retains in the last analysis very little. He is not interested in history of which Montaigne is so fond that he gets lost in it for an entire chapter. He disdains the travels on which Montaigne embarked by proxy in his geographical works. Pascal never travels even in his dreams. We scarcely find in the *Pensées* more than a few scattered observations on war and tyranny, virtually nothing about suffering, tears, blood, and only two or three references to death. What is most striking in Pascal is his complete silence about the most bestial of human vices, sadism and cruelty, which on several occasions are vigorously denounced by Montaigne. Pascal appears to overlook the moral maladies of humanity: its sufferings, the tortures and aberrations of love, the hell of Sodom and Gomorrah, the rivers of blood and slime which flood the earth. Not from lack of feeling, but from an obvious intention of being more sober than Montaigne. He is naturally much more sober than the Christian moralists, than the Fathers of the Church, and *a fortiori* than Jansen. If we want to measure the distance between the *Pensées* and the *Augustinus* all we have to do is to place side by side Pascal's description of man and Jansen's horrifying, passionate, blood-soaked page on human wretchedness in the first chapter of Book II, Volume II of the *Augustinus*:

From the moment of its origin the human race bears the full burden of its condemnation and its life, if it can be called such, is totally bad. Do we not arrive in the world in a horrible state of ignorance? From the womb does not the child lie in thick darkness? Is he not ignorant of who he is? What he is? Who created him? Who engendered him? Already guilty of a crime and incapable of virtue, so enveloped and smothered in darkness that it is impossible to arouse him from a state of torpor of which he is unaware? And this form of intoxication lasts for months and years. From this dark obscurity come all the errors of human life which gathers to its bosom all the sons of Adam. . . . What a love of vain and harmful things, what gnawing cares, worries, sufferings, fears, unhealthy joys, disputes, struggles, wars, pursuits, rages, hostilities, lies, flatteries, pains, thefts, rapine, perfidies, pride, ambitions, envy, homicides, parricides, cruelties, sadism, wickednesses, lusts, boastings, impudences, impurities, fornications, adulteries, incests, infamies against the nature of both sexes which are too shameful to mention, what sacrileges, heresies, blasphemies, perjuries, oppressions of the innocent, slanders, swindles, frauds, false witnesses, iniquitous judgments, violence, larcenies! It is impossible to imagine any form of turpitude which is not to be found in life.

As for children . . . what masters, canes, whips and beatings are not found necessary? What purpose do they serve if not to put the brake on the imbecilities and evil desires which we bring with us into the world? What an evil thing to remember! Without work, we forget. Without pain we should remain ignorant. What pain in order to act. . . .

As for our body, what is there that it does not fear? Heat, cold, storms, rain, floods, sunburn, lightning, hail, fire . . . plants, animals, mad dogs, etc.

As for the righteous . . . error tempts them in order to break them, sadness in order to cast them down. . . . Who can describe the yoke that weighs on the sons of Adam? The flesh never ceases to wage war against the spirit and the spirit against the flesh in order to prevent us from doing what we want; we must always be on the watch in order not to be deceived by appearances, not to become the prey of cunning, not to fall into error, not to confuse good and evil . . . not to succumb to a shameful sloth, to ingratitude, to evil desires . . . in short, not to put our trust in our own strength rather than in the grace of Jesus Christ in order to secure victory.

It is easy to see what separates the harmless picture of the *Pensées* from this hell of screams of rage and slaughter. It is commonly said that Pascal exaggerates the wretchedness of man. That is absurd. Compared with the picture presented by Lucretius, Sade, Dostoevsky, Proust or Kafka, Pascal's vision of humanity is that of a choirboy.[6] He never concerns himself with the evil done by man, but simply with the ridiculous spectacle of his activities. In the *Pensées* man never assumes the appearance of a savage and lubricious ape whose instincts civilization tries in vain to camouflage. For Pascal it is sufficient to express astonishment that a judge laughs during a sermon, that a doctor puts on a gown, that a philosopher trembles on a plank suspended over an abyss, that a king dances a minuet. He finds man merely grotesque and not wicked. A glimpse of the Courts of Justice or people coursing a hare is sufficient for his demonstration. What is more, in both spectacles he suppresses the sight of blood and torture, and only preserves the comic element.

[6] See the comments of A. Béguin, *Pascal par lui-même*, p. 61.

CHAPTER III

Contradictions of Man

PASCAL would not have been himself if he had stopped after this preliminary work, which consisted in reducing Montaigne's field of observation, classifying his scattered comments, imposing a discipline on the tendency to wander, cutting away the rather straggling undergrowth of the *Essays* in order to give them the trim shape of a French garden; nor again if he had failed in the task of rejuvenating Montaigne, curbing his slightly diffuse style and brushing the coat of the country gentleman before putting it on. Pascal not only stabilizes the volatile Montaigne, he also excavates his work in depth and wrecks the elegant garden so that he can sink a mine shaft.

The distortions of the imagination, for example, divert Montaigne who describes them amusingly and thinks the tricks used by the wanton to play with man as a cat plays with a mouse are vastly entertaining. Pascal blots out Montaigne's comments and produces an epic picture. This time it is less a question of the rogueries of a woman than the diabolical plotting of a great witch, the "empress of the infernal marshes",[1] the mistress of dreams, "error and falsehood, and all the more treacherous because it does not always deceive".[2] For Pascal admires imagination which creates poets and madmen, conquerors and murderers. He is perfectly ready to see in it one of the signs of man's creative powers. It would be a mistake to interpret his description as nothing but a speech for the prosecution: it is a passionately warm, interesting, gripping examination in which imagination is invested with the austere beauty of a magic face. And we are a very long way from Montaigne. It was sufficient to vary the lighting for the atmosphere to change.

[1] Villon, "Ballade à Notre-Dame".   [2] Laf. 81: Br. 82.

236

The same thing happens in questions of politics and law. We remember the ironical way in which Pascal doffed his cap to triumphant force. According to him man is capable, from time to time, of catching a glimpse of absolute justice which would consist in equality of goods, power in the hands of the man most capable of wielding it, the suppression of war, slavery and tyranny. But the force is there which creates positive laws and imposes them. Justice becomes a weathercock. "If the temperature at the pole went up by three degrees, it would turn jurisprudence upside down; a meridian determines truth . . . According to reason, nothing is just in itself; everything varies according to the weather."[3]

Is this a Machiavellian justification of the theory and practice of tyranny and the right of force? Far from it. It is simply the recognition of a pathetic state. By attacking it, the utopians provoke revolutions and civil wars and the people end by paying the price. Pascal had lived through the Fronde. He knows that there is no more horrifying misfortune than civil war. He detests war, finds it absurd and obscene. If it is necessary to make war, it must be done; but to make war in order to abolish war is sheer lunacy. It is preferable to bow before the man dressed in crude brocade and followed by four lackeys.[4] Doffing hats, yes! Respect, no! Only the body inclines.

Up to this point Pascal has followed Montaigne, but the political ideas of the author of the *Essays* came from his wish not to be disturbed. First and foremost, let us have peace. Pascal saw further. He honours Plato and Aristotle "for writing about politics . . . with the idea of drawing up rules for running a madhouse. And if they pretended to take it all seriously, they knew perfectly well that the madmen to whom they addressed themselves thought themselves kings and emperors."[5] Behind these declarations we catch a glimpse of a theory which belonged peculiarly to Pascal: the theory of the three orders of greatness. The greatness of conquerors, dictators and masters of the world is not worth a second's thought in the order of the spirit. Pascal goes beyond Montaigne in placing politics on the lowest rung of the scale of values: the rung dominated by the great pachyderms, the

[3] Laf. 108: Br. 294. [4] Laf. 56: Br. 318, 319. [5] Laf. 196: Br. 331.

animals. Above the tyrant, he sets the man capable of showing contempt.

In short, if human entertainments merely amuse Montaigne by their oddity, they inspire Pascal to write a page which is the equal in nervous power of the meditation on the two infinites. Man's taste for noise is a problem which has to be solved. It is not enough to laugh at it. We must discover the cause and guess why we are so enthusiastic about this attenuated form of intoxication, this light-headedness, this substitute for spiritual joy. And the *Essays* put Pascal on the track of a fascinating problem that Montaigne had not even noticed.

It leads him to undertake an extraordinary analysis of *ennui*. Here, to be sure, is something new: the detection of this poison, this secret vice which rots human nature. We shall have to wait for the nineteenth century, for Chateaubriand and Baudelaire, to find anything as profound as Pascal's soundings.

> That [he writes] is how the whole of our life slips away. We seek repose by battling against a few obstacles, and if we overcome them, repose becomes unbearable because of the boredom it generates. We have to get away from it and go round begging for excitement. . . .
>
> For we either think of the miseries which are ours or of those which threaten us. And even if we found ourselves adequately protected all round, boredom would, of its own accord, soon come welling up from the depths of our heart, where it has its natural roots, and fill the mind with its poison. Thus man is so wretched that, owing to his peculiar disposition, he would still be bored even if he had no cause for boredom. . . .[6]

It is the *acedia* of the medieval cloisters, the disgust with life, the spleen of the *Fleurs du mal:*

> *Dans la ménagerie infâme de nos vices,*
> *Il en est un plus laid, plus méchant, plus immonde*
> *. . . C'est l'Ennui. L'Oeil chargé d'un pleur involontaire*
> *Il rêve d'échafaud en fumant son houka . . .*

Pascal will go further still. How is it all possible? he will ask

[6] Laf. 269: Br. 139.

himself. The power of the imagination, diversion, madness, politics, *ennui*? Why is man so grotesque? Why are his antics so pathetic? It is because man thinks. He is ridiculous, feels the need of distractions, and is bored simply because he thinks. All our miseries and all our sufferings are the result of thought. So, too, is all that makes man great.

For all of a sudden human wretchedness lights up and Pascal rejoices for mankind with an immense, an almost lyrical pride. Man is a great aristocrat, a dispossessed monarch, but nevertheless a monarch. A marvel! A prodigy! Intoxicating greatness! Man becomes a giant who rediscovers by the power of his thought that he has something in common with infinite space: "By means of space the universe contains me and swallows me up like a speck; by means of thought I comprehend the universe."[7] We must understand the word "comprehend" in the sense of "envelope", "dominate", "grasp".

Without man's power of thought, all his chatter, all his follies would be nothing but amusing games like those of puppies or monkeys. Thought turns everything upside down and the stage on which the human comedy is performed is illuminated by flashes of lightning. Like a backcloth appears the meditation on the two infinites. The play has turned to tragedy and we watch the smile grow rigid on the atheist's lips.

The tragedy lies in the fact that man sees himself under two aspects, sees himself dance, go hunting, fall in love, use his imagination. It comes from man's astonishing power of knowing himself, of measuring his stature in infinite space and the duration of his life in time, of reliving the past, of foreseeing the future, of knowing the time of his death. The tragic figure is the one who knows that he will die before the curtain falls and who changes the subject of conversation. When the animals dance or go hunting, they behave like beings who will live for ever, whereas the dance and the hunt of men are the dance and the hunt of men who will die. Their pleasures are no more than the last cigarette of the man condemned to death. Every instant of their life carries them consciously towards their inexorable fate.

Man knows that his imaginary happiness is a sham. What does

[7] Laf. 217: Br. 348.

it matter! He always pretends to believe that it will last for ever. He wants to cure himself of thought which puts the spectacle of death constantly before his eyes; thought is his only malady, his only form of anguish. He diverts himself and grows heady. Politics, amusements, appointments, wealth, gambling and love delight him because in so far as he surrenders to them he ceases to be a man. Or better, because man is incapable of supporting with impunity the continued exercise of his proud privilege. Anyone who wanted to think all the time would go mad. Man has to play the fool, divert himself, and if one can apply intelligence to the task of wearing oneself out, all is for the best! Thought is no longer concerned with anything but troubles which paralyse thought.

Only man does not resort to suicide as easily as that. Even when he is taken up with amusements, egoism, dreams and follies, it is the pursuit of God, that is to say, of happiness, on which he embarks. In his own eyes man is a "bottomless gulf" which he tries to fill.

What is he seeking when he makes himself the centre of the universe? Nothing less than God. "The basest thing in man is his thirst for fame, but that in itself is the clearest sign of his excellence. . . . He sets such high store on reason that, whatever his worldly advantages, unless he is well endowed with it he is not satisfied. He may have the best position in the world, but nothing can deflect him from this wish, and that is the most indelible quality in the heart of man."[8]

And what does man seek outside himself? Nothing other than God. By amusements, unceasing activity, travel, action, war and love, he tries to quench an infinite thirst. He is not interested in the kill, but in the hunt. He is caught in an endless current. He feels that he should flee himself, that the infinite good lies outside him; but he only finds a wandering prey which drives him back to his task of Sisyphus. He will never open "the door of repose" for himself.[9]

The impossibility of stopping and finding fulfilment in a being or state of mind without anxiety shows that unless he accepts an animal repose, man desires the infinite.

[8] Laf. 91: Br. 404.　　　　[9] Laf. 269: Br. 139.

Baudelaire is the greatest of Pascal's disciples. We know how frequently he speaks in his work of that pursuit of the infinite which drives the condemned man along a path which has no bounds. The introduction to the supreme art of distraction known as "the artificial paradise" is Pascalian in its very style.

Alas! The vices of man, however horrible we may suppose them, contain the proof (if it were no more than their infinite expansion!) of his thirst for the infinite; only it is a thirst which causes him to mistake the path. . . . The lord of the visible world (I am speaking of man) has therefore attempted to create Paradise by means of drugs, alcoholic drinks, like a maniac trying to replace solid furniture and real gardens by scenes painted on canvas and hoisted on to a frame. In my view, this degeneration of the sense of the infinite is responsible for all the criminal excesses, from the concentrated and solitary intoxication of the man of letters who, compelled to seek relief from physical pain in opium and who having thus discovered a source of morbid delight, gradually turns it into his sole form of personal hygiene and, as it were, the sun of his spiritual life, to the most repellent forms of drunkenness of the back streets where with their minds filled with fire and glory men wallow fatuously in the filth of the gutters.[10]

And the same theme appears in the poetry:

> Faites votre destin, âmes désordonnées,
> Et fuyez l'infini que vous portez en vous!

It is somewhat odd that the sense of sin should be less acute in Pascal than in Baudelaire because in the eyes of Pascal distraction is less a sin than a form of unavoidable stupidity.

For the past three hundred years all sorts of people have protested against Pascal's picture of the human condition. Voltaire blamed Pascal for not appreciating sufficiently the douceur de vivre. He has been echoed by theologians who maintain that human unrest is a myth, that God might well have created man as he is without raising him to the supernatural order, that the effects of original sin are not a fact of experience and that human life does not conceal any mystery. Does this mean that Pascal was

[10] Baudelaire, Oeuvres (Bibliothèque de la Pléiade), I, pp. 274–6.

the inventor of gambling, war, suffering and death? Once again, he scarcely mentions them.

These attacks are based on a misunderstanding of Pascal's thought. He makes no attempt to prove original sin. He simply observes man, watches him live his life and think, counts the obstacles in the way of this same thought with the same rigour that he had applied a short time ago to the observation of the effects of the vacuum. He preserves the same impartiality as an usher handling an affidavit or an accountant examining a balance sheet.

Since 1660 the evolution of humanity has proved him right with a vengeance. The rationalist humanism and the optimism of the century of enlightenment, science, international organizations have ended in fraudulent bankruptcies. All that counts in psychology from Nietzsche to Proust, from Stendhal to Dostoevsky, from Kakfa to Malraux and Camus, develops, elaborates and extends the intuitions of Pascal. It seems that all the great voices echo his own. As Aldous Huxley has amusingly observed: "In the beginning and in the state of nature, human beings were not, as the philosophers of the eighteenth century imagined, wise and virtuous; they were apes". Pascal would merely have added: "In so far as they were already human beings, they were thinking apes, and they remain so".

CHAPTER IV

The Use of Thought

" A THINKING animal, such is man." This is admitted by the
atheist at Pascal's invitation. Is not thought given to man
to enable him to resolve the fundamental problems of his
origin, nature and destiny, and to find happiness?

Pascal at once reverts, for the instruction of his atheist, to the
conclusions of his dialogue with Lemaistre de Sacy on Epictetus and
Montaigne which was at the same time a dialogue on Descartes.
He urges the atheist to interrogate the philosophers, consult the
doctors who are divided into two tribes: Doctors So-much-the-
worse and Doctors So-much-the-better.

The So-much-the-worse are the sceptics. In order to discover
what they think, all you have to do is to gather an armful of the
arguments scattered through the *Essays*: "We have no certainty
of the truth of (first) principles. . . . No one can be sure . . .
whether he is awake or asleep. . . . Since we often dream that we
are dreaming, piling one dream upon another, it could well be that
the half of life when we think we are awake, is no more than a
dream . . . from which we awake at death. . . ." Pascal recalls
Montaigne's discourse "against the impressions created by habit,
education, the manners of countries and other similar things . . .".[1]
On the credit side of the sceptics' account he draws up an inventory of everything in which men have believed they have
discovered the Sovereign Good: "stars, sky, earth, elements,
planets, cabbages, leeks, animals, insects, calves, serpents, fever,
pestilence, war, famine, vices, adultery, incest".[2] Have not the
most high-minded of philosophers often ended in deviations and

[1] Laf. 131: Br. 434. The passage is partly crossed out by Pascal.
[2] Laf. 300: Br. 425.

follies similar to those of the most degenerate forms of religion? The result is that underneath each of these little observations which Pascal borrowed from Montaigne we could put the name of a contemporary thinker or writer.

The dogmatic reply to this universal scepticism is an appeal to good faith. "We cannot doubt natural principles," they say. "The sceptics only have one objection to this: the uncertainty of our origins which includes that of our nature: to which the dogmatists have been busy replying since the world began. So it is open warfare between men in which each of us must inevitably take sides."[3]

For we have to take sides. Everything is at stake. Pascal insists on this, but he shows that the views of both sides are without justification: absolute scepticism arouses a spontaneous protest on the part of human nature. Men cannot doubt everything. "I take it as axiomatic that there has never been a completely dyed-in-the-wool sceptic. . . ." Pushed to its extreme limits, scepticism would lead to a complete paralysis of thought, to suicide in a state of pure insanity. "Nature lends its support to tottering reason and prevents it from pushing its lunacy to such lengths as that."

Is dogmatism any more solid in its unbending pride? It, too, comes into conflict with an insurmountable obstacle: our uncertainty "whether man is created by a good God, a wicked devil or by chance . . .".[4] Descartes bases his whole system on the divine veracity. Belief in reason ultimately means belief in God. The atheist who is a disciple of Montaigne's regards this as begging the question: Cartesian dogmatism implies the autonomy of philosophy and a possibility of its grasping the Sovereign Good—a thing to which Pascal cannot give his assent.

Without concluding in favour of either of the two great families into which thinking men are divided, Pascal brings them face to face: the race of men who doubt and the race of those who believe. In the last analysis, the sceptics' doubts involve them in a perpetual state of contradiction with themselves. Their very gestures are affirmations and they always finish by acting as though they possessed the absolute. As for dogmatists, they base their

[3] Laf. 246: Br. 434.   [4] *Id.*

reasoning on non-existent foundations. Reason cannot justify its ambition to become the cornerstone of the universe and to solve the riddle of the world. Pascal thinks that Cartesianism is "the romance of nature, more or less similar to the story of Don Quixote".[5]

Pascal felt within himself the rift between scepticism and criticism on the one hand, moral dogmatism and metaphysics on the other. He himself experienced the twofold need to assert and to doubt, to produce a synthesis of Descartes and Montaigne. He had re-read the *Essays* too often to put his entire trust in reason. He was too sincere to base his faith on a philosophical system. Faith did not come to crown metaphysics. It was the answer to an appeal of the soul. By destroying an excessive confidence in reason, scepticism creates a necessary vacuum.

But Pascal was too deeply versed in the sciences not to know what marvels reason is capable of discovering by its own unaided powers. He puts too much poetry into his eulogy of the mathematician. Reason can accomplish everything except give us the Sovereign Good which does not depend on it. Everywhere it ends by coming up against mystery and must resign itself to the fact: "Reason's final step is the recognition that there are an infinite number of things which are beyond it; it is merely feeble if it does not go as far as to grasp that."[6] Powerful reason becomes conscious of its limitations when it reaches them; weak and soft though it is, it is nevertheless convinced that it is capable of resolving the mysteries but does not even touch their fringe. It prides itself on a fictitious power: "There is nothing which is so much in conformity with reason as the rejection of reason."[7] It is therefore not in the name of faith, but of reason itself that Pascal rejects with a shrug of his shoulders the absurd pretensions of rationalism.

But Pascal goes further than this disillusioned analysis which ends in the rejection of both sceptic and dogmatist. Nature, he says, prevents us from being so extravagant that we end up in a state of absolute doubt. What nature? And how can dogmatism be possible? If pure reasoning is incapable of fertilizing thought,

[5] Laf. 1,008 (Luxembourg ed.).   [6] Laf. 373: Br. 267.   [7] Laf. 182: Br. 272.

where does thought look for strength and support? In fact, answers Pascal, in order to live and think all men appeal to a power which is not the faculty of reasoning: it is the heart or intuition. The heart enables us to understand and to feel simultaneously. It offers certitudes which have nothing in common with those of syllogisms:

We come to know truth not only by reason, but even more by our heart; it is through this second way that we know first principles, and reason, which has no part in it, tries in vain to undermine them. The sceptics, whose only object it is, toil away at it fruitlessly. We know that we are not dreaming; however powerless we may be to prove it by means of reason, our powerlessness demonstrates nothing except the feebleness of our reason and not, as they maintain, the uncertainty of the whole of our knowledge . . . . And it is just as useless and just as ridiculous for reason to demand of the heart proofs of its first principles in order to concur in them, as it would be for the heart to demand of reason an intuitive knowledge of all its propositions before accepting them.[8]

Pascal sets great store by the intuitive knowledge of the heart. It is direct and absolute. It places us in contact with things and beings, while reason only apprehends ideas and concepts. The heart is the organ of intuition of the sensitive minds whom Pascal contrasts with the pure mathematician. The relations between one person and another depend on it. And that is why the faith of simple people is a gift of the heart which operates with the assistance of an upright will. In his *Traité de l'oraison* Nicole wrote of truth: "It is nothing but the old law as long as it remains only in the mind: it becomes the new and evangelical law when it is engraved in the heart."[9]

There is no sentimentality in Pascal's appeals to the heart. What he means by heart and feeling is only the most vivid form of intelligence, but an intelligence continually guided by an experience of life and by moral effort. The heart is incapable of constructing systems like the abstract logic of the metaphysicians, but it enables us to transcend them. In his analysis of the highest form of thought Pascal opened the way for the profound *aperçus*

[8] Laf. 110: Br. 282.   [9] 2nd ed., Paris, 1684, p. 278.

of Newman. The heart is the "illative sense" of *The Grammar of Assent*.

> It is a capacity [writes Newman] of entering with instinctive correctness into principles, doctrines, and facts, whether they be true or false, and of discerning promptly what conclusion from them is necessary, suitable, and expedient. . . . It is an intimate understanding of an assemblage of intellectual data. . . . I have already ventured to say that our belief in the extended material world follows on an inference from our perception of particular objects through their phenomena, as those phenomena actually come before us, or even . . . from our experience of the sensible phenomena of self. It is by the illative sense that we come to this conclusion, which no logic can reach.[10]

Bergson, in his turn, extends and elaborates Pascal's *aperçus*. He transforms intuition into "something subtle, very light and almost airy which flees as soon as you approach it, but which we cannot look upon, even from a distance, without becoming incapable of attaching ourselves to anything else."[11] But Bergson, who used these words of Spinoza, turns intuition into the true philosophical method. "It is not necessary," he declares, "in order to reach intuition, to move out of the sphere of the senses and consciousness. Kant's mistake was to think that it was. . . . Let us go back to the origins of our power of perception and we shall find that we possess knowledge of a new kind without there being any need to appeal to new faculties . . . ."[12]

He ended by recognizing the knowledge of the mystics as the highest form of intuition and identifying himself very closely with Pascal.

Thus Pascal, the precursor of Newman and Bergson, returning to the subject of the discussion on Epictetus and Montaigne, develops in a fragmentary way in the *Pensées* the observations contained in the treatise called: *That there are other proofs as certain as those of geometry*. To deny the great value of those proofs known as moral or intuitive would amount to paralysing thought and preventing the very exercise of reason.

[10] *An Essay in Aid of a Grammar of Assent* (London, 1870), pp. 353, 354–5.
[11] H. Bergson, *La Pensée et le mouvant* (Skira, Geneva), p. 123.
[12] *Ibid.*, p. 138.

Pascal is absolutely bent on convincing the atheist of the necessity of intellectual humility—Bergson would have used the word "simplicity"—which is nothing but a submission to facts. Whether we like it or not, human thought operates in this way: intuition of principles by the heart, reasoning, accession to mystery and illumination of the mystery by a fresh intuitive penetration. Before discovering mysteries in the universe outside him, man discovers them in the deepest part of his own nature. Thus, thought comes into conflict not only with the obstacles of distraction, madness and death, but in its exercise man rediscovers his own fundamental ambiguity. Torn between pride and laziness, human reason is enclosed in an inescapable vicious circle.

Rationalists of the extreme right and the extreme left, from Charles Maurras to Albert Bayet, have accused Pascal of scepticism or fideism. They are guilty of a contradiction. Pascal allows scepticism its place. He would think today in terms of Voltaire, Renan, Anatole France and André Gide, but as he did not feel that he had the right to refuse a hearing to the dogmatism of Epictetus and Descartes, he would find a place for the heroic morality of Nietzsche, Proudhon and Malraux and above all for the splendid efforts of the scientists which have simply deepened the mystery of the universe. He would begin all over again to construct a synthesis between doubt and affirmation seeing everything "more clearly and from a greater distance".[13] As F. Droz put it with felicity: "There, where people saw in the *Pensées* the contradictions of a system, we should see rather a system of contradictions."[14] Today Pascal, as an advocate of experiment, would regard himself as being under an obligation to consider man as a whole. Having pushed the thinking faculty to its limits, the atheist would be in a position to open his eyes and take a look at the universe.

[13] Laf. 472: Br. 285.
[14] F. Droz, *Études sur le scepticisme de Pascal*, 176–7. On the importance of this book, see B. Amoudru, *La Vie posthume des Pensées* (Paris, 1936), p. 120, and also A. Vinet, *Études sur Blaise Pascal*, 4th ed., 1904, pp. 233–59.

CHAPTER V

The Infinite

I T HAS been said that, as a thinker, Pascal was an exponent of interiority, of immanence. This is not entirely true. If he considers that the metaphysical proofs of the existence of God are no longer valid, he does not think it a waste of time to confound his atheist with the infinity of the cosmos. The summit of the *Pensées* from which one looks down on the panorama of the work is the meditation of the two infinites.

Pascal's scientific studies led him to devote a large amount of space in his book to the idea of the infinite. He had probably toyed with a microscope in its primitive form and the astronomical telescope, both of which had been invented a hundred years earlier. In mathematics he was a convinced upholder of the theory of the infinity of numbers. He had pushed his study of infinitely small quantities a very long way, which had enabled him to solve the problem of the centres of gravity of solid bodies created by the cycloid.

The problem was one of the fashionable ones of the day. At the time of the ancient Greeks Democritus had maintained that the universe was infinitely large. Descartes was of the same opinion and Pascal might have come across the following sentence in the *Principes de la philosophie* published in 1647: "We shall also see that this world or the extension of which the universe is composed has no limits because whatever we may pretend, our imagination can still stretch beyond the idea of space indefinitely extended."[1]

The world therefore opens on to the infinite, but Pascal expresses the idea with a power and warmth which is far removed

[1] *Les Principes de la philosophie*, Pt. II, Section 21.

from the dryness of Descartes. He takes up the ancient formulas on the infinite spheres which had been brought to his attention by Montaigne's *Essays*.

Moreover, he believed that it was possible to divide space and matter into an infinite number of parts just as easily as to multiply them. In this he was an opponent of the views of Democritus, as accepted by Cavalieri and Descartes, who admitted the existence of indivisible atoms. Against this, Pascal recalls certain burning pages of Père Mersenne which he had read as a young man. In one of them, the *Quaestiones celeberrimae in Genesim*, he found a description of the dissection of an insect: "What, I ask you," said Mersenne, "is more worthy of admiration, if we look at it attentively, than a fly in which there is certainly a liver, a heart, a brain, with veins and arteries. . . . What space exists between the joints of the feet of ants, what nerves are intended for each leg, what is the pattern of their nerves and arteries, what a size their eyes must be, what a variety of coloured tunics they have and what a length their optic nerve must be. . . ."

When it came to inorganic matter, Mersenne was no less decided than Pascal; it was divisible to the infinite: "If all the angels went on dividing a drop of water from now until the Day of Judgment, so that every minute they divided it into a thousand million parts, what remained of the drop on the Day of Judgment would still possess an infinity of parts."[2]

In a less unusual and more attractive passage Pascal writes: "I will describe [for man] not only the visible universe, but the whole inconceivable vastness of nature enclosed in the abridgement of an atom. Let him see it in an infinity of universes, each of which has its firmament, its planets, its earth in the same proportion as the visible world: in this earth animals and finally mites, in which he will find again what he found in the first. . . ."[3]

In short, instead of imagining like Fontenelle a plurality of universes juxtaposed in the infinitely large, Pascal conceives as possible universes enclosed in one another, in a chain stretching to infinity.

[2] *L'Impiété des déistes*, vol. II, p. 345. Cf. R. Lenoble, *op. cit.*, p. 251, and E. Jovy, *Études pascaliennes*, VIII, pp. 29–32.
[3] Laf. 390: Br. 72.

Méré reacted vigorously when Pascal discussed the infinitely small with him: "Can you decide", he wrote, "in this small space how much faster the Sun travels than Saturn, or whether the Sun is motionless as some people are convinced? Could you estimate, either you or Archimedes, in a space so narrow, by how much the velocity of a cannon surpasses the speed of a tortoise? . . ."[4] Pascal must have laughed over the absurdity of an intelligent man who sees in imagination the span of the universe. It was Pascal who was the defender of the future of science. He had never intended to say that in the universe of the infinitely small a mathematician named Pascal was debating the tininess of mites with another microscopic being named Méré; but by means of an insight in which there was an element of genius he had sensed that atoms obey the same laws as the planets and the nebulae.

Pascal asserted the reality of this ideal double infinity of the universe much less definitely than some of his expressions appear to suggest. He speaks of the immensity that we *may* conceive. There is one fragment which clarifies his thought on this point: "Nature repeats the same things over and over again: the years, the days, the hours: it is the same with space, while numbers are placed end to end, one after another. Thus a kind of infinite and eternal is created. It is not that there is anything which is infinite and eternal about it, but these finite objects multiply indefinitely. Thus it seems to me that the number which multiplies them is infinite."[5]

The infinite appears much more as a law of the mind which makes the calculation than as a property of the universe. In theory, everything is infinitely divisible and multipliable. In fact, for practical purposes the universe is infinite, because the mathematician can go on dividing and multiplying without reaching its limits. If anyone today works out the equation of the radius of curved space or the diameter of punctiform ether, the numbers obtained will not correspond to anything in the imagination of man and will overwhelm it. Apart from their mathematical value, they are unthinkable in concrete terms and in figures mean that the human being is lost between two abysses.

This perception provides a firm starting-point for Pascal's

4 *G.E.*, IX, p. 220.   5 Laf. 347: Br. 121.

meditation: "This is as far as innate knowledge takes us. If it is not true, there is no truth in man."[6] He clings to this hard saying. He wants the atheist to consider it "seriously and at leisure", to chew it over, to spend his time "contemplating [it] in silence". "He will tremble at the sight of these marvels."[7]

From this break with the intelligent, ordered, comprehensible and measured world of the Ancients and the middle ages, from this penetration into a monstrous universe which no longer has anything reassuring about it, Pascal draws his first conclusion, the definition of man: "A void in comparison with the infinite, a whole in comparison with the void, a middle term between nothing and all."[8] What a *trouvaille* this formula turns out to be: "a middle term between nothing and all", and it is amusing to see how Havet protests in the name of good sense.[9] In the eyes of Pascal it is sufficient to situate man physically for him to appear a mysterious hybrid: "Infinitely far from grasping the extremes, the end of things and their origins are completely hidden from him in impenetrable mystery; he is equally incapable of seeing the void whence he comes and the infinite in which he is engulfed."[10]

That is a serious situation. The evidence of mystery has been translated into a formula. All the learned men who boast that they have discovered the secret of the world see the infinite slamming the door in their faces. And three centuries of intense scientific effort and astonishing discoveries have simply reinforced Pascal's proposition. The learned subscribe to his conclusion and, as they themselves are very well aware, do not attempt anything more than "to catch a glimpse of the middle of things, in an eternal despair of ever knowing their origin or their end."[11]

Does this mean, then, that man will be able to codify and delimit an exhaustive knowledge of the phenomena which are within his comprehension, construct a science of beings which are finite like himself? He will not be able to do so any longer. The infinite, which a short time ago was described as being at the extremities of the universe, now insinuates itself into the mind of

[6] Laf. 390: Br. 72 (passage deleted in both).   [7] *Id.*   [8] *Id.*
[9] "In nature there is no infinitely small which is a void, for the void does not exist" (*Pensées de Pascal*, 2nd ed., Paris, 1866, I, p. 14).
[10] Laf. 390: Br. 72.   [11] *Ibid.*

man. The sciences that deal with finite objects are "infinite in the range of their researches".[12] We shall never exhaust all the implications of the least experience. The scientist deduces a law which can never reach the ultimate reality of things any more than the name of a town suggests its image to someone who has never been there. "We distinguish grapes from other fruits and among grapes, muscatels, then Condrieu, then Desargues, and then this cutting. Is that all? Has it ever produced two bunches alike? . . ."[13] "A town and a stretch of country, when seen from afar, are a town and a stretch of country, but as we draw near we see houses, trees, tiles, leaves, grass, ants, the legs of ants, and so on to infinity. All of it is included in the term country."[14]

As for man himself: "Why is my knowledge limited? My height? My span of life to a hundred rather than to a thousand years? What was nature's reason for making me like that, for choosing this number rather than that, because out of the infinity of numbers that exist there is no reason for choosing one rather than another because no one of them is more tempting than another?"[15]

If this is the position with the objects of experience, it is the same with the sciences which develop outside our experience: "Who can doubt that geometry, for example, has an infinity of infinites of problems which await solutions?" That, one might venture to say, is infinity filled to the brim. Man reaches it in his own creations which transcend him. Pascal never ceased to probe and explain this fertile and original train of thought. Mathematics, physics, philosophy, psychology, all the sciences are infinite "in the number and subtlety of their principles" as well as in the number of their conclusions. "Our intelligence", he concludes, "occupies the same position in the realm of intelligible things as our body in the realm of nature."

This gives us a better idea of the role played by the heart in Pascal's thought. It is the power of grasping in a flash the first principles on which reasoning is founded, of stopping the endless chain of doubts and deductions, of finding a "solid basis" in a world in which reasoning and experiment are endowed like space

[12] Laf. 390: Br. 72.
[13] Laf. 983: Br. 114.
[14] Laf. 113: Br. 115.
[15] Laf. 385: Br. 208.

and time with a coefficient of infinite divisibility and multiplicity.

What is still more serious than the infinity of the world and the sciences is the perpetual movement of our stream of consciousness. Pascal did more than anticipate the analysis of Bergson. He depicts a world which is in a continual state of flux. "Nothing stops for us."[16] Before our eyes the universe emerges at every moment from the void in order to soar towards the infinite. Pascal speaks of the "astonishing processes" of things. It is true that he somewhere contrasts the fixity of the world with our duration in it: "The eternity of things in themselves or in God must still be a source of astonishment in our little life. The fixed and unchanging immobility of nature compared with the changes continually taking place in ourselves ought to produce on us the same effect."[17] But he struck out this sentence. In our efforts to solidify the world of appearances, we are always dupes: "We burn with the desire to find a stable position, a solid base for building a tower which will rise to infinity; but our entire foundations crack; the earth opens like a vast abyss. Therefore, let us not look for security and stability. Our reason is always cheated by deceitful appearances; nothing can stabilize the finite between two infinites which enclose it and fly from it."[18]

This last sentence must be taken literally. We are imprisoned in a world which is constantly shifting. It is the flux of "fragile things passing, as they are swept away by the current".[19] And we slip away with them.

The final consequences of the infinity of the world which according to Pascal prevents our mind from embracing the whole of reality, whether inside or outside us, whether applying to matter or to man, and the multiple reactions of phenomena on one another: "As all things are caused and causing, supported and supporting, mediate and immediate, and all held together by a natural and imperceptible link which joins the most distant and diverse, I am convinced that it is impossible to know the parts

[16] Laf. 390: Br. 72.   [17] *Id.*
[18] *Id.*   [19] Laf. 696: Br. 458.

without knowing the whole, any more than we can know the whole without the parts."[20]

In another place Pascal states even more succinctly the imperceptible link which joins the different parts of the universe to one another: "A stone can change the whole surface of the sea."[21]

In short, apart from the infinity of the physical and psychological worlds there is, according to Pascal, a "moral infinite". Observing that the Bible is intended for people of all social classes, he adds: "Nature seems to have accomplished the same result with its two infinites, natural and moral: for there will always be higher and lower, more and less astute, people who are more elated and more wretched."[22] Human organs, he remarks, "are odd, fickle."[23] We can go up and down infinite scales: "Chance provides us with thoughts, and chance obliterates them. . . ."[24]

The moral infinite forbids extremes; it progresses in opposing directions, and man finds himself torn asunder. "When we try to push virtues to extremes in either direction, vices appear which insinuate themselves imperceptibly into them; by invisible ways in the direction of the small infinite; and a swarm of vices from the direction of the great infinite, with the result that we are lost among the vices and no longer see the virtues."[25]

In fact, one of the moral consequences of the meditation on the two infinites in all the different orders is that man must avoid excess of every kind. What do his social position, his higher or lower degree of learning matter? He is a little better off and sees things from a greater height. But what does it amount to in face of the infinite? The first lesson we must learn is the need for great detachment, a perfect indifference towards the finite, and an attitude of enlightened prudence towards mortal excesses. Excess is the enemy of the good. Man goes wrong in all orders, even in the moral order, if he relies on his own strength to reach the infinite.

But cannot the infinite descend to the level of man? Would man dare to impose limitations on the action or being of the infinite God? In his driest tone Pascal teaches the atheist a lesson in

[20] Laf. 390: Br. 72.   [21] Laf. 749: Br. 505.   [22] Laf. 260: Br. 532.
[23] Laf. 103: Br. 111.   [24] Laf. 952: Br. 370.   [25] Laf. 943: Br. 357.

humility: " 'Do you think that it is impossible for God to be infinite
and indivisible?' 'Yes.' 'Then I will try to show you something
that is infinite and indivisible. It is a point moving everywhere at
an infinite speed. For it is one wherever it is.'" (Einstein would
translate this by saying that a point moving at a greater speed than
light would be present everywhere in the world.) " 'May this
effect of nature, which previously seemed impossible to you
[Pascal continues] make you realize that there might be others
which you do not yet know. Do not assume that after your
apprenticeship there is nothing left for you to learn.' "[26]

Pascal is obviously giving an example simply to show how the
infinite, when it makes an irruption somewhere, turns the rules
of logic, which are designed for a measurable world, inside out.
Voltaire naturally missed the point completely. He gives these
comments in a footnote to the thought: "It contains four things
which are palpably false: (1) that a mathematical point can exist
in isolation; (2) that it can move to right and left at the same time;
(3) that it can move at an infinite speed, for there is no speed so
great that it cannot be increased; (4) that it is completely whole
everywhere."[27]

As soon as it was a question of the infinite or poetry, mysticism
or moral delicacy, Voltaire lost the thread of his conversation with
Pascal. He understood no better than a blind man would if somebody talked to him about red and green.

But Pascal was addressing himself to an atheist with an adequate
knowledge of geometry. His arguments carry weight. His genius
foresaw the partial eclipse of the discursive reason that we have
witnessed during the past century. The man without God appears
isolated in a universe which has lost its proportions. The splendid
burst of optimism of the Renaissance and the eighteenth century
collapse before the spectacle of an empty, inhuman world. The
divine and beneficent watchmaker dreamed of by Voltaire, who
made man a present of pleasure, does not exist any more than
Descartes's metaphysical God. In fact, outside Christian faith
modern man only discovers for himself in the world an absurd

[26] Laf. 344: Br. 231.
[27] Voltaire, *Remarques sur les Pensées de M. Pascal*, Oeuvres, Ed. Beuchot,
Paris, 1829, Vol. XXXVI, p. 84.

fate which ends with the void. He may make the statements which Pascal is far from accepting, but which he puts into his mouth:

> I do not know who placed me in the world, what the world is, what I myself am; I am in a state of terrible ignorance about everything; I do not know what my body is, what my senses are, what my soul is or the very organ that thinks what I am saying, which reflects on everything and on itself, and does not know itself any more' than the rest of me. I see the terrifying spaces of the universe which imprison me, and I find myself planted in a tiny corner of this vast space without my knowing why I happen to be here rather than in some other place. . . . I see only infinities on all sides which enclose me like an atom and like a shadow which only lasts for a second that will not return. . . . Just as I do not know whence I came, so I do not know whither I am going.[28]

It is the atheist and not Pascal who cries out: "The eternal silence of these infinite spaces terrifies me."[29] It is he, too, who declares: "It is a horrible sensation to feel that everything we possess is slipping away."[30] He who says: "What must I do? I see everywhere nothing but obscurities. Am I to believe that I am nothing? Am I to believe that I am God? All things change and succeed one another."[31]

According to Pascal, the meditation on the infinite at the beginning of the *Pensées* assumes a unique importance. It leads the atheist to admit the existence of the irrational and of mystery.

What is more, the infinity of the world is, in the order of bodies and space, the closest symbol of what are, in the moral order, spiritual realities. The contemplation of the infinity of greatness and smallness is an admirable exercise for anyone who wants an insight into what a person is talking about when he speaks of God and to avoid unreasonableness through trying to be too rational. A look at the infinite is a look at the signature of God in the universe, a look at what with the exception of thought most closely resembles the divine greatness and the divine obscurity. It is a necessary prelude to the examination of faith.

[28] Laf. 11: Br. 194.   [29] Laf. 393: Br. 206.   [30] Laf. 152: Br. 212.
[31] Laf. 25: Br. 227.

CHAPTER VI

The Wager

THE meditation on the infinite has driven the atheist into agnosticism. The wager is a whole cluster of arguments designed to force the agnostic to live to all intents and purposes in conformity with Christian morality. That is all. It is frankly absurd to try to turn it into an argument intended to prove the existence of God. Pascal was too exacting, had too high an opinion of intellectual probity to have suggested such a piece of mathematical juggling. "Our soul", he writes, "is tossed into the body where it finds number, time, dimensions. It argues about them, calls them nature or necessity, and cannot believe in anything else."[1]

Now, as we have seen, number is infinite; time and space can be multiplied by this infinite number. And the infinity of the physical world alone is sufficient in itself to annihilate us. Without understanding it, all we know is that it exists.

How will it be with the infinite God whose existence is posited by Christianity? He escapes verification in the same way as infinite number. Pascal does not deny that in theory the atheist can arrive at the existence of the philosophical God of Descartes, but for the moment it is outside his perspective. He is concerned with the God of Christians whose existence is bound up with a supernatural order. This God cannot be reached by reason alone. "Reason can determine nothing: there is an infinite chaos which divides us."[2] It is not only the chaos of the infinity of the physical world; it is "the infinitely more infinite distance between minds and charity".[3] Now "a coin is being spun at the extreme point of this infinite distance which will turn up heads or tails"—heads or

---

[1] Laf. 343: Br. 233. [2] *Id.* [3] Laf. 585: Br. 793.

tails we say, meaning that the Christian God either exists or he does not exist for us at death, which is the only problem that concerns us. "What is your bet? If you rely on [pure] reason, you cannot settle for either, or defend either position."[4]

It must be clearly understood that by following Pascal in his observations on the infinite, the agnostic has lost all rational objection to the existence of the Christian God; in this respect he differs from the atheist. He is in the dark. "Nature offers me nothing that is not a source of doubt and anxiety. If I saw nothing in it which was a sign of the Divinity, I should answer in the negative; if I saw everywhere the signs of a Creator, I should live at peace in the faith. But seeing too much for denial and too little for certainty, I am in a state which inspires pity."[5]

It is clearly the agnostic and neither the Christian nor Pascal who sees in faith a wager on the unknowable.

"Do not therefore accuse those who have made their choice of bad faith because you know nothing about it." "No, I do not blame them for their choice [replies the agnostic], but for making a choice at all." It is always a mistake to choose. "The right course is not to wager."[6]

When he has reached this point in the discussion, Pascal aims not at making the existence of God depend upon a game of chance, but at inducing the unbeliever to take a decisive step which will put him in a position to perceive the proofs of the faith. If you act as though God existed, it does not mean that you have the faith (if this attitude were maintained it would be nothing but a caricature of faith, a form of religious agnosticism which Pascal would reject with horror), but it is an indispensable preliminary in preparing yourself for the faith and for studying the proofs. For the unbeliever is imprisoned in a vicious circle. On the one hand, his egoism prevents him from perceiving the force of the proofs of the existence of the Christian God, but on the other, his ignorance of the Christian God prevents him from ridding himself of his egoism and his passions. Pascal will try to break down this egoism by using it to produce not a new conviction, but a practical approach, the opening up of a soul which will allow an inrush of faith.

[4] Laf. 343: Br. 233.   [5] Laf. 13: Br. 229.   [6] Laf. 343: Br. 233.

Since he has become an agnostic, the unbeliever no longer accuses faith of absurdity, but considers that it is to blame in so far as it comes to a decision about the unknowable. To be sure, replies Pascal, "you have to wager; you are not a free agent; you are committed."[7] Life involves choice. If you refuse to act as though the Christian God exists, you are acting as though he did not exist. You think like an agnostic, but live like an atheist. Now, in the case of the pure agnostic, the infinite God of whom we are speaking has one chance in two of existing. What will happen on the death of the Christian and the atheist?

If God does not exist the atheist will have gained nothing because after his death he will disappear into the void and his life will be as though it had never been. The Christian will have lost nothing because he will no longer even be able to remember the pleasures which he has foregone.

If God exists the atheist will be deprived of him for ever, which will be an infinite loss. The Christian, on the contrary, will be united to him for ever, which will be to gain the infinite. By deciding provisionally to live as though God existed, the agnostic has nothing to lose and everything to gain.

In this very simple form the wager reminds us of the reply attributed to the Abbé Mugnier. An unbeliever said to him with a malicious smile:

"Monsieur l'Abbé, you will be disappointed after your death if God doesn't exist."

"And what about you, if he does exist?" retorted the Abbé.[8]

As long as Pascal keeps to the fundamental rule of his game, which consists of sticking to the rigid principles of agnosticism and giving to the existence of God one chance in two, his calculations emerge triumphantly. Should we not be wrong, for example, if we refused to risk 5,000 francs when there was one chance in two of winning a million? Who would refuse to take the risk? It would have been even more stupid to refuse to risk one franc to gain a billion when the odds were even. What are we to say when the prize is the infinite, when the value of what we stand to win exceeds anything we can imagine? The value of the

[7] Laf. 343: Br. 233.
[8] The same *boutade* is mentioned by F. Droz, *op. cit.*, p. 12.

stake is reduced by comparison to nothing. We risk a *sou* to win billions of billions. We should feel that it was no longer gambling, and in his triumph Pascal asserts that "our argument is of overwhelming force when the finite must be staked in a game in which there are even chances of winning and losing, and the infinite is the prize".[9]

Up to this point, provided that you accept the rules of the game and the state of mind of the people who are taking part in the dialogue, it is difficult to see what objections can be brought against Pascal. But in a passage written in an elliptical style, he tried to go further and modify something that was fundamental to his argument: the equal chances of loss and gain. He declares that, even if there were an infinite number of chances of losing, it would still be right to wager because there were an infinite number of chances of winning. What you risk is nothing in comparison with what you may win. The introduction of the infinite as a stake makes every bet reasonable provided that there is at least one chance of winning.

This is plainly false. And if it had to be understood in that sense, Pascal's thought would contain its own refutation. The one chance of winning is reduced to nothing in comparison with the infinite number of chances of losing. Any reasonable man would refuse, on such conditions, to wager even a single franc in order to win a million because he would feel that for practical purposes he was bound to lose. That is the reason why the State is certain to win in the National Lottery. It is Fontenelle's objection. According to Lachelier's summary:

He puts on the stage a Chinaman whom a missionary is trying to convert by showing him what a poor thing our personal life is and the infinite greatness of the happiness to come. But, replies the Chinaman, it is as though you invited me to wager a piastre against the Chinese Empire on condition that I should only win if a child who was amusing himself by putting in their places the twenty-six letters of the alphabet without knowing them put them in their right order at the first attempt. Now according to Fontenelle, the Chinese Empire is worth a hundred billion piastres; but the emperor who wagers it against one piastre has only one chance of losing

[9] Laf. 343: Br. 233.

against a number of chances of winning which can be represented by the figure 13 followed by thirty-two noughts. . . . The Emperor of China's stake is thirteen thousand billion billion times higher than that of his opponent.[10]

In short, to bet in such conditions spells certain loss. In reality, it seems that in this obscure passage Pascal meant to say that by risking his life in order to gain another and infinitely happy life, the two infinites cancelled out: that of the chances of losing and that of the happy life; that what the wager offered was reduced mathematically to risking our life for another similar but completely happy life with even chances of winning. The proportion of chances is essential from the beginning of the wager to the end. It is this that turns Fontenelle's objections into so much sophistry. It alone expresses the complete uncertainty of the agnostic. It is confirmed by an interesting correction in the manuscript. Pascal had begun by writing "*as much chance of winning against a finite number of chances of losing*".

The wager does not end there. Pascal went further. He thought that when betting our stake would be returned to us during the session and before the result was known. What has the agnostic risked by wagering for God? Has he had to accept instant death? Not at all. Risking his life means no more than abandoning "poisonous pleasures, fame, lust". Is it really a loss? At most it is an exchange because the agnostic has bartered these false values not only against one chance in two of winning an infinity of lives which are infinitely blessed, but also against the other material worldly goods: "You will be faithful, honest, humble, grateful, beneficent, genuine, a true friend." God will reward you. "You will gain in this life", adds Pascal.[11] A wager in favour of God does not mean buying a lottery ticket; it means living a life of perfection; staking one's life in order to give the absolute every chance of revealing itself.

To this the other party might reply that he already possesses these goods, that he is upright, sincere and genuine. But that

---

[10] *Oeuvres de Jules Lachelier* (Paris, 1933), II, p. 61. Lachelier's notes "Sur le pari de Pascal" are with those of Père Valensin in *Balthazar* (Paris, 1934), the best on the subject.
[11] Laf. 343: Br. 233.

simply shows that he had already wagered in favour of God. Let him not halt on the way. The moral infinite is opening up before him. Let him go to meet it. Little by little he will come to see it. Pascal guarantees that he has ceased to gamble on the uncertain. He will discover that the chances of losing are nil, that is to say, that there is no possible doubt about the existence of the Christian God. "You will find that you have gambled on something that is certain, infinite and has cost you nothing."[12] You will see that, from a practical point of view, we do not reach this degree of certainty by the study of metaphysics, but by a moral effort. "Try therefore to convince yourself not by multiplying the proofs of the existence of God, but by overcoming your passions."[13]

> I should soon have given up pleasure, they say, if I had had the faith.
> But I tell you: You would soon have had the faith if you had given up pleasure.
> Now it is up to you to begin. If I could, I would give you faith; I cannot do so and for that reason I cannot test the truth of what you are saying; but you can very well give up pleasure and test the truth of what I am saying.[14]

For faith is not a matter of reasoning, but of intuition of the highest intelligence which is known as the heart and whose exercise is only possible through an effort of supernatural charity.

The agnostic has understood the nature of faith perfectly clearly. He knows that for the true Christian it is not a matter of a chancy bet, but a certainty which is as absolute as that of his own existence and completely disinterested. In short, it is an act of love. The unbeliever desires it without being able to attain it. "I am made in such a way", he admits, "that I cannot believe."[15]

This was the admission for which Pascal was waiting. The whole aim of the *wager* was to provoke this inadvertent, this despairing appeal. In order to achieve it, Pascal wanted to prove to his interlocutor by means of a mathematical formula that agnosticism, and still more atheism, are forms of suicide and of a plunge into the void, that his illusions prevent him from seeing clearly, make him impervious to the proofs of faith. Pascal was out to break a

---

[12] Laf. 350: Br. 240.   [13] *Ibid.*   [14] *Ibid.*   [15] Laf. 343: Br. 233.

misplaced pride, a concern for "what people would think", the secret pride of the man who arrogates to himself the right to hate the infinite God like an accused person before the tribunal of reason. He wanted to make an end, as though he had foreseen it, of the frivolity of a Renan and his countless followers.

The agnostic claims that he is incapable of making an act of faith. "Take holy water, have masses said," Pascal retorts brutally. "That will naturally make you inclined to believe and will stupefy you."[16] You may fly off the handle, dumbfounded by the cynicism of the suggestion, but what a blinding beam of light has been turned upon the most secret workings of the human soul. "Holy water and masses"—it sounds as though he said it to shock the Protestants. He has no use for a religion which is supposed to be "pure" or wholly spiritual.

"That will stupefy you." It is quite true: he himself borrows the language of the agnostic. He forestalls Voltaire and the people who scorn the externals of religious worship: crosses, chasubles, holy water, masses, statues of St Anthony. Do the externals of the faith shock you? Do you think they are stupid? Ought we to be cunning with the infinite? Is it less stupid to drink water than to put our fingers into it? To play tennis, go hunting and be present at His Majesty's *petit lever*, than to go to mass? With faith, as with everything else, even with love, man is neither angel nor beast, and whoever tries to play the angel ends by playing the beast. The stupidest person of all is the one who imagines that he can escape the human lot. Let us muzzle the beast by using its own weapons against it and perhaps we shall get used to the angel. The man who manages to overcome self-esteem will try to win over the Infinite by dipping his fingers into a holy water stoup.

We cannot fail to admire the harsh and brutal manner in which the argument of the wager is conducted by Pascal. Some people like to be treated with more consideration and feel that they are being badgered. The hint of triumph that we detect in Pascal's voice gets on their nerves. We have to make our choice; Pascal is no "wet". There is nothing unctuous or timid or soft about his manner. He does not possess Fénelon's exquisite courtesy or the

[16] Laf. 343: Br. 233.

art of turning Christianity into the supreme ornament of a distinguished life. He goes full tilt, enjoys giving scandal and sometimes bursts out laughing.

But there are people who enjoy the exhibition of brutal strength in which they discern a whole tradition of Catholic writers who are determined to present the truth crudely with all its tears and resistance. Salvation lies in the wound: the deadly abscess must be uncovered. God loathes the lukewarm, and death is a nasty story which is well worth thinking about for ten minutes or so. In one sense Pascal is both the Léon Bloy and the Bernanos of the seventeenth century. Without the insults, to be sure, but he also thrusts man without the slightest compunction and with both hands into the middle of the spiritual battle with the infinite: a cruel battle with sweat and tears. In dialogue form the wager is the history of a decisive step by the wretched waverer in the direction of the tragic game in which he goes under in order to rise again. It is crossing the frontiers of a Kingdom where amid the flashes of lightning on Sinai the God of blood and thunder speaks.

For the wager opens the way to something else. The gamble is not sufficient in itself; we must look at the other side of the cards. The atheist is ready. Pascal at last opens his Bible.

CHAPTER VII

The Bible[1]

"CAN'T I see the other side of the cards?" asked the atheist.[2] "We must look at it closely; we must produce the documents."[3]

"We must be sincere," writes Pascal when he reaches the crucial stage of the Apology: the examination of the value and meaning of the Bible.[4]

He was sincere. He did produce the documents. He tried to look at everything closely. He read a great deal, took notes on the *Pugio Fidei*, a large volume by a Dominican devoted to the exegesis of the rabbis. He studied and compared the different Greek and Latin versions of the Bible. Like Bossuet at the end of his life, it seems that he even attempted to learn Hebrew. And he put down in his notes the results which were original and almost staggering.

In order to be fair, we must ask about his equipment as an historian and his methods of exegesis. What did the people whom he frequented, the people at Port-Royal, know about the Old Testament?

Anyone who feels like making some interesting discoveries and judging the sacred hermeneutic of Pascal's friends only needs to open the fourth volume of Lemaistre de Sacy's folio Bible. So far as typography, illustrations, the quality of the paper and binding are concerned, it is a majestic looking tome. It was published in 1717, fifty-five years after Pascal's death, but it is a faithful

---

[1] On Pascal and the Bible, in addition to the thesis by J. Lhermet, *Pascal et la Bible*, see M.-J. Lagrange, "Pascal et les prophéties messianiques" in *Revue Biblique*, 1906, pp. 533–60; E. Jovy, *op. cit.*, VIII, pp. 152–94: "Pascal et la Bible", "Pascal exégète et philologue"; A.-M. Dubarle, "Pascal et l'interprétation de l'Écriture" in *Les Sciences Philosophiques et Théologiques*, 1941, pp. 346–79, and "Quelques Allusions Scripturales des *Pensées* de Pascal", *ibid.*, pp. 84–95.
[2] Laf. 343: Br. 233.   [3] Laf. 421: Br. 593.   [4] Laf. 425: Br. 590.

reflection of the ideas of the master who taught him about the Bible.

When we open the fourth volume devoted not to the translation of the text, but to history, sacred chronology, the geography of the East, the language and religious institutions of the Jews, we have the feeling that we must be dreaming. Six magnificent maps, due to the talent of Sieur Moullart Sanson, geographer-in-ordinary to the King, unfold. The first is a map of the earthly Paradise. It is round with a diameter of 20,000 yards. Bordered by trees, adorned by little mountains and an almost square lake, it lies to the east of a country named Ethiopia and to the north of another called Assyria, between two shores which we assume are more or less those of the Hellespont and the Caspian Sea. The map of Palestine is no less strange. We should take it today for the drawing of an eight-year-old child. The coastline buckles and flattens, changes from one map to another. Before Abraham the Black Sea did not exist. As for Sinai, on the same map the geographer gives it two very different shapes, each as inconsequent as the other. In short, we find the same fantastic cartographical blunders as in Olivetan's sixteenth-century Bible which makes Italy look like a squashed acorn.

Although less obvious, the surprises that sacred chronology has in store for us are no less entertaining. The history of the world is divided into seven ages. God created the heavens and the angels on 23rd October 4004 B.C. Adam and Eve were brought into the earthly Paradise on 30th October. Adam knew Lamech for fifty-six years and the antediluvian patriarchs lived altogether in one family for several centuries. The Flood occurred in year 1656 of the history of the world. Noah was born in the lifetime of Enos, Canaan, Malaleel, Jared, Methuselah and Lamech. In short, the authors of the book took the Bible absolutely literally as though it were a technical history. They extracted from it a rigid chronology which they expounded with disarming candour. Whether they are discussing currency or the form of cherubim, the complete, absolute and unique authenticity of Moses' authorship of the Pentateuch, the attribution of the authorship of the books of the Bible to those whose names they bear, not the faintest doubt assails them. They regard the Bible not so much as containing a specifically religious revelation as being the book of the history of men, family memoirs written down day by day since Adam. Such, for that matter, was Bossuet's opinion. We plunge into a world radiating kindness, order and naïve security.

Now, Pascal subscribed to this view completely. Although he displayed such unjustified scepticism about Homer—"No one", he said, "supposed for a moment that Troy and Agamemnon had really existed any more than the golden apple"—he accepted without question the six ages of the world, the chronology of the Bible and the longevity of the patriarchs.[5] He even regards it as a valuable historical argument: "The Creation and the Flood are so close together that they almost seem to touch:"[6] He repeats to satiety that the Bible is "the oldest book in the world"[7] and that it contains "the most authentic history".[8] He was undoubtedly of the opinion that Hebrew was the language of the first men. He dismisses the histories of the Chinese and the Egyptians as myths. To believe the Chinese would be tantamount to calling Moses a liar, for "Sem, who saw Lamech, who saw Adam, also saw Jacob, who saw those who had seen Moses."[9] It was a choice between Moses and the Chinese and he gives his reasons for choosing Moses: "I only believe histories whose witnesses are ready to let themselves be torn to pieces."[10] Pascal read Genesis as he read a treatise on geometry with the naïveté of a man of the Middle Ages.

Things might have been different. It was only an accident which prevented Pascal from catching a glimpse of the truth, at any rate in so far as it related to the meaning and style of the Bible. The very year he died, a young ecclesiastical student, son of a blacksmith at Dieppe, entered the Oratory. He intended to study oriental languages, learnt Hebrew properly, made friends with a rabbi and carried out all the work that Pascal had hoped to undertake. His name was Richard Simon. In 1678 he published his *Histoire critique du Vieux Testament*. It was a very different book from the fourth volume of Lemaistre de Sacy's Bible. It was distinguished by prudence in matters of science, conscientiousness in matters of detail, and pertinent judgments. Richard Simon knew the Massoretic

5 Laf. 415: Br. 629.   6 Laf. 569: Br. 624.   7 Laf. 552: Br. 620.
8 Laf. 458: Br. 622.   9 Laf. 573: Br. 25.   10 Laf. 421: Br. 593.

Hebrew text, that of the Versions. He compared them carefully. This meant that he had all the necessary documents at hand. What is most striking is that in the critical examination of them he displayed precisely the same qualities that Pascal, in his treatises on physics, had recognized as being those of the scientist, the experimental worker. When we read him it seems as though we are reopening the Preface to the *Treatise on the Vacuum*. "We must never go against experience", he declares.[11] And in another place: "We should not allow ourselves to be prejudiced in favour of the ancient interpreters as though their Jewish exemplars were better merely because they were older. . . . It is necessary to examine with care all the different Readings of the Hebrew Text that the ancient Interpreters can provide; and then judge according to the rules of Criticism, without paying too much respect to antiquity, which are the best and which should be preferred; but this discernment requires a perfect knowledge of the Hebrew Language."[12]

And Richard Simon's results—for example, his observations on the first chapters of Genesis and the method of translating them— are pure masterpieces of exegesis. His ideas on chronology, the origins of the Hebrew language, the authenticity of the Pentateuch completely differ from Pascal's. They are almost the same as our own. He already senses the anonymity and pseudonymity of many of the books of the Old Testament, the role of the interpolators, the difference of literary genres. Following Rabbi Isaac Abravanel, he adopts the hypothesis of the scribes of Moses. "There are", he says, "an infinite number of repetitions of the same thing in the Pentateuch which are apparently not by Moses. . . . Moreover, I doubt whether we can attribute to Moses or the Public writers of his time the lack of order to be found in several places in the Pentateuch. . . . The diversity of style which is found in the books of Moses also seems proof that they are not all by the same author. . . ."[13] Speaking of some of the Sapiential books, he writes: "Some people have thought that the books of Job, Tobias and Judith were not so much history as books written in the manner

[11] R. Simon, *Histoire critique du Vieux Testament*. New ed. Rotterdam, 1685, p. 37.
[12] *Ibid.*, p. 111.   [13] *Ibid.*, pp. 33–9.

of parables and sacred fiction which have their usefulness."[14] Whereupon he concludes judiciously: "For the rest, whether a book is history or a simple parable, it is not on that account less true or less divine."[15] And we can find elsewhere in the *Histoire critique du Vieux Testament* a hundred other equally judicious observations.

Richard Simon agrees with Pascal only on one point: the obscurities of the Bible of which he speaks continually in the *Histoire critique*, so much so that the title of Book III reads: "In which the author deals with the manner of translating the Bible correctly and in which he shows at the same time how obscure Scripture is." As for Pascal, he declares bluntly: "I agree that [Scripture] has obscurities which are as odd as Mahomet's."[16] But Pascal and Simon would cease to agree as soon as it came to defining what constituted the obscurities. For Simon they were the result of the time that had elapsed between the period of the sacred writers and our own, of the mistakes of copyists, of the forms of biblical style, above all of the precise meaning of rare or difficult Hebrew words, of the grammatical value of particles and the tenses of verbs. In his opinion the texts were perfectly clear for the contemporaries of the sacred writers.

For Pascal the reasons were different. He was shocked by the old Semitic content of the Bible: ritual gestures like circumcision and promises of military victories made by the Prophets. The whole of the political, human and bloody aspect of the cult of Jahveh scandalized him no less than the nymphs of the Mohammedan paradise in the Koran. And if Richard Simon patiently attempts to clarify the difficulties of the text of the Bible, at one swoop Pascal tries to reduce the religious obscurities and does so by the theory that it was a code. "The Old Testament", he proclaims, "is a cipher."[17] We must discover the key.

What are the proofs of the existence of the cipher? First, the Bible itself says so: the rabbis who know what they are talking about all agree. In short, the study of the text convinces us. We find side by side "obscure" and "carnal" pages while others are clear and "angelic".

[14] *Ibid.*, p. 58.   [15] *Ibid.*   [16] Laf. 412: Br. 598.   [17] Laf. 510: Br. 691.

According to Pascal therefore we should set about it as though we were dealing with a message in code.[18]

You proceed from the known to the unknown, from signs whose meaning is definite to those whose meaning has to be discovered. It will be observed that some Biblical discourses are equivocal and that certain words are used in place of others: the law, sacrifices, circumcision, manna, relationship with Abraham, the promised land, monarchy, the levitical priesthood are expressions with a "twofold meaning" which stand for grace, deliverance from sin, the Eucharist, the spiritual reign of the Messiah. They are "figures".

In order to develop these "figures" or symbols, which reintroduce the essential of the New Testament into the Old, Pascal follows two masters: St Augustine and Jansen, who are themselves the defenders of an allegorical interpretation put forward by the most illustrious of the Fathers of the Church: Origen, Ambrose, Jerome. It is a method which goes back to the New Testament and beyond to the rabbinical tradition which was anterior to Christianity, and was developed chiefly in Egypt under Philo of Alexandria. In the middle ages all the doctors indulged in allegorical interpretations. And in our own time Claudel, who applied to the study of the Bible the symbolist principles of Mallarmé, tried with the assistance of some of the theologians to continue this noble line in spite of the triumph of historical exegesis within the Church.

Pascal, to be sure, did not adopt all the absurdities of the rabbis who found as many as seventy-two different meanings in Scripture. He did not possess the learned, amusing and unbridled imagination of Claudel. He remains balanced and reasonable, concedes that certain images "seem to be too fine spun" and announces that he will speak "against those who use too many symbols".[19] But in essentials he sticks to his discovery. He believes that it will enable him to reconcile all the contradictions in the text. He has the reassuring impression of possessing the key to the code. "Once the mystery has been revealed, it is impossible not to see it."[20]

---

[18] "An unknown language can be deciphered" (Laf. 989: Br. 45).
[19] Laf. 411: Br. 650; Laf. 488: Br. 649.   [20] Laf. 501: Br. 680.

Thus from the first line of Genesis until the last line of the last book, the Old Testament teaches nothing but the spiritual and mystical theology of the Church, the existence of the God of charity and renunciation, the coming of the spiritual Messiah who will deliver souls: "Moses", he writes, "was the first to teach the doctrines of the Trinity, original sin, the Messiah."[21] And Pascal concludes with his golden rule: "All that does not tend towards charity is symbolical. The sole object of Scripture is charity."[22]

It remains to explain the reasons for the existence of the code. Why was not God clear from one end of his message to the other? Why these Mohammedan obscurities? Why this marked taste for worldly goods which seems to emerge from the Bible, the slaughter, the stench of blood that we breathe in it, the whole of the "carnal" side of Scripture? They are traps, ambushes set to catch the human passions which God seems to encourage. What! Could God have intended to deceive individual men? Yes, replies Pascal without hesitation, and for two reasons. If God has strewn the Bible with "rat traps", it is because he is the hidden God: *Deus absconditus*, he whom we must seek patiently. It is up to us to find him. The Bible like the universe is a mixture of light and shadow. We must love the light in order to make the shadow disappear. God can only deceive those who allow themselves to be caught by their taste for earthly things. In the promises of the Old Testament "each of us discovers what lies in the depths of his heart; temporal and spiritual blessings, God or creatures".[23] His interpretation is like the crucial test of our most secret desires.

The second reason for the existence of the code of the Bible was the necessity to entrust it to impartial witnesses. By the game of double promises, which is something of supreme skill, God made the most "carnal" people who exist the repository of his spiritual message. In face of the promises of universal domination which they thought had been made to them, the "greedy", "gross" Jewish people displayed an "exceptional regard for their prophets" and became the witnesses "least likely to favour us . . . and

[21] Laf. 592: Br. 752.   [22] Laf. 504: Br. 670.   [23] Laf. 519: Br. 675.

showed themselves the most scrupulous and zealous that can be described".[24]

Pascal's thesis holds together. There is no crack in the system. All the objections are foreseen provided that we confine ourselves to the subject of the Bible, to the knowledge that he possessed, to what was to be found in Lemaistre de Sacy's folio edition.

Obviously he is wrong. Pascal's chronology is false. The Bible is not obscure in the sense that he intended. It is not in code. It is not true that everything not related to charity is symbolical. And all these symbols are, as Richard Simon happily expressed it, "applications [rather] than explanations".[25] Scripture is clear; its obscurities are due to our ignorance of the past. They cannot be resolved by Pascal's arbitrary principles. What he lacked—he cannot be blamed for it—was a knowledge of the history of the text, the language and the style of the Bible. He died fifteen years too soon to be a pupil of Richard Simon's. For once through lack of the necessary data he turned his back on experiment and flung himself into the *a priori*.

Nevertheless, not everything is lost in the unfinished cathedral represented by the fragments of exegesis that we find in the *Pensées*. On the contrary, if we pull down the artificial scaffolding of the theory of symbols, we find the votive chapels dedicated to the Prophets, the Evangelists and Jesus Christ. And here Pascal is in full possession of his powers again. He is no longer at grips with problems where the real unknown quantities and the rudiments of a solution were lacking. Prophecy, sanctity and the redemption of man were things that he experienced passionately. He breathes in the clarity of Scripture. His genius shines once more. He forgets about his rabbinical and Claudelian games with images, traps and figures in order to become once more an incomparable reader of the Bible.

When this happens, he is far above Richard Simon. For in spite of his critical genius Richard Simon got no further than the prolegomenal reading of the Bible; he cleared the ground, laid the foundations, but did not go beyond that. In order to understand the Prophets we must possess something of the prophetic

[24] Laf. 518: Br. 571.   [25] *Histoire critique* . . . , p. 405.

spirit ourselves, feel their poetry like a call, share their indignation, join in their prayers. Jahveh is still there. It is time to stop
treating the sacred books like dead letters. We must not think
that the significance of the human destinies whose course unfolds
before us in the Bible is exhausted by history. We must read the
Bible as Péguy read *Antigone* or *Polyeucte*, linking each section to
its future echoes, seeing it as part of the vast religious *élan* progress-
ing steadily along a path leading to Christianity in which all its
hidden powers come to fruition. That circumcision, the sign of a
blood alliance, is continued by the Last Supper, the Cross, the
Mass; that the ritual ablutions of Leviticus ended in baptism;
that the combined figures of David and the suffering Servant
of the Second Isaias culminate in Jesus Christ—these are true
symbols. There is no longer anything artificial or arbitrary.
The Old Testament prefigures the New as the acorn prefigures the
oak which emerges from it. Chart of a religion opening on to the
infinite; the infinite alone came to satisfy the ancient aspirations
to which it bore witness.

Pascal tried not merely to translate the Prophets into his warm,
beautiful, poetic and supple language, but to group the messianic
prophecies in clusters. He constructed them and made them
converge, he became their architect. And his work was impressive
in its results as we see it preserved in fragments in the Brunschvicg
edition of the *Pensées* numbered 713, 722 and 726.[26] In the autograph manuscript the texts, with the exception of the last which
only occurs in the Copy, are written out with particular care.
The lines are short, well written, and set in the middle of the
pages in columns with very occasional corrections.

Pascal himself retranslated extracts from the Prophets because
at that time no satisfactory translations existed: the Louvain
version had a sixteenth-century tang and Lemaistre de Sacy's was
still in preparation. The majority of the clergy and educated
people could read the Bible in Latin with ease. Now, Pascal's
translation stands apart from others owing to its perfection of
style. It is a fine measured prose without odd turns of phrase or
technical terms and much less servile in its handling of Hebraisms

[26] Laf. 664, 662, 661.

than Bossuet's translations. Pascal sometimes tightens up the style, suppresses repetitions, sacrifices something of its oriental suavity to French clarity. In short, instead of transcribing he translates.

Pascal's style was wonderfully adapted to that of the Bible. If he had known Hebrew and had had the time he might have become the official French translator of Scripture, have provided a classic French version, the equivalent of Luther's for Germany and of the Authorized Version in England. It would have saved us from the imposition of Lemaistre de Sacy's dull, slovenly, wordy translation, the barbarisms of Segond's version and the Abbé Crampon's pidgin version. Pascal would have done for the Bible what Amyot did for Plutarch.

The care with which Pascal translated and copied them out in his notes shows what importance he attached to the prophetic passages. They are the pivot of his whole *Apology*. In them the atheist hears the voice of the infinite God without parts whose greatness he began to sense in the meditations on the infinity of the world and the wager. God explains in his own words the origin of man's wretchedness and the reasons for his greatness. He promises forgiveness and the Redeemer. All the characters in Scripture point towards Jesus Christ "whom the two Testaments regard, the Old as its hope, the New as its model, both as their centre".[27] Truly when it was a matter not of symbols, but of prophecies promulgated with complete clarity and of the eternal message of the Bible, the sense of the supernatural which guided Pascal did not lead him astray and his religious genius opened the door wide to the profound meaning of the Scriptures.

[27] Laf. 600: Br. 740.

CHAPTER VIII

Jesus Christ

THE presence of Jesus Christ shines at the very heart of the *Pensées*. When he speaks of Jesus Pascal becomes lyrical: humble and radiant, tender and triumphant. "The *Pensées*," wrote Sainte-Beuve, "when looked at as a whole, are so clothed in light, so rigorous and forbidding from the outside, so tender and appealing from within, that they appear to me like an ark of cedar with seven folds which are covered with sheets of gold and impenetrable steel and yet at their very centre enclose naked, loving and joyful, the bleeding heart of the sacrificial Lamb."[1]

The overture of this poem to the glory of Jesus Christ is devoted to his human role in history. The atheist picks up the Gospels. Pascal intends to begin by making him feel their tone and style. The people of the seventeenth century who had been brought up on the secular literature—Greek and Latin—of Antiquity and were therefore imbued with the idea of eloquence were far removed in taste from the literary style of the Gospels. They were in general devout Christians, regarded the Gospels as sacred books and accepted them as such. So did Pascal, but in addition he was too fond of naturalness not to appreciate it in the perfect simplicity of word and gesture in the Gospels. "The style of the Gospels is admirable in many ways, among them the fact that they never use invective against the murderers and enemies of Jesus Christ . . ."[2] This simplicity appears pre-eminently in the words of Jesus: "Jesus Christ said things so simply that it seems that he did not think them; and yet so clearly that we see quite well that he did think them."[3] All the more so because the beauty of this naïve language, which is so far from striving after effect, contains

---

[1] *Port-Royal*, IV, pp. 270–1.   [2] Laf. 428: Br. 798.   [3] Laf. 586: Br. 797.

something that is infinitely greater: the moral grandeur of Jesus Christ: "Who taught the Evangelists the qualities which belong to a completely heroic soul to enable them to depict it so perfectly in Jesus Christ? Why were they weak during his agony? . . . They show him as capable of fear before the necessity of facing death had arisen, and afterwards completely steadfast."[4] "[Jesus] is fond of his relatives, but his charity is not confined within these limits; it extends to his enemies, then to the enemies of God."[5]

The moral perfection of Jesus owes nothing to the apathy of the Stoics: it remains human and moving.

Pascal really touches on a serious question here. Sainte-Beuve was right when he wrote: "Take the greatest of the modern anti-Christians . . . anyone who has *completely* misunderstood Jesus Christ, and look at him carefully: you will see that something is lacking either in mind or heart."[6] A sincere admiration for Jesus is the gulf that separates Renan from Voltaire. Voltaire, who was the idol of a frivolous century, scoffed at Jesus and Joan of Arc, treated Pascal as a madman and dismissed all poetry with a sneer. "A century of geese", as André Breton would say. On the other hand, in spite of his scepticism, Renan like Jean-Jacques Rousseau regarded Jesus as the moral hero of humanity. He respected and venerated him. In our own time it was possible for André Gide not to be a Christian: it was impossible for him to re-read some of the parables without tears. When they were in prison, Oscar Wilde and Dostoevsky were continually reading the New Testament. Aldous Huxley discovered in Jesus that childhood of the heart which is more precious than anything. In the sphere of pure philosophy, Bergson saw in him the perfect example of the mystical hero, the one who sounds the most effective appeal to a religion opening a window on to the infinite. Yes, an appreciation of the Gospels remains the touchstone of a certain delicacy of heart.

Obviously, Renan and his followers who have a profound respect for the Gospel, place Jesus among figures who are partly legendary. Pascal did not foresee this kind of sceptical admiration. Nevertheless, from time to time we come across brief observations in the *Pensées* which have a bearing on the matter:

[4] Laf. 593: Br. 800.   [5] Laf. 671: Br. 767.   [6] *Port-Royal*, IV, p. 270 note.

The Apostles were either deceived or deceivers; either is difficult
to accept because it is not possible to imagine that a man has been
raised from the dead.[7]

The hypothesis that the Apostles were frauds is absurd. Let us
follow it to its logical conclusion; let us imagine those twelve men
coming together after the death of Jesus Christ and conspiring to
say that he had risen from the dead. It would have been an attack on
all the powers. The heart of men is strangely prone to levity, to
change, to promises, to wealth. If a single one of them had denied
it under the influence of these seductions or more probably under
the pressure of imprisonment, torture and death, they would have
been lost. Follow that to its conclusion.[8]

Pascal would have elaborated these jottings with his customary
verve, his shrewd good sense. He would have turned the veracity
of the disciples into a problem of psychology. He was ignorant
of some of the difficulties of Biblical criticism, but he rose above
them because he was carrying on a dialogue with an honest man,
and in his opinion honesty was more important than erudition
when it came to judging questions that science left unanswered.
For in our own time Renan's *a priori* refusal to admit the possibility
of miracles must be rejected by anyone who accepts even the
hypothesis of the existence of the God of Christians.[9] A century
of strenuous work in the field of criticism has led to a vast extension
of our knowledge of the historical background of the Gospels and
shed fresh light on the circumstances in which they were written;
we are none the less still obliged to rely on "hindsight" when it
comes to making up our minds about the content: miracles, the
supernatural, the Resurrection.

Pascal saw very clearly that the common objection of his day,
as of our own, lay in the facility with which legends come into
being, in the existence of innumerable stories of marvels and
miracles. But, he said, "Instead of coming to the conclusion that
there are no genuine miracles because there are so many spurious
ones, we should argue that there are some genuine miracles because
there are so many spurious ones, that the only reason why there

---

[7] Laf. 599: Br. 800.   [8] Laf. 587: Br. 801.

[9] See pp. xcvi–xcviii of Renan's introduction to the standard edition of his
Vie de Jésus which are astonishing and unintentionally comic.

are spurious ones is that there are some genuine ones."[10] Chesterton expressed this more lightly: "A false ghost disproves the reality of ghosts exactly as much as a forged banknote disproves the existence of the Bank of England—if anything, it proves its existence."[11]

According to Pascal, the most significant of the miracles of Jesus was neither his Resurrection nor any of the miracles of healing, but the position and range of the Gospel, its inexplicable triumph in fulfilling the prophecies. It would be possible to contest the meaning he attributed to the visions of Daniel, and it would be right to do so. Two facts cannot be gainsaid: several centuries before the Christian era the Jews were permeated by messianic expectations and the religion of Jesus completely conquered the civilized world. It never ceased to be a matter of astonishment to Pascal and nothing today prevents us from sharing his astonishment.

The consonance of these two facts clarifies the paradox of the Gospel: the victory of Jesus by methods which were diametrically opposed to those of all the world conquerors. For there exists outside Christianity the case of another religious triumph—that of Islam. Pascal deals with the objection. For Mahomet's victory was achieved "by killing, that of Jesus by causing the deaths of his own followers . . . they are so opposed that if Mahomet, humanly speaking, chose the path of success, Jesus Christ, humanly speaking, chose that of death: and instead of concluding that, since Mahomet succeeded, Jesus Christ could have succeeded, we must say that, since Mahomet succeeded, Jesus Christ was bound to die."[12]

Pascal takes pleasure in insisting on the lowliness of Jesus' fate as a man. This disproportion between the life of Jesus and the grandiose position he occupies in human history is a source of satisfaction to him:

What man ever had greater fame? . . . And yet what man ever enjoyed his fame less? Of his thirty-three years, thirty were spent

[10] Laf. 478: Br. 818.   [11] *Orthodoxy* (London, 1909), pp. 281–2.
[12] Laf. 403: Br. 599.

without any public appearance. In three years he passed for an impostor; the priests and the leaders of the people rejected him; his friends and closest relations scorned him. Finally, he died, betrayed by one of his own disciples, denied by another, and deserted by them all. What share had he then in this fame? Never has a man had greater glory, never has a man suffered greater ignominy. ... [13]

Of all that is on earth, he only participates in what is unpleasant and not in what is pleasant.[14]

He arouses violent opposition.

All that is great on earth united: the scholars, the sages and the kings. Some wrote, others condemned, others slew. And notwithstanding all this opposition, simple, powerless people [the Apostles] resisted all those powers, compelled the kings, the scholars, the sages to submit, and banished idolatry from the face of the earth.[15]

In this extraordinary success Pascal saw the action of a super-human power and like Bossuet he gave a meaning to History. The spirit of man is irresistibly led to it, and if he refuses to accept the Christian mystery, he is left with the choice of accepting the myth of human evolution or that of periodic cataclysms and the eternal return. Pascal knew that the design whose pattern he read in History was the vision of faith. "How marvellous it is to see with the eyes of faith Darius and Cyrus, Alexander, the Romans, Pompey and Herod, working without realizing it for the glory of the Gospel."[16]

But Pascal does not confine himself to the analysis of the human greatness of Jesus in the sphere of morality and History. He sets out to discover the place of Jesus in an order in which he appears unique. He seeks to establish between the atheist, to whom his *Apology* is addressed, and Jesus a man-to-man relationship which is not affected by the passage of time.

The atheist is now torn by uneasiness. He knows that the physical world is infinite, empty and silent, "that the heart of man is hollow and full of vileness",[17] that society is only a lunatic asylum. He has accepted the wager which has committed him to

---

[13] Laf. 605: Br. 792.   [14] Laf. 671: Br. 767.   [15] Laf. 642: Br. 783.
[16] Laf. 594: Br. 701.   [17] Laf. 272: Br. 143.

making an effort to rid himself of his passions. He has read the Bible, has discovered the code which conceals the presence of the hidden God. If he does not yet dip his fingers into holy water, at least he holds out his arms in a gesture of supplication: "I hold out my arms to my Saviour."[18] What a marvellous surprise it would be to be able to wait for death in peace, filled with hope and joy!

With lyrical enthusiasm Pascal draws a picture of the atheist's discovery of Jesus Christ, "the true God of men".[19] He has only to recall the night of 23rd November 1654: "Jesus Christ is the object of everything and centre towards which all things gravitate. Whoever knows that, knows the reason for everything."[20] "We only know ourselves through Jesus Christ. We only know life and death through Jesus Christ."[21] "Without Jesus Christ the world would not continue to exist; it would either be destroyed, or would be a sort of hell. . . ."[22] And everything is concentrated in the meditation on the three orders of greatness suggested to Pascal by his mathematical discoveries. This time the human infinite takes on meaning. Here is the Pascalian hymn to charity, the song of the mystic kingship of Jesus:

The finite distance between bodies and minds symbolizes the infinitely more infinite distance between minds and charity; for charity is supernatural.

The blaze of fame has no attraction for people who are engaged in intellectual pursuits.

The greatness of men of intellect is invisible to kings, to the rich, to captains, to all those who are great according to the flesh.

The greatness of wisdom, which is nothing if it does not come from God, is invisible to the sensual and to the men of intellect. They belong to three different orders.

The great geniuses have their empire, their splendour, their greatness, their victory, their glamour, and have no need of greatness according to the flesh with which they have no connection. They are seen not with eyes, but with minds; it is sufficient.

The saints have their empire, their splendour, their victory,

[18] Laf. 466: Br. 737.   [19] Laf. 380: Br. 547.   [20] Laf. 17: Br. 556.
[21] Laf. 602: Br. 548.   [22] Laf. 17: Br. 556.

their glamour; and have no need of material or intellectual greatness
with which they have no connection, for they neither add nor take
away anything. They are seen by God and the angels, and not by
bodies or inquisitive minds: God is sufficient for them.

Archimedes, without any outward show, would be held in the
same veneration. He did not stage any visible battles, but he made his
discoveries available to all minds. O how he burst upon men's minds!

Jesus Christ, without possessions and without any outward display
of knowledge, stands in his order of holiness. He made no discoveries;
he did not reign; but he was humble, patient, holy, holy, holy unto
God, terrible to devils, and without sin. O with what great pomp
and vast magnificence he came in the eyes of the heart, which
perceives wisdom!

It would have been pointless for Archimedes, prince though he
was, to play the prince in his mathematical works.

It would have been pointless for Our Lord Jesus Christ to come
as a king, in order that his reign of holiness should dazzle; but he
certainly came with the splendour which belongs to his order!

It is quite ridiculous to take offence at the lowliness of Jesus
Christ, as though his lowliness were of the same order as the greatness which he came to reveal. When we consider the greatness that
he showed in his life, in his Passion, in his obscurity, in his death,
in the choice of his disciples, in their desertion, in his secret resurrection, and the rest, we shall see that it is so great that there is no reason
to be scandalized by a lowliness which is not there.

But there are some who are only impressed by worldly greatness,
as though there were no spiritual greatness; and others who only
admire spiritual greatness, as though there were not other forms of
greatness which stand infinitely higher in the order of wisdom.

All bodies, the firmament, the stars, the earth and its kingdoms,
are not equal to the least among minds, for the mind knows it all and
itself; and bodies, nothing.

From all the bodies put together we should not be able to extract
one little thought: it is impossible and belongs to another order.
From all the bodies and minds we should not be able to extract a
single spark of true charity: it is impossible and belongs to another
order which is supernatural.[23]

And Pascal goes on to develop these functions, "the offices"
of this kingship that Jesus exercises in the order of charity:

[23] Laf. 585: Br. 793.

He and he alone would produce a great people, an elect, a holy
and chosen people; guide them, nourish them, bring them into a
place of peace and holiness; make them holy for God; make them
the temple of God, reconcile them with God, save them from the
wrath of God, deliver them from the bondage of sin which
clearly reigns in the heart of man; give his people laws, engrave
the laws in their hearts, offer himself to God for them, be a victim
without blemish and himself the high priest: having to offer up himself, his body and blood, and nevertheless offer bread and wine to
God. . . .[24]

And under the influence of the presence of Jesus Christ the
world lights up, the social comedy becomes holy liturgy, the
wretchedness of man is transformed into divine greatness, all
corruption distils glory. "Reflect on the role of Jesus Christ in
everybody, and in ourselves: Jesus Christ as father in his Father,
Jesus Christ as brother in his brothers, Jesus Christ as a poor
man in the poor, Jesus Christ as rich in the rich, Jesus Christ as
doctor and priest in priests, Jesus Christ as sovereign in princes,
etc. For he is by his glory all that is great, being God, and is by his
mortal life all that is stunted and abject."[25]

If Pascal preserved the text of *The Mystery of Jesus* it was perhaps
because he would have revised it and used it to move the listener
by the spectacle of the communion of the Christian and his
Saviour at the moment of his deepest distress and his most
appalling sufferings. He would perhaps have given us a glimpse of
his heart broken in prayer, joy, sacrifice and tears.

But was there not a risk of Jansenism casting its shadow over the
radiant perspectives of redemption? In no sense. The text of the
Pensées proclaims: "Jesus Christ for all. . . . It is Jesus Christ who
is universal; the Church herself only offers the sacrifice for the
faithful; Jesus Christ offered up the sacrifice of the Cross for all
men."[26] And in another place: "Jesus Christ the Redeemer of all?"
he asks in a dialogue. "Yes, because he made his offer as a man who
redeemed all those who were willing to come to him. As for
those who die on the way, that is their misfortune; but so far as
he is concerned, he offered them redemption."[27]

[24] Laf. 585: Br. 793.   [25] Laf. 560: Br. 766.   [26] Laf. 423: Br. 774.
[27] Laf. 771: Br. 781.

But Pascal was no Protestant. The salvation of Jesus Christ is through the Church which man must accept and the Church does not hold a lower place in his soul than Jesus Christ. The Church and Jesus Christ cannot be separated.

Pascal does not deal with the Church *ex professo* in the *Pensées*. But he has several profound insights about her. His ecclesiology is derived from Bérulle and Saint-Cyran, and by way of them goes back to St Augustine, the great doctor of the Catholic idea.

In Pascal's view the Church is Jesus Christ himself, incarnate and continuing to fulfil his functions as Saviour, doctor, father, and prolonging on earth his passion, death and Resurrection: "I am present to you", says Jesus Christ to Pascal, "by my spirit in the Church, by my power in the priests, by my prayer among the faithful."[28]

The miracles belong to the history of the Church and bear witness to the divine solicitude for her which is constantly renewed; the seals which authenticate her mission, the lights which are planted along her route keep her from error and guide upright souls to her. The light is such that Pascal declares: "It is impossible that those who love God with all their heart should fail to recognize the Church, so evident is she."[29]

In fact, the Church alone teaches the truth: "The history of the Church should, properly speaking, be described as the history of truth."[30] Pascal knew very well that it was from her that Scripture comes, that the sacraments come which restore man to his supernatural destiny. He denounces the Reformation vigorously for rejecting confession.[31]

With the Church he is at pains to emphasize first and foremost, as belonging to her very essence, her perpetuity in time and her union in space. He constantly insists on her perpetuity. In his opinion the Church was already in existence at the time of the Patriarchs; she goes back to the origins of man, to the promises made to Adam; and if Pascal exaggerates the link between the Old Testament and the New, his theory of "figures" enables him to stress the unity of the Church throughout time and to bring

---

[28] Laf. 739: Br. 553.   [29] Laf. 902: Br. 850.   [30] Laf. 562: Br. 858.
[31] Laf. 99: Br. 100.

into her all the Jews who lived before the coming of Jesus Christ. He glorifies her eternity: "Religion is adapted to every sort of mind. The first stop at its foundation alone, and our religion is such that its foundation alone is sufficient to prove its truth. The others go back as far as the apostles. The most fully instructed go back to the beginning of the world. The angels have a still better view and from a greater distance."[32]

Moreover, in order to explain the unity of the Church more clearly, Pascal takes up again and with great brilliance deepens the allegory of St Paul who compares the Church to the human body: "Imagine", he said, "a body composed of thinking members."[33] Christians ought to feel the joy of being part of a body. "Their happiness no less than their duty lies in accepting the guidance of the whole soul to which they belong, and which loves them better than they love themselves."[34]

In one or two notes on the Pope, Pascal recalls the commandments of the Gospel on authority-service: "The Church, properly speaking, is in the body of the hierarchy", he remarks incidentally.[35] But "plurality, which is not reduced to unity, is a form of confusion; unity which is not dependent on plurality is tyranny".[36] The Church therefore offers a true image, but always threatened in her purity, of a society dominated and animated by the law of charity. She offers the rarest form of equilibrium between authority and freedom, between plurality and unity. She is the Gospel which endures.

[32] Laf. 472: Br. 285. [33] Laf. 687: Br. 473. [34] Laf. 676: Br. 482.
[35] Laf. 838: Br. 889. [36] Laf. 848: Br. 871.

CHAPTER IX

The Style and Poetry
of the "Pensées"

PASCAL is the only author among the classics whose drafts
have been preserved. Thanks to this, we can watch the very
genesis of his thought. Beneath the innumerable alterations
in the text, we can reconstruct the different states of some of the
greatest passages in the *Pensées*. There are occasions when whole
pages are crossed out. On other occasions, Pascal will rewrite a
sentence a dozen times until at last he hits on the precise and
pungent turn of phrase which alone satisfies his exacting taste
and his heart.

Let us look carefully at the following page in which all the
rejected words and phrases are printed in parentheses and in
italics.

Let man therefore (*consider*) contemplate all nature in her full and
lofty majesty; let him turn his eyes away from the lowly objects
which surround him, (*let him extend them to those innumerable fires
which roll so proudly over him, that this immense extension of the universe,
vast path which the sun follows in its turn, may appear to him—make him
consi . . .*—) let him look upon the dazzling light, placed (*in*) like an
eternal lamp (*in the centre of*) to illuminate the universe, (*that the*) let
the earth appear like a point compared with the vast circle that
(*it d . . .*) the orb describes (*make him look on the earth as a point—
around—in s—and that the vast circle itself be not considered as a point*),
and let him be filled with amazement that the vast circle itself (*is not
—is taken for a tiny point*) is only a tiny point in relation to the course
traced by the stars revolving in the firmament. But (*will his gaze
halt there—if he—let our eyes not come to a halt there*) if our eye comes

to a halt there, let (*his*) imagination go further; it will be more likely to grow weary of forming ideas (*of the immensities of space*) than nature of providing (*any*) material. The whole of the visible world is no more than (*a little atom*) an imperceptible speck, in (*the va— th̄e immense*) the ample (*itude*) bosom of nature. (*We*) None of our ideas comes anywhere near it (*we do not imagi . . .*), we waste our time in pushing our ideas beyond the (*imaginary*) imaginable confines of space; we produce only atoms compared with the reality (*this infinite vastness*) of things. Nature is an (*astonishing*) infinite sphere whose centre is everywhere, whose circumference is nowhere. In short, it is the greatest (*of*) tangible sign of the omnipotence of God that our imagination boggles at the thought of him (*Incomprehensi . . . —but to recover oneself*).

Let man when he recovers (*from a cer . . .*) himself consider what he is compared with what is; let him look upon himself as though he had strayed (*in the immense expanse of things and housed in the little dungeon which only gives him a sight of the universe that appears to him— if—of such astonishing size—he w . . . —instead—that he—that it is only an insensitive point—atom—in the true immensity of things—in this backwater of na . . . —turned away from nature—and let him be astonished at the fact that in this little dungeon where he is housed he sees nothing but the universe—astonished by—that the universe which he sees—admired from the dungeon where he was housed—and fou . . . —in that way he will learn*) and from the little dungeon where he is (*stray . . . —housed*) housed—I mean the universe—let him learn to judge (*the whole earth—this—the universe that he discovers*) the earth, kingdoms, towns, houses and himself at their proper value.

What is a man in the face of (*nature*) the infinite?[1]

The manuscript of the *Pensées* contains a score of similar pages. When we examine the writing we can distinguish two kinds of correction. One consists of unfinished words or sentences which were crossed out the moment they were written down. The other is the result of re-reading the text and the discarded passages are usually struck through with a vertical line. It follows that Pascal did not write from memory, as Marguerite Périer maintained, but put his thoughts straight down on paper. His thought was modified in the actual process of writing and became more complex. It has been said that there were as many as ten or fifteen

[1] Laf. 390: Br. 72.

drafts of some of the *Provincial Letters*. He was therefore quite the reverse of the spontaneous writer. If his conversation was undoubtedly picturesque, full of fire, vitality, unexpected sallies, if the rhythm of his written work was breathless as the evidence of his handwriting—it sometimes attained the speed of shorthand—suggests, he continually corrected as he wrote. He was a merciless critic of his own work. He was determined to achieve perfect fluency combined with absolute precision. We are greatly indebted to scholars like Lafuma whose masterly edition enables us to follow Pascal's pen in its least movements: those movements which reveal the secret processes of the immensely powerful intellect of the man who held the pen.

If Pascal had merely been endowed with an exact mind he would have written like Descartes. If he had simply possessed an unbridled imagination, he would have written like Montaigne. He was Pascal. This means that he possessed an exceptionally subtle and penetrating mind as well as a powerful imagination and a highly developed sense of verbal music. The fact is that he was a poet.

> It was characteristic of the conversation of Napoleon as of Pascal [said Sainte-Beuve] that whether they liked it or not, it imprinted itself in the minds of those who listened . . . . I have mentioned Pascal; of all modern writers he is perhaps the one to whom Napoleon, when he is at his best and most characteristic, comes closest in the quality of his style. . . . His style normally bears the imprint of his will power. Pascal, in the immortal *Pensées* which were discovered after his death in note form and which he wrote down in this form for himself alone, often recalls by his abruptness, by the despotic tone of which Voltaire complained, the tone of the notes dictated by Napoleon or that of his correspondence. There was something geometrical about both of them. Their words are engraved, as it were, with the point of a compass.[2]

Pascal possessed the first great virtue of the poet: the gift of wonder, the sense of amazement, of unending astonishment when confronted with himself, with the workings of his unconscious,

[2] *Causeries du lundi*, I, pp. 181–2.

with the world, reason, imaginative power, the wraiths and phantoms that belonged to his dreams. In comparing his attitude with the placidity of an Aquinas or a Descartes, it has been pointed out that there is something in him of the man who greets everything with the victorious cry of Christopher Columbus when he reached the shores of America. That is true. The theorems of Euclid, the existence of the vacuum, the mysterious presence of the Christian God in a soul, the fatuous propositions of the casuists, the divisibility of matter, the power of imagination and reason, love and death, filled him with amazement. He was a poet. Not even God himself was a source of surprise to St Thomas or Descartes. A tile, a grape stone, children who clout one another in the street, struck Pascal as something novel and released a cluster of images. He was a poet.

He possessed the secondary quality of the poet which is completely negative: he detested rhetoric, despised Cicero and loathed emphasis. He made fun of the inflated vocabulary, the flashiness and preciosity of the verbal trumpery that the Jean Cocteaus of his time called poetry. He himself had given very little thought to such matters, but they aroused an instinctive revulsion in him. He would have laughed at Pradon whom his contemporaries rated far more highly than Racine. He was determined to be a prose-writer who forged his own style—a style which was brutally effective.

His thought was calculated to insulate him from what we should today describe as "pure poetry". Philosophy and poetry are naturally on bad terms. The scholars and the philosophers have a poor opinion of poets. They distrust a Plato or a Bergson who expressed their ideas poetically or clothed them in a variegated garment of myths and colours. Most of the great poets—the Hugos and the Claudels—are content to make words flash like jewels. But to be moved, to weep and tremble as you evoke what for other people remain empty abstractions, is proof that you are an odd fellow, a Lucretius, a Dante, a Shakespeare or the author of the Book of Job. Pascal belongs to this hybrid race. "If he possessed the requisite sense of language and the impelling desire to express himself in terms of beauty," said Aldous Huxley, "Einstein could write the most intoxicating lyrics about relativity and the pleasures of pure mathematics."[3] Pascal is exactly like that. The *Pensées* are a great poem which swarms with religious and philosophical ideas clothed like the characters in Hofmannsthal's *Jedermann* or the medieval allegories. For Pascal philosophical reflection becomes a powerful and disturbing drama. He makes Man, the Infinite, Madness, Religion, Charity and Scripture perform like actors in a play. We see re-enacted the experience "which tricks" men;[4] see the spread of "impenetrable darkness" which blinds them;[5] watch rising up before us self-love which is "a marvellous instrument for closing our eyes to realities in the pleasantest possible manner."[6] We see Reason appear. We hear it "shout".[7] It is "unhinged".[8] The Senses arrive to trick it and it "takes its revenge on them".[9] It is a fools' comedy. Pascal would like to "finish off" Reason.[10] But when it has become weak and tottering, we find it propping itself up with "knowledge of the heart and senses", "humiliating itself".[11] The heart then opens and shows that it is "hollow and full of vileness".[12] Suddenly there arises the Spectre of Ennui which "of its own accord . . . comes welling up from the depths of our heart, where it has its natural roots, and fills the mind with its poison".[13] A poisonous plant growing wild. Finally, Imagination enters the scene: the mad creature wearing the garment of madness. "Mistress" of the world, the "haughty power" trailing behind it its court of miracles, its collection of "healthy men, sick men, rich men and poor men".[14] It has its accomplices. In order to make a grave-faced judge laugh during the sermon, it has mobilized Nature which has given the preacher a hoarse voice, a barber who has "shaved him badly", and Chance which has made him look "scruffier than usual". As soon as day breaks, it compels men "who have been refreshed by sleep" to leap out of bed to continue "the pursuit of its phantoms and submit to its impressions". It gives an outrageously inflated value to little things and reduces the value of great. It dresses up judges, barristers, doctors, and

---

[3] *On the Margin* (London, 1923), p. 30. This essay, "On the Stuff of Poetry", applies strikingly to Pascal.

[4] Laf. 300: Br. 425.   [5] Laf. 312: Br. 427.   [6] Laf. 81: Br. 82.
[7] *Id.*   [8] *Id.*   [9] Laf. 82: Br. 83.
[10] Laf. 124: Br. 73.   [11] Laf. 214: Br. 282.   [12] Laf. 272: Br. 143.
[13] Laf. 269: Br. 139.   [14] Laf. 81: Br. 82.

turns them into gesticulating dummies at some monstrous and grotesque *kermesse*.

The moment that Religion is about to make its appearance, man hears frightful voices rising all round him. It is a Witches' Sabbath. "What then does this chaos, this monstrous confusion proclaim? . . . What then are avidity and impotence crying out to us? . . ."[15] Like a veritable Hamlet among these shrieking ghosts, the shattered man interrogates himself: "Let man now appreciate himself at his true worth. Let him love himself . . . let him despise himself . . . let him hate and love himself . . ."[16] Finally, divine Wisdom like Piety in the prologue to Racine's *Esther* arrives to deliver its admirable monologue: "Do not expect, O men," it says, "either truth or comfort from men. I am that which created you, and alone can tell you who you are. But you are now no longer in the state in which I created you. I created man holy, innocent, perfect; I filled him with light and intelligence; I showed him my glory and my wonders. The eye of man then beheld the majesty of God."[17]

Except for the ending, the Pascalian tragedy is marked by a violent, caustic tone, an element of exasperation, a "brusque and vehement" style, as Montaigne would have said.[18] "[Indifference] astonishes and appals me: I find something monstrous in it . . . inevitably . . . horrible . . . indubitable . . . extravagant creature . . . incurable unhappiness . . . terrible ignorance . . . terrifying spaces . . . monstrous thing . . . strange insensitiveness . . . incomprehensible form of bewitchment . . . strange confusion . . . such contemptible people . . . horror."[19] The words finish by creating an atmosphere of tension and tragedy until the moment when Pascal himself, drowning the tumult, cries out: "Humble yourself, impotent reason; be silent, dullwitted nature. . . . Listen to God."[20]

But the rudest shock that we get from this "terrorist" style, as a schoolboy would have described it at the time of the Resistance, comes from the knife-edge proverb, the short, stark images which implant themselves in our minds. There is a sudden flash

[15] Laf. 402, 300: Br. 435, 425.
[17] Laf. 309: Br. 430.
[19] Laf. 11: Br. 194.
[16] Laf. 234: Br. 423.
[18] *Essais*, Ed. Villey, I, p. 329.
[20] Laf. 246: Br. 434.

of claws: "If the nose of Cleopatra had been shorter . . ."[21]
"A picklock boasts and expects to have his admirers."[22] "What a
happy life from which we deliver ourselves as though it were
the plague! . . ."[23] "The power of kings is based on reason and on
the folly of their people, and much more on folly."[24] "The
final act is bloody, however fine the rest of the play: you end by
dropping a handful of earth on the head and that is the end for
ever."[25] "Let someone put it to the test: let him leave the king all
by himself. . . ."[26]

The inventor of aphorisms and proverbs is not invariably a
poet. He may be a poet as Lucretius, La Fontaine and Péguy were,
but Pascal's proverbs are very different from La Fontaine's. The
morality of the *Fables* is prose in verse: that of Pascal is poetry in
prose. Original, newly created proverbs which crystallize in
images. Compare

"One 'take it', it is said, is worth more than two 'you shall have
its' "[27] and "A tree does not know that it is wretched."[28]

In the first example we hear echoes of Molière; in the other,
Descartes as a poet. It reflects the precise difference between the
style of the *Pensées* and that of the *Caractères*. La Bruyère draws his
portraits with minute accuracy; Pascal lays on the colours,
emphasizes the features, darkens the shadows, throws everything
into relief by the harshness of the stroke. He cuts out the padding
and the verbiage. It is prose in the manner of Rembrandt.
In each of these aphorisms there is a strong word that cuts like
the lash of a whip. And in the cry of pain the poetry is born.

The brutal mingling of hard, naked philosophical thought, the
tone of a passionate controversialist, the imaginary characters in a
drama, and finally the savage stream of harsh, biting aphorisms—
such is Pascal. In turn, he displays a macabre humour, sounds a
kind of death knell, trembles with fervour, with weariness, with
mortal tension, or surrenders himself with a pacific smile to joy.
He belongs to the front rank of those prophet-visionaries whose
triumphant appearance was celebrated by Rimbaud.[29]

[21] Laf. 90: Br. 162.　　[22] Laf. 94: Br. 150.　　[23] Laf. 299: Br. 361.
[24] Laf. 63: Br. 330.　　[25] Laf. 341: Br. 210.　　[26] Laf. 270: Br. 142.
[27] La Fontaine, "Le Petit poisson et le pêcheur".　　[28] Laf. 218: Br. 397.
[29] Letter to Paul Demeny of 15th May 1871. (This is the famous "Lettre du
Voyant".—Trans.)

Pascal used a rhythm which was naturally poetic: stanzas, refrains, *pantoums*. Strowski picked out a *pensée* set out in this way at the bottom of Folio 47 of the original manuscript:

> Nothing is so intolerable
> to man as to be
> in a state of complete repose,
> without desires, without work,
> without amusements, without occupation.
> He then feels his nothingness, his abandonment,
> his inadequacy, his dependence,
> his emptiness, his futility.
> Then at once wells up from the depths of
> his soul, weariness,
> gloom, misery,
> exasperation, frustration,
> despair.[30]

If the *Pensées* had been printed in his lifetime, Pascal would have arranged the three sentences in prose form. But in the autograph manuscript, where he had plenty of room, he unconsciously followed the rhythm marked by the two nouns in each line. A simple rhythm that we can find in Tertullian, St Augustine, St Bernard and in the liturgical prose of the low Latin of the middle ages and even in certain pages of Jansen. It would be possible to rearrange some of the minor works of Cardinal de Bérulle in their entirety in this rhythmic prose because the Cardinal, too, wrote in a language depending on assonance.

There are many passages in the *Pensées* which can be treated in the same way to bring out the cadence:

> We float over a vast expanse,
> always uncertain and drifting,
> tossed hither and thither.
>
> Whatever the point to which we seek
> to attach ourselves to consolidate our position,
> it shifts and leaves us;
> and if we follow it,

---

[30] *Les Pensées de Pascal,* étude et analyse, p. 128.

it eludes our grasp,
  slips away
  and flies from us in unending flight.[31]

What is more, Pascal's style relies heavily on antithesis:
intentional, deliberate antithesis, which is a sort of transposition of
Semitic parallelism into French:

What sort of a portent then is man? What a novelty!
What a monster, what a chaos, what a mass of contradictions!
What a prodigy! Judge of all things.
A ridiculous earthworm, repository of truth, sink
of uncertainty and error, the glory and the scum of the world.[32]

In some of the greatest passages Pascal uses Claudel's versicle
(*verset*). There is nothing particularly surprising about it because
both Pascal and Claudel found the form in the Bible.

None of the books of the Bible is written in the versicles that a
number of writers began to use about 1830: Lamennais in
Paroles d'un croyant, Mickiewicz or Edgar Quinet. But Hebrew
is such a concise language in comparison with French that a single
line of one of the prophets or psalmists often takes up two or
three lines in Latin or French. It so happens that five words of
Isaias can only be translated by a dozen words in French. Hence
the versicle.

The Mystery of Jesus and the meditation on "the order of
charity" are written in versicles and probably the fragment
numbered 556 in Brunschvicg of which there is no autograph
manuscript.[33] In these cases Pascal begins a fresh line after a
versicle and inserts a dash on the left-hand side to separate it
clearly from the next. And the links that join the moments
of the meditation on the agony of Jesus or on his greatness are not
based on logic, but are repetitions of a theme which seem to
result from the emotion, the expansiveness, generated by the
meditation.

In this form of poetry in which Pascal rediscovers the style of
the Psalms and the Gospels, we find the refrains, the constant
repetitions, the whispered litanies that belong to all prayer:

---

[31] Laf. 390: Br. 72.   [32] Laf. 246: Br. 434.   [33] Laf. 17.

Jesus sought some consolation at any rate in his three dearest
friends, and they were asleep. . . .
It did not even prevent them from dropping off to sleep. . . .
But he did not receive any because his disciples were asleep. . . .
We must not sleep during that time. . . .
Jesus, while his disciples slept . . .
Jesus, seeing them all asleep . . .
Jesus finding them still asleep . . .
Jesus seeing all his friends asleep . . .[34]

In the meditation on the "three orders" the word "greatness"
takes the place assigned to the verb "sleep" in the *Mystery*. It
recurs in almost every line. We also observe the repetitions and
refrains: "All the bodies, the firmament, the stars, the earth and
its kingdoms. . . . All the bodies together and all the minds
together. . . . From all the bodies together. . . ."[35]

It is in these marvellous versicles rather than in the involuntary
alexandrines, which sometimes turn up, that we find the supreme
beauty of the *Pensées*, their strangeness and audacity, the way in
which, going beyond the seventeenth century, Pascal anticipates
the twentieth and becomes the ancestor of *The Satin Slipper*, *The
Mystery of the Charity of Joan of Arc* and the litanies of Péguy.

[34] Laf. 739: Br. 553.   [35] Laf. 585: Br. 793.

Epilogue

Pascal possesses the threefold greatness of the scientist, the poet and the saint. He suffered the threefold humiliation of the poor man, the sick man and the sinner. He paid the threefold tribute of ink, tears and blood.

The influence of Pascal, whom Barrès describes as "the most venerable of French heroes", is less in danger than at any time of eclipse. Living at the moment of the greatest revolution in human knowledge, the birth of science, Pascal is completely modern in his conception of mathematical, psychological and historical truth. In these three "orders" he was an innovator. He foresaw the most important results; he established the principles of the mechanism. The exact sciences provided the inspiration for many of the pages of the *Pensées*. He led the way along the path followed by the philosophers and the scientists who came after him, whereas Descartes embarked on a metaphysical path in which Kant was to create havoc. There is nothing archaic about Pascal. Alone in his century he drew up the inventory of the eternal problems.

He is the author of an *Apology* founded on psychology and historical criticism; he was in exactly the position in which we find ourselves after the collapse of metaphysics. More than this, Pascal's fame is partly the result of an event that he did not foresee: the abandonment of Christianity by a section of the intelligentsia of the great Western nations during the eighteenth and nineteenth centuries. By what paradox has their apostasy been responsible for making the fortune of an *Apology* for the Christian religion? It is this: that while never himself doubting the truths of the Christian faith, Pascal found a way of expressing the doubts of the unbelievers whose numbers were minute when he wrote, but were destined to grow enormously. Now, Pascal did not cheat, did not minimize their difficulties like Nicole or

Bossuet. He did not adopt a superior attitude towards them, but he was vividly aware of the tragedy of their position. To the eighteenth century the break with religious faith appeared as a liberation. Men lived by the illusion of the goodness of human nature, by the illusion of the moral progress which would follow the growth of scientific knowledge, by the benefits of absolute freedom. We have long ago got over that. And Pascal had so clearly foreseen it that in 1962 he, the believer, the man of faith, is far closer to the contemporary unbeliever than Voltaire the sceptic. Voltaire's reasons for his unbelief are those of a Radical-Socialist local councillor. Now the modern world is eaten up by anxiety. Man feels that he is caught up in some monstrous drama. He is lost. He faces death alone.

If Christendom had survived with all its medieval panoply, Pascal might have been less well understood today because he professed the Christian faith in all its starkness. He isolated it from the social and metaphysical ties to which it seemed to have become irrevocably committed under the Ancien Régime. Unlike Aquinas and Descartes, Pascal was no metaphysician; there is no infantile cosmology in his work, no throne supporting the altar as there is in Bossuet's. In a century of absolutism in which faith was bound up with the social order, as it had been in the past with the Roman Empire, and with the physics of Aristotle, Pascal brought to bear on politics and metaphysics a judgment which was ruthless in its lucidity. His blistering sentences plant, in front of Christ represented by a Church whose weaknesses are never concealed, a man who is stripped of all his masks and subterfuges, who is shivering with cold in an empty universe and who is forced to choose between two extremes: the Crucified Christ and the void.

Index